ULTIMATE JOURNEYS
for TWO

ULTIMATE
JOURNEYS
for TWO

Extraordinary Destinations
on Every Continent

MIKE & ANNE HOWARD

NATIONAL
GEOGRAPHIC
WASHINGTON, D.C.

CONTENTS

Previous page: Zambia's serene Zambezi River in sunset hues, before it plummets down Victoria Falls
Top to bottom: Grevy's zebra in Samburu, Kenya; monks in Chiang Mai, Thailand; fisherman in Canoa Quebrada, Brazil; bungalows over Coron Bay, Philippines; Franz Josef Glacier, New Zealand; Árbol de Piedra in Department of Potosí, Bolivia

Top to bottom: Buddhist art along the trails of Emeishan, China; chill, cheery bungalows on Caye Caulker, Belize; chubby gentoo penguins on the Aitcho Islands, Antarctica; tandem ziplining in Samaná, Dominican Republic; the salt-dusted Moon Valley in the Atacama Desert, Chile; scuba diving in the Great Barrier Reef, Australia

Diani Beach, Kenya

INTRODUCTION

On our way to one of the deepest canyons in the world, hugging the curves of the Andes and yielding to cows, a fiesta of elderly Peruvians appeared in the middle of the road. We crept forward, assuming they'd move to the side, but instead a woman wearing a traditional embroidered dress knocked on our window. "Come dance!" she said in Spanish with a smile. "You may not pass, until you dance!" Mike and I looked at each other, and then simultaneously swung open our doors. The partygoers cheered and the band of wooden instruments got louder. She took our hands and pulled us into a circle of twirling ladies. Around and around we went, with leg kicks and hip shakes, until the shot master appeared with an earthen jug. He poured us an overflowing chicha corn brew, and we toasted with an exuberant, *"Salud!"* Arm in arm with our new amigos, we danced until dark and happily never made it to the famed canyon.

How It All Began

When we started planning our honeymoon, we took out a piece of paper and wrote down our dream trips: ice climb in Patagonia, hike Machu Picchu, dive the Great Barrier Reef, go on safari during the great wildebeest migration, and more experiences than we could fit on the page. It felt impossible to choose. Then Mike asked me, "What if we did them all?" It seemed unfathomable, and I chuckled at the thought. "No seriously," he said. "We've got our health, some savings, and each other. Will there ever be a better time to explore the world?" That night we

Dancing with new friends at an unexpected street party in Achoma, Peru

set the "HoneyTrek," our honeymoon and journey around the world, in motion.

We saved, researched, and prepped like mad for 16 months. Then on January 22, 2012, we boarded a one-way flight from New York City to the Amazon jungle. Saying goodbye to our home, jobs, family, and friends, we stepped into the great unknown. All the fears ran through our heads as we waited at the gate. What about our careers? Our nest egg? What if we get sick, robbed, or worse—go crazy spending 24 hours a day together? Plenty was telling us to just stay home. Though after seven continents and over five years of continuous travel, we have a million reasons why this was the best decision we've ever made.

We have sipped tea with a Laotian medicine man, ridden a grape harvester in Marlborough wine country, drummed in a Xhosa initiation ceremony, befriended a geisha in Kanazawa, taught impromptu English classes in a Hmong village, and experienced a kindness from strangers that has truly touched our souls. None of these things were on the original bucket list, but they top the charts as some of our most unforgettable experiences.

The first step is to get out there, be it for two weeks or two months, and even if you don't make it to the deepest canyon in the world, you'll have one heck of a ride.

Adventure Travel for Couples

There are many books on romantic travel, showcasing the destinations with the finest candlelit dinners, couples massages, and silkiest sheets. And, hey, we like those things too, but lasting memories run deeper than a few nights in a fancy hotel. When you discover a beach cove without a footprint, a temple covered in vines, or a waterfall nestled in the forest, and the only person around is the one you love . . . it's sweeter than a chocolate on your pillow.

The adventures highlighted in this book would also be great for solo travelers, but there are plenty of books about them. This book is about the both of you, the love of travel and each other. It's about enhancing relationships through action and making adventure a part of your lives.

When you share a travel experience that transcends words, it connects you. Things you could never quite explain to other people are instantly understood with a sound, smell, or quick glance. And even the snafus bring back fond memories. Like that time our bus broke down in Mozambique and we hitched a ride on top of a banana truck; or when we took a wrong turn on Mount Kenya and got escorted out by armed rangers; or when we accepted a dinner invitation in Norway only to be served sheep's head with eyeballs (and thank goodness, aquavit). When we recount these stories, they all end in laughter. The bumps in the road make the sunset richer, red wine finer, and bedtime spoons that much closer.

Exploring your curiosities, actualizing dreams, and celebrating life—this is the ultimate journey for two.

Open the Heart and Mind

We're serial adventurers, and always want to see and do more. Though after countless excursions across the globe, we can tell you, the times we have aimlessly wandered the backstreets, struck up conversation with a fruit vendor, joined a pickup volleyball game, or spent the evening in a local's home—these moments of immersion rival the wonders of the world.

From the Beijing couple we met on the way to the Great Wall of China to the Rastafarians at Victoria Falls, the people have made each place so special. We've had heartwarming chance encounters around the globe, but we won't give luck all the credit. We always learn a little bit of the local language to greet the people that cross our path. (If you can tell a Turkish grandma that her food is *lezzetli*—delicious—you've made a friend for life.) We've honed our street smarts, followed gut instincts, and tried to approach every situation with an open mind and a smile.

Plan Less, Get More

Leave room in your itinerary to seize unexpected opportunities. If there's a local festival in the

An artsy interpretation of our initial around-the-world honeymoon route

field, a religious ritual by the river, or a pig roast in the town square—you want to be there. With limited days, it's tempting to schedule every moment of a vacation. Although some planning is necessary, give yourself time to follow the rhythms of a place. Let the destination unfold, and the serendipitous moments may just become the main event.

Taking the public bus with Maasai warriors, eating enchiladas at the market stalls, and sleeping in Buddhist monasteries—these are invaluable experiences that barely cost a thing. Forgo a few of your creature comforts and do as the locals do. Better than affordable, it's as authentic as it gets.

This free-wielding approach might sound risky to some, but on this eternal honeymoon, we've never had any significant illness, robbery, or injury. And with all the street food, chicken buses, and roadside guesthouses we've sampled, this must be proof that the world's not so scary after all. Sure, it may be safer to stay home, though missing these life-enhancing experiences is a far greater risk.

Road to El Chaltén, home to Patagonia's iconic Fitz Roy

What's in This Book

When people ask us to name our favorite place, we always respond, "What types of places do *you* like?" We've explored over 500 destinations and love them all for different reasons, but if you let us know you are a beach or mountain person, we'll have your ideal answer. We've organized the chapters of this book with that same principle in mind. We want you to discover destinations based on your passions and find new adventures, too. We didn't put major cities in the book, because you know those already, and though we did include some well-known sites like Angkor Wat and the Sacred Valley, we're sharing a fresh approach to shake the crowds. (Ever seen Niagara Falls encrusted with icicles? Did you know there is more than one Inca trail to Machu Picchu?)

To ensure we offer the best possible destinations and tips for couples travel, we've called in 11 of our favorite globe-trotting duos to add their favorite places and tried-and-true advice. Each chapter features a "Power Couple's Pick," and between the thousands of places we've

A family of elephants crossing our path in Samburu, Kenya

Saying goodbye to our apartment in Hoboken, New Jersey

collectively visited, you know this is a solid selection. When we wanted more road trip suggestions, we asked Lisa Gant and Alex Pelling of 2people1life, who've driven 150,000 miles across 70 countries. Our contributors range in age from the intrepid millennials Elayna Carausu and Riley Whitelum of the popular YouTube channel Sailing La Vagabonde, to the wise Kristin Henning and Tom Bartel of the blog Travel Past 50. They come from a variety of backgrounds as well: From award-winning Canadian travel writers, to nomadic house sitters from Australia, to American speakers at TEDx, we've got every couple covered when it comes to finding travel inspiration.

This is not your typical nitty-gritty guide; we strive to share the essence of each place and ways to make it shine. We've included our off-the-track finds, tested-and-approved activities, and a few things we're dying to go back and do. We're sharing insider tips, along with fun facts, and stories from behind the scenes. You'll find transit blunders, comical encounters, touching moments, and a look at real life on the road.

Let the Journey Begin

This book is made for dreaming big. Most of these places aren't in your backyard, and some of the activities might put butterflies in your stomach. This book is not for the average tourist, but you are not the average couple. You're intrepid, inquisitive, and up for a challenge. And because we like that about you, we've also found some of the most decadent and luxurious experiences to reward your adventurous spirit. We strive for that blissful balance, to not just bring you home relaxed, but invigorated. In passing on these stories, we're letting you in on our secrets, in hopes that they inspire your own exploration, and that someday we might get to hear yours in return.

Western Greenland
Greenland
170

Norwegian Fjords
Norway
136

Churchill
Canada
96

North Coast
Ireland and Northern Ireland
208

Olympic Peninsula
United States
188

Rhine Gorge
Germany
56

Ghent
Belgium
116

Mount Rainier
United States
34

Central Vermont
United States
172

Lauterbrunnen Valley
Switzerland
32

Moab
United States
142

Niagara Falls
United States and Canada
174

Sintra
Portugal
118

The Southwest
United States
206

Kaua'i
United States
66

Durango
Mexico
148

North Eleuthera
Bahamas
68

ATLANTIC

Guanajuato
Mexico
114

Western Cuba
Cuba
214

Samaná
Dominican Republic
78

OCEAN

NORTH

AMERICA

Mesoamerican Barrier Reef
Belize
126

St. Lucia
Lesser Antilles
190

Tortuguero
Costa Rica
100

Monteverde
Costa Rica
186

EQUATOR

Galápagos
Ecuador
84

Volcano Avenue
Ecuador
212

Yasuní
Ecuador
192

Manaus
Brazil
194

Jericoacoara
Brazil
150

PACIFIC OCEAN

SOUTH

AMERICA

Urubamba Valley
Peru
38

Lake Titicaca *Bolivia and Peru*
52

map key

- ■ Mountains
- ■ Lakes, Rivers & Falls
- ■ Beaches & Islands
- ■ On Safari
- ■ History & Architecture
- ■ At Sea
- ■ Deserts & Dunes
- ■ Snow & Ice
- ■ Jungles & Rain Forests
- ■ Road Trips
- ■ Supernatural

Department of Potosí
Bolivia
220

Atacama Desert
Chile
154

Iguazú Falls
Argentina and Brazil
46

Los Glaciares
Argentina
174

Torres del Paine
Chile
40

Antarctic Peninsula
Antarctica
160

OCEAN

EUROPE

ASIA

PACIFIC

OCEAN

INDIAN

OCEAN

AUSTRALIA

ANTARCTICA

Tromsø
Norway
166

Central Georgia
Georgia
210

Cappadocia *Turkey*
108

Pamukkale *Turkey*
224

Cyclades Islands
Greece
135

Ladakh *India*
230

**Annapurna
Sanctuary**
Nepal
24

Emeishan
China
28

Bagan
Myanmar
106

Wulingyuan *China*
234

Fenghuang *China*
112

Nam Ou River Valley *Laos*
60

Inle Lake
Myanmar
48

Siem Reap
Cambodia
232

Khao Sok
Thailand
182

Railay
Thailand
74

Mũi Né
Vietnam
144

Cordillera Central
Philippines
26

Northern Palawan *Philippines*
130

Mekong Delta *Vietnam*
58

Tioman *Malaysia*
76

EQUATOR

Samburu *Kenya*
94

**Virunga
Mountains**
Rwanda
36

Crater Highlands *Tanzania*
92

Zanzibar *Tanzania*
72

South Luangwa *Zambia*
98

Livingstone
Zambia
54

**Namib
Desert**
Namibia
152

Kruger
South Africa
88

Western Cape
South Africa
200

Central Flores
Indonesia
222

Komodo
Indonesia
132

Top End
Australia
86

Daintree
Australia
180

0   2000 km

0   2000 mi

Rotorua
*New
Zealand*
228

Westland
New Zealand
162

South Island
New Zealand
202

**Tasman
District**
N.Z.
124

TRAVEL STYLE

Everyone has a unique travel style, though putting two together can take some finessing. Find your commonality. Try your partner's passion; you just might like it. Conquer fears—nothing is that scary when you have each other. Discovering your dream destination, striking the right balance of activities, and adding romance to each day—that is the path to a happy medium, and your happy place.

CHOOSING DESTINATIONS

"What are we looking for in our next vacation?" It's an important question that many couples forget to ask one another. Too often, the conversation jumps straight to "Where do we want to go?" and then the region's offerings and experiences come as an afterthought.

Instead, talk about your vacation goals and let them be your guide. Before you default to that spot everyone's talking about or return to a place you've enjoyed in the past, ask: Do we want to discover new cultures? Hike the wilderness? Take to the sea? Hone a skill? Or attempt something completely new?

Put each of your goals down on paper, see where you overlap, and seek out the places that satisfy your travel cravings, as individuals and as a couple. This simple exercise of gathering your thoughts and comparing notes will not only build excitement for your trip and inform the decisions you make—it's also a chance to learn something new about each other.

Prioritize Adventures

Today is the youngest you will ever be. Let that inspire you to travel farther, hike higher, stay longer, dive deeper, and do more now. When picking destinations for our around-the-world honeymoon, our guiding philosophy was: Go places too far for a week's vacation and too rugged to tackle with creaky knees. Hiking 95 miles round-trip to Annapurna Base Camp and staying in rustic Himalayan teahouses is one of our favorite adventures. Though would we have felt the same way, or even attempted it, a decade or two later?

Ask yourself: What are my limits, and what adventures lie at the edge of those boundaries?

We don't care what age you are—it's never too late to get out there. As time ticks on, you'll inevitably need more comforts and the less likely you'll be to reach these authentic and adventurous corners of the world. Challenge yourself to get off the cushy tourist track, before anything convinces you otherwise.

Kicking back at Casa Lucila in Mazatlán, Mexico

Consider Developing Countries

We adore world-class cities; you just won't find them in this book. You don't need us to tell you that Paris and Kyoto are fabulous. What's more, they don't ring with a sense of urgency. Most of those cities have incredible standards of historic preservation, along with Western comforts and infrastructure. It would be easy to visit them later in life, and they will likely be similar, if not enhanced. Places like Inle Lake and Volcano Avenue, on the other hand, are changing fast. They are ripe for adventure and rich with culture, untainted by mass tourism. To see them in this state, time is of the essence.

Another fantastic benefit of developing nations? They're affordable. The cost of an average three-star hotel in Hanoi is two-thirds less than London. So, don't let the pricey airfare deter you from far-flung places. These trips are often cheaper in the end, and your chance to experience them may never be the same.

Destinations to Fit Your Budget

If there is a place you are dying to visit, make it happen! One-of-a-kind experiences, like paragliding over Pamukkale's Roman ruins or World War II wreck diving in the Philippines, are worth every penny. As the saying goes, "Travel is the one thing you buy that makes you richer," and it's so true. Before you let price deter you, remember you can always find a clever way to experience a place affordably. Never rule anything out and see the Travel Smart chapter (p. 239) for ways to lower the price of your dream vacation.

Although you can always "travel hack" for better deals, it's nice to know some places are less expensive out of the gate. Central America, eastern Europe, and Southeast Asia are a few of the culturally rich and stunning regions of the world where "budget" doesn't mean lower quality. Consider countries that will bring your costs down while enhancing your travel experience.

Country Status

Odds are good your desired destination is a safe place, but it's always smart to check for any recent instability. Visit *Travel.State.gov* for advisories, read the regional news, and check the travel forums (with a grain of salt) to determine if you should go now or perhaps wait for a later date.

THE WELL-ROUNDED TRIP

Travel is a way to explore your interests—try a new water sport, practice a language, take a traditional cooking class, summit a volcano, and do the things you cannot do at home. With a whole world to choose from, there are plenty of places to suit your interests. If you love trekking, go to the Himalaya, but don't stop there. Continue to the medieval cities, world-class rapids, and rhino-filled jungles in the foothills.

We see travel as an opportunity to experience another country's exotic treasures and little-known delights. If you can do it any given Sunday (that is, eat a burger by the pool), skip it, and push yourself to do something different, like feast on Turkish mezes in a Byzantine cave or sample craft beers in a Cistercian monastery.

Get Perspective

Eat at a city's street carts and you'll see where the fancy fusion restaurants get their flavors. Spend time with the hill tribes and find out where boutiques get their ethnic design inspiration and many of their accessories. Snowshoe between mountain huts for a couple days and those high-thread-count hotel sheets will feel a whole lot softer. Having a range of experiences—fancy to budget, urban to countryside, relaxation to adventure—will give a place context and make a trip richer overall.

Mix Local and Luxury

It's your vacation; you deserve a little pampering. Gourmet meals, ocean-view suites, spa treatments, and other decadent delights should absolutely pepper into your holiday. We love a boutique hotel that draws inspiration from the regional style and makes it shine with storied antiques, menus rooted in tradition, and cultural elements at every turn. Enjoy that dreaminess; just don't let a plush resort shelter you from life outside its gates. Wander the streets without a guide and eat a few meals at the hole-in-the-wall restaurants. For a couple nights of your trip, try a private room at an Airbnb or homestay. It might not have an in-room espresso maker or bellhop, but the authenticity and heartwarming local interactions will be a priceless upgrade.

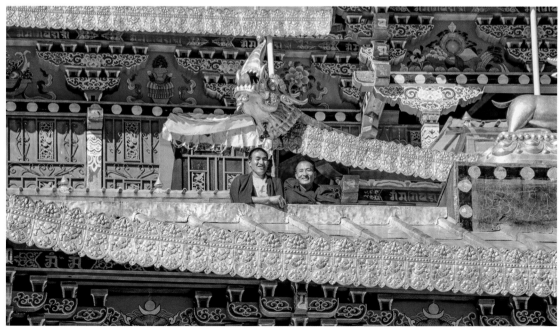

Tibetan monks enjoying Benzilan's Gedong Mask Festival, China

Planning Versus Spontaneity

With limited vacation days, we all want to maximize our time off. Fearful that space will fill up, many people prebook their tours, hotels, and ground transportation. This is entirely understandable, and if you are dying to experience certain activities (particularly in high season), you should secure those in advance. Though whenever you can, avoid locking in reservations; you'll find a myriad of benefits:

- It's often cheaper and better for the local economy to book on-site.
- Many of the most authentic options aren't listed online, but quickly present themselves once you arrive.
- You can gauge ideal timing for weather-dependent activities.
- Local events, festivals, and invitations often pop up with little notice, and you wouldn't want to miss them due to a prior reservation.

Determine your must-do activities and make them happen, but leave room for the unexpected, so you can seize unique opportunities as they arise.

Finding Balance

People often come back exhausted from a whirlwind trip saying, "I need a vacation from my vacation." Although we think that's better than, "I got sunburnt and gained five pounds at the buffet," we want to help you find the perfect balance of adventure and relaxation. Rather than feeling the need to explore from dawn until dusk, stagger your activities throughout the day and week.

One morning, stroll the streets at sunrise, watching the markets open and the town come alive. Get in an activity or two, and then recharge with an afternoon siesta. Wake up refreshed and find out what the nightlife is like. Seeing a town at different times of day will give you a holistic perspective on a place.

The day following a big adventure, find an inviting bench in the town square or sip coffee at a mom-and-pop café. People-watching and striking up conversations with locals are highly underrated travel activities, and can sometimes offer more cultural insight than a museum. At the end of every day, take the time to enjoy sunset and each other's company.

TRAVELING AS A COUPLE

According to an African proverb, "If you want to go fast, go alone. If you want to go far, go together." Travel is an incredible bonding experience at every stage of the process. Brainstorming your ideal destinations. Working together to plan an itinerary. Reaching a distant land, navigating the unknown, and experiencing things you've only dreamed about—that shared accomplishment is worthy of a champagne toast.

In an exotic setting, romance is inevitable, but so are the challenges. Tour cancellations, stomachaches, uncooperative weather, getting lost in an urban jungle—some less-than-dreamy things are bound to happen. And when they do, it's good to know how to deal with them so you can get back to having fun.

Finding Compromise

Make your shared interests the focus of your itinerary. That will likely be enough to fill your vacation days. But when your wish lists don't quite match up, be receptive to your partner's interests. Showing you care through action is more powerful than words. Take turns picking activities. A night at a soccer game is a fair trade for an opera performance. At the first grumble, gently remind each other, trying new things is what travel is all about.

Take a Little Time Apart

Having different interests is natural, so it's okay to explore a few of them on your own. Travel is a great opportunity for self-reflection; giving yourself the space to do that is good for everyone. Take a day or an afternoon to try the things that call your name. Plus, as the adage goes, absence makes the heart grow fonder—especially when you have exciting stories to share at the end of the day.

Freedom camping alongside Lake Alexandrina, New Zealand

Roll With the Punches

Vacations are built up as the "perfect" escape (did someone say paradise?), so when there's a bump in the road, we're often caught off guard. Avoid this pitfall by accepting that some stuff will go awry, and make a pact to get over it quickly. When unforeseen circumstances alter the game plan, see what new opportunities present themselves—you may discover something even better. And if nothing else, find the humor in the hiccups and remember it's all part of the adventure.

Be Prepared

Hunger, heat, and a dead phone are all ingredients for a squabble. Taking basic precautions, like packing snacks, water, and a charger, will help. But when all else fails, dig deep and find composure; getting mad never helps. Remember not to lash out at each other over something a granola bar could fix, and don't confuse a bad mood with true feelings.

Make Time to Do Nothing

In a whirlwind attempt to enjoy as much as we can, we often forget to take a moment to appreciate the little things. For a day or two, ditch your itinerary. Hold hands as you wander charming alleys, follow the smell of fresh baked goods, pop into antique stores, and chat with the locals along your way. It's also important to just be still sometimes. Sleep in, have breakfast in bed, and look into each other's eyes a little longer.

Ways to Add Romance

Northern lights dancing overhead, sun setting into the sea, mist enshrouding ancient temples—travel sets the stage for romance. With incredible natural beauty and a vacation vibe on your side, you don't need to lean on five-course meals and theater tickets. A few thoughtful gestures and simple surprises can elevate any place to your special spot. When you're looking for a little romance, try these tips . . . and don't forget to lean in for the kiss:

- Pack votive candles, massage oil, and bubble bath.
- Take dessert anywhere but the table.
- Stargaze in a hammock for two.
- Savor a sunset picnic with local delicacies.
- Plan a date night and don't reveal the details.

CHOOSE YOUR OWN ADVENTURE

Not just your standard "things to do," this book is filled with one-of-a-kind experiences. Find the activity that gets your heart racing—dogsledding, microlight flying, wreck diving, polar bear safaris—and see where it is in the world. Flip to its corresponding page; perhaps it will lead you to a country you've always dreamed about or a destination you're discovering for the first time. Open your mind, indulge your wild side, and let adventure be your guide. And if you're ever bored of the same old thing, turn here to spice things up:

Opposite: Mushing a dogsled team on Tromsøya Island, Norway

Torres del Paine, Chile

"We are now in the mountains and they are in us, kindling enthusiasm, making every nerve quiver, filling every pore and cell of us."

—JOHN MUIR

Chapter One

MOUNTAINS

Mountains emerge from the horizon with indescribable intrigue. Trails meander in all directions, along a river, through a forest, into a valley. Each offers a fresh adventure. Choose the path toward a 20,000-foot peak and the landscape can evolve from a tropical jungle with swinging monkeys to hanging glaciers with snow leopards looming. Follow the snaking stones of an ancient aqueduct and it can lead you to a lost civilization and clues to the past.

Pushing your muscles, lungs, and determination to new heights, you reach an amphitheater of jagged peaks. Sit back and revel in your accomplishments or press on—the summit is the holy grail for many adventurers. Mountains, across continents and cultures, have long been considered sacred, and many are still worshipped. Trek from temple to temple in China, hike to the cliff-carved altars in Peru, or find your own spiritual place in Patagonia. Walk, climb, cave, paraglide, kayak—just go. The mountains are calling.

Descending from Annapurna Base Camp with our local guide

ANNAPURNA SANCTUARY
Nepal

ASIA
NEPAL Annapurna Sanctuary

When eight of the world's 10 highest mountains are packed into one country, it's time to go big or go home. Enter the heart of the Himalaya via the narrow pass between Machapuchare and Hiunchuli mountains. Follow the trail along the glacial-fed Modi Khola River into the ring of 20,000-foot peaks at Annapurna Base Camp (ABC). Ascending 7,000 vertical feet from pink rhododendron forests to icy moraines, the diversity of landscapes is astounding. Not just for trekkers, these ancient footpaths connect remote mountain villages and are a window into traditional Gurung and Magar cultures. The route to ABC is dotted with teahouses offering home-cooked meals, cozy beds, and enough provisions to skip the camping gear and wilderness survival school. In five or six unforgettable days, you'll reach the 13,546-foot base camp and the majestic panorama of the Annapurna massif. Wake up to sunrise over the ring of sacred peaks and feel every ache in your body vanish into thin air.

 WHEN TO GO

October–November offer optimal hiking weather, as do April–May, with a rhododendron bonus.

WHERE TO STAY

Jhinu Guest House: Basic but perfectly positioned near the must-soak hot springs. **Chomrong Cottage:** A beacon of Western comforts, days deep in the Himalaya, offering chocolate cake, burritos, and top-notch views. *Note:* Most trailside villages have teahouses with booking on arrival.

 GET ROMANTIC

Pack a tiny bottle of massage oil. Nightly rubdowns will become a romantic (and necessary) ritual.

HONEYTREK TIP

Don't prebook your trek with a Western company. Head to the Annapurna trekking capital of Pokhara, where quality local guides abound for a fraction of the price.

Soaking in Jhinu Hot Springs off the Modi Khola River

COUPLES ADVENTURES

Gurung Traditional Museum ▲

The local Gurung people believe the Annapurna Sanctuary to be a sacred place, home to various Hindu, Buddhist, and animist gods. Visit the museum in Ghandruk to learn about the fascinating traditions of the residents here and their surprising history as a fearless wing of the British Army.

Jhinu Hot Springs ▲

Twenty minutes from the village of Jhinu, natural springs are channeled into a scenic stone pool alongside the lush Modi Khola River. Relax your weary muscles with a long soak after the day's trek.

Beyond Base Camp ▲▲

Pay your respects to fallen climbers at the prayer-flagged stupa, roam the craggy sheep pastures, rock scramble the moraine of the South Annapurna Glacier, join a pickup volleyball game with the ABC

✣ Hiking Fuel: Dal Bhat

The signature dish of Nepal and your ABC power food is undoubtedly *dal bhat*. Translated, it's a simple lentil and rice soup, but in reality the dish's variety of spices and vegetable curries serve as an expression of each region. Ginger, chili, tamarind, turmeric, or mango pickle may kick up your dal bhat on any given day, but one thing is constant: It's always served bottomless. Eat seconds and thirds. You earned it.

A classic serving of bottomless *dal bhat*

caretakers, and toast your trekking accomplishment with a glass of raksi millet wine.

Sunrise Over Poon Hill ▲▲▲

Wake up an hour before dawn, put on your beanie and headlamp, and hike from Ghorepani to Poon Hill. Watch the Annapurna Range and the Dhaulagiri massif turn from a glowing silhouette to a snowy panorama of jagged peaks. The stand-alone trek to Poon Hill (about 5 days) is also a great time-crunch alternative to ABC (about 10 days).

TO EXPLORE MORE ON THIS CONTINENT, CHECK OUT:
» Lakes: Inle Lake, Myanmar...p. 48
» Supernatural: Wulingyuan, China...p. 234

CORDILLERA CENTRAL
Philippines

ASIA **Cordillera Central**
PHILIPPINES

Although impressive in size, it's the spirit of resilience that makes Luzon's most prominent mountain range so captivating. In a country that's been occupied by the Spanish, Americans, British, and Japanese, the people of Cordillera Central never surrendered their mountains or way of life (even if they had to do some headhunting). Cultivating their steep slopes into thriving rice terraces for the past 2,000 years, they worked with the landscape's natural contours and hand-built a network of rain forest–irrigated paddies with stone and mud walls, plus enough stairs to encircle half the globe. The harmony they created between nature and humankind is so impressive it prompted a new UNESCO recognition category: cultural landscapes. The communities are connected by this agricultural history, but vary with unique religious, artistic, and cultural expressions, across the Kalinga, Mountain, and Ifugao Provinces. Hike to the hanging coffins of Sagada, partake in a lunar harvest in Batad, or get a tribal tattoo in Buscalan. Wherever you go and whatever you do in the Cordillera, it will be an adventure.

WHEN TO GO
April–June and September–November skirt most of the rain while still yielding radiant green terraces and a chance to watch the harvest.

WHERE TO STAY
Native Village Inn: Traditional thatch huts with friendly service and top-notch views of the Banaue rice terraces. **Misty Lodge:** Cozy wooden rooms and a great café in a serene forest setting just outside of Sagada village.

GET ROMANTIC
Take afternoon tea at the Sagada Lemon Pie House. The cheery yellow cabin with high ceilings, big windows, and floor cushions is an intimate spot for sweets and mountain tea.

HONEYTREK TIP
Instead of sitting 10 to a bench inside the Jeepney bus, ride on the roof for more space, fresh air, jaw-dropping views, and some fun banter with the locals. Use your jacket as a seat cushion and hang on tight.

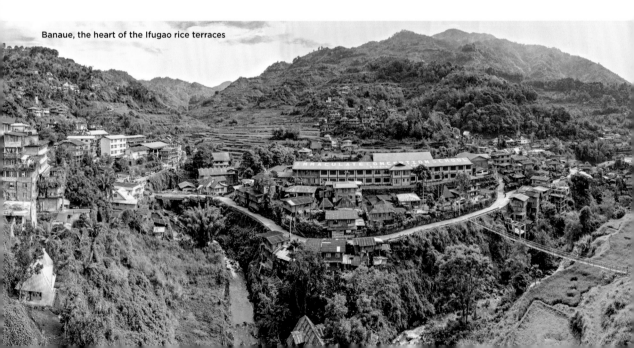

Banaue, the heart of the Ifugao rice terraces

Hiking break above the terraces of Batad village

COUPLES ADVENTURES

Rice Terrace Trekking ▲▲▲
Go deep into the Ifugao rice terraces with a two-day hike along the Awan-Igid Trail to the traditional villages of Pula, Kambulo, and Batad. If short on time, beeline to spectacular Batad. Explore the cascading paddies, the village of stilted homes, and the 200-foot Tappiya waterfall.

Tribal Tattoos in Buscalan ▲▲▲▲▲
With tattoo artist Whang-od's recent nomination for the Philippines' National Living Treasures designation, the 1,000-year-old Kalinga tradition is having a resurgence in her remote village. Watch master tattooists use ink-soaked thorns to hammer tribal designs at 100 taps a minute, or get in line for your own permanent work of art.

Echo Valley Hanging Coffins ▲▲
Walking above St. Mary's church in Sagada and down to the lookout point, you'll see painted wooden coffins nailed high into the cliffs. This stunning Igorot burial ritual has been practiced for nearly two millennia and continues today.

Spelunking Sumaguing Cave ▲▲▲
Follow the underground waterfalls, cascading hundreds of feet down a limestone cavern. Bouncing from pool to pool, playing with light and shadow, and rappelling on otherworldly formations make this one of the Philippines' best caving experiences.

⟐ My Way or the Highway

Jeepneys are a purely Filipino phenomenon and one of our favorite modes of local transportation. These vehicles were constructed from U.S. military jeeps left over from World War II, and have since been stretched and customized into regional buses with personal flair. No two Jeepneys are the same and each bears the artistry, humor, and pomp of its driver. Jokes, family photos, pickup lines, and biblical verses are often displayed on the inside; outside, anything goes, as long as it turns heads.

Philippines' public transit and cultural icon

TO EXPLORE MORE ON THIS CONTINENT, CHECK OUT:

» **At Sea: Northern Palawan, Philippines...p. 130**
» **Supernatural: Central Flores, Indonesia...p. 222**

Xixiang Chi temple appears after a day's trek.

EMEISHAN
China

ASIA
□Emeishan

f you can picture a classical
Chinese painting of a mist-shrouded mountain carved
with stone stairs leading to red pagodas, then you
can picture Mount Emei. This sacred Sichuan peak is
where Bodhisattva Puxian reached enlightenment, and
where one of China's founding Buddhist temples was
built in the first century. Pilgrims and Chinese tourists
come in droves to see the main monuments, but for
those looking to trek the 10,000-foot mountain and
enjoy its 150 monasteries, temples, and pavilions,
it's a heavenly two-day ascent. Walking through the
bamboo forests, tea plantations, and limestone passes,
you will see a temple peek through the trees every
hour or so. Their presence paces the journey with
Zen-filled breaks to admire the religious art, take a
heady whiff of incense, and hydrate to the sounds
of chanting monks. Reach the much anticipated
Golden Summit, a temple complex perched on the
sheer cliffs, and join the devotees in their excitement
for this divine place.

✕ WHEN TO GO
Find pleasant temperatures with the aza-
leas from March–May, and red maple
leaves in September–October.

🏨 WHERE TO STAY
Emeishan Hostel C: A good English-
speaking base camp before your trek, plus
storage for your heavier bags. **Hongchun-
ping Monastery:** Simple mid-mountain
accommodations elevated by the sacred
surroundings, and nearby Hard Wok Café.

♥ GET ROMANTIC
Engrave a lock with your names and fasten
it to the railings of Qingyin Pavilion. It's a
symbol of good luck and everlasting love.

✓ HONEYTREK TIP
Take the Baoguo Temple trail, ascending
from the west side for the most scenic
route. Give yourself two days to cover
the 36-mile trail, ending with a night at
the Golden Summit.

Beautiful yet mischievous Tibetan macaque monkey

COUPLES ADVENTURES

Baoguo Monastery ▲▲
Spend your first night in this Buddhist monastery at the base of Mount Emei. Wake up to the sounds of monks chanting during their sunrise ritual, wander the extensive 17th-century structures and gardens, stock up on water, and let the hiking commence!

Qingyin Pavilion ▲
Seven miles into the Baoguo Temple trail, a red pavilion with a swallowtail roof appears between two waterfalls, arced wooden bridges, and lush fir trees. *Tip:* For the best pictures of this Tang dynasty beauty, dip down to the riverbank.

Niuxin Pavilion to Xianfeng Temple ▲▲▲
Hang a left at the Qingyin Pavilion for the prettiest section of the trail. Walking the cliffside paths and suspension bridges of the Heilongjiang Plankway, past troops of Tibetan macaque monkeys, you'll reach the Jiu Lao Taoist caves, the beautifully maintained Xianfeng Temple, and dramatic limestone cliffs.

The Golden Summit ▲▲
Sitting atop sheer cliffs at around 10,000 feet, the site of the first-century temple is the spiritual and physical pinnacle of the trek. Watch the sunset shimmer off the gilded architecture, celebrate with a hearty meal at the Golden Summit Hotel, then wake up for sunrise and marvel at the sea of clouds rolling over the valley.

✣ Side Trip: Yangtze River Cruisin'

With the third longest river in the world just a few hours from Emeishan, we had to cruise a few of the Yangtze's 3,915 miles. And when we say "cruise," we mean on a triple-decker riverboat, complete with one karaoke parlor, four electronic mahjong tables, 498 Chinese tourists, and two Westerners. We joined the tour to experience the beauty of the Three Gorges, mountain pagodas, and unique history along this ancient trade route, but it turned out that spending time with the passengers was half the fun. Though we only met one other couple that spoke English, a combination of hand signals, Tsingtao beer, and endless smiles were enough to make a boatful of friends.

Impromptu mahjong lessons on a Yangtze cruise

TO EXPLORE MORE ON THIS CONTINENT, CHECK OUT:
» Rivers: Nam Ou River Valley, Laos...p. 60
» History: Fenghuang, China...p. 112

Shepherd Traditions

Hiking through the Andean villages, with houses made of stone and warmed by fire, we wondered if they would ever change. The residents know of the modern conveniences in the foothills, but the simple life has been thriving here for centuries. Next time we hike the trails of the Sacred Valley, we hope to meet this shepherd as a grown man, still contemplating the majesty of the mountains.

A young Andean shepherd along the Cachicata Trail, Peru

LAUTERBRUNNEN VALLEY

Switzerland

EUROPE

Lauterbrunnen Valley
SWITZERLAND

Where the Bernese Alps drip with 72 waterfalls and hand-carved chalets nestle in the cliffs, the Lauterbrunnen Valley appears as a Swiss fairy tale. Just an hour from the country's adrenaline capital of Interlaken, Lauterbrunnen's villages are hidden in one of the deepest and narrowest valleys in the European Alps and one of Switzerland's largest nature conservation areas. They are connected by cable cars, mountain railways, and footpaths, and are happily (if not deliberately) off the beaten track. Having turned away development opportunities for ski resorts and car-ready roads, many locals opt for a simpler life, and they savor it with a glass of Chasselas wine and a pot of fondue. As they say, "If heaven isn't what it's cracked up to be, send me back to Gimmelwald." Among the plethora of picturesque villages are Mürren, Stechelberg, and Lauterbrunnen itself, with the 13,642-foot Jungfrau peak as their loftiest neighbor. Traveling from one cliff town to the next can be thrill enough, though it's easy to amplify your mountain high with paragliding, BASE jumping, and other wild rides.

WHEN TO GO
The valley is ablaze with flowers in May, and hiking is fantastic until October.

WHERE TO STAY
Hotel Staubbach: A traditional B&B in Lauterbrunnen village with spacious rooms and hearty breakfast. **Hotel Alpenruh:** In the carless hamlet of Mürren, this mid-priced chalet gives you the Alpine village experience and access to top adventures.

GET ROMANTIC
Play James and Bond girl with sunset martinis at the Schilthorn mountain's revolving restaurant. As seen in the film *On Her Majesty's Secret Service,* the Piz Gloria also serves stunning views of the many mountain peaks and gleaming glaciers.

HONEYTREK TIP
Fill your rucksack with regional delicacies for spontaneous mountaintop picnics. You'll get the best views at the best lunch prices in Switzerland.

Timeless villages nestle into the Lauterbrunnen Valley.

House-proud locals vie for the most beautiful garden.

COUPLES ADVENTURES

Climb the Via Ferrata ▲▲▲▲
Get geared up in Mürren, then scale the series of iron rungs, pegs, ladders, and bridges to the ultra-charming Gimmelwald (sounds crazy but it's a classic way to get between steep Alpine villages). Along the 1.4-mile route on the Lauterbrunnen Wall, stop at the platforms to watch the BASE jumpers take flight from 1,200 feet.

Paraglide the Peaks ▲▲▲▲
Soar past the Schilthorn, taking in epic views of the Jungfrau, Eiger, and Mönch mountains, not to mention the French Alps and Germany's Black Forest. No windows, no doors, no motors, just the crisp updraft and wind in your hair.

Enter Trümmelbach Falls ▲
Millennia of glacial runoff has burrowed its way in and out of a Lauterbrunnen mountain via this 10-part waterfall. To access the circuitous cascades,

✣ The BASE Jumper Bar
Adjacent to the Staubbach Falls in Lauterbrunnen, the Horner Pub seemed like a quaint place for a pint. We opened the carved door and a dozen boisterous dudes, a few of them with crutches and casts, filled the traditional Swiss tavern. Overhearing stories about parachute malfunctions and near misses with cliffs, we soon realized it was the eve of the World Wingsuit Championships and clinked glasses with the craziest of bar mates.

Cows grazing between mountain villages

Swiss engineers have built a veritable labyrinth inside the walls of the slot canyon, allowing you to catch a new vista with every twist and turn.

Overnight in Timeless Obersteinberg ▲▲
From Stechelberg, hike two hours along the river Lütschine and hanging glaciers until you reach Obersteinberg Lodge, a 19th-century chalet frozen in time. Enjoy farm-fresh cuisine with views of a 1,000-foot waterfall, then cozy up by candlelight (the only illumination available). For an extended hike, begin or return via the charming Gimmelwald or Mürren.

TO EXPLORE MORE ON THIS CONTINENT, CHECK OUT:
» **At Sea: Norwegian Fjords, Norway...p. 136**
» **Road Trips: Central Georgia...p. 210**

Mount Rainier's summertime wildflower spectacular

MOUNT RAINIER
U.S.A.

NORTH
AMERICA
□ **Mt. Rainier**
UNITED
STATES

One of the most dangerous volcanoes in the world is also one of Washington State's most irresistible attractions. Warnings be damned, when the clouds vanish from the 14,410-foot peak and the sun shimmers off its two dozen glaciers, Mount Rainier beckons all nature lovers to its slopes. Day hikers, mountaineers, backcountry skiers, bird-watchers, and botanists can find plenty of adventures in this national park, just two hours southeast of Seattle. Rainier has two main access points: Sunrise and Paradise. Paradise is one of the snowiest places on Earth, averaging 54 feet annually. From November through May, snowshoeing, AT skiing, and sledding opportunities abound. Come July, wildflowers burst onto the scene in a riot of color, waterfalls gush, and temperate rain forests evoke spellbinding hikes. Trek the legendary Wonderland Trail, or enjoy an easy loop around an island of 1,000-year-old trees. You won't find revolving restaurants or alpine slides on Rainier, but you will find pure beauty left wild.

WHEN TO GO

The full park is open from July–September, while snow bunnies can romp around Paradise year-round.

WHERE TO STAY

Paradise Inn: A historic hotel, as close you can get to the peak without a tent. **Packwood Lodge:** Recently renovated and just four miles from the park's southeast entrance.

GET ROMANTIC

Road-trip to Crystal Mountain for stunning views of Mount St. Helens and Glacier Peak, then ride the gondola to Summit House restaurant or enjoy a picnic at Suntop Lookout.

HONEYTREK TIP

To beat the Seattle day-trippers, visit midweek and start your long hikes at dawn and your short hikes mid-afternoon.

Sunbeam Falls flowing from the glaciated Rainier

COUPLES ADVENTURES

Wonderland Trail ▲▲▲▲▲

Follow the glacial valleys and volcanic ridges around Mount Rainier for an epic 93-mile trek. The 22,000 feet of elevation change ushers you from temperate rain forest to high alpine meadows, to cascading waterfalls, to snowfields, to a Technicolor dreamcoat of flowers.

Grove of the Patriarchs ▲

The Ohanapecosh River saved this island from centuries of wildfires, leaving many trees to grow to a ripe old age of 1,000 years. Cross the suspension bridge and stroll the 1.5-mile loop in the company of ancient Douglas firs, red cedars, and western hemlocks. Continue hiking to Stevens Canyon Road to see the glorious Silver Falls.

Skyline Trail ▲▲▲

To get the big mountain experience on a time crunch, this 5.5-mile loop gives you Rainier's craggy slopes, Nisqually Glacier, the rugged Tatoosh peaks,

✢ Surprise Sledding

It was a sunny spring day and the Skyline Trail was calling our name. With our sneakers laced tight, we followed the path, though it quickly vanished under a blanket of snow. Burly men in backcountry ski gear swooshed past us, further affirming how unprepared we were. We climbed the bootpack trail, sinking knee-deep every few steps. When we reached Panorama Point, we clinked our water bottles in a victorious toast, then contemplated how the heck we were getting down. Our only option was to make a sled with our jackets and giggle our way home.

Marmots are common—especially at lunchtime.

and views all the way to Oregon's Mount Hood. Stop for a picnic at Panorama Point, keeping an eye out for cheeky marmots, and dip down to the photogenic Myrtle Falls before returning to Paradise.

Snowshoe Slumber Party ▲▲▲

Snowshoe or cross-country ski into the evening on the groomed Mount Tahoma Hut-to-Hut Trail System. Spend the night cooking in an equipped cabin or yurt, cuddling by the fireplace, and waking up in bed to snowy views. Continue on this 50-mile network, or just hibernate for a few days. Also open in the summer.

TO EXPLORE MORE ON THIS CONTINENT, CHECK OUT:

» **Rain Forests: Olympic Peninsula, U.S.A....p. 188**

» **Road Trips: The Southwest, U.S.A....p. 206**

Hiking to see the golden monkeys of Volcanoes National Park

VIRUNGA MOUNTAINS

Rwanda

BY BRET LOVE & MARY GABBETT

AFRICA

RWANDA□ **Virunga Mountains**

When you're surrounded by the majestic Virunga Mountains—a chain of towering volcanic peaks straddling the border of Uganda and the Democratic Republic of the Congo—you can see why Rwanda's nickname is "the land of a thousand hills." The East African nation is widely known for its devastating 1994 genocide, which left over 800,000 Tutsis and sympathetic Hutus dead after decades of civil unrest. But Rwanda has undergone a radical transformation, with increased political stabilization, dramatic infrastructure improvements, and economic growth fueled by its burgeoning ecotourism industry. Most travelers come to see the critically endangered mountain gorillas. Nine hundred remain in the wild, half of which are in Rwanda's Volcanoes National Park. These dynamic landscapes, stretching from Lake Kivu in the south to Uganda's Lake Edward in the north, rank among the most beautiful we've ever seen, offering plenty more adventures for active travelers and nature lovers.

WHEN TO GO

The long dry season from June–September is the most popular time to visit. Try the shorter dry season from December–February to avoid crowds.

WHERE TO STAY

Sabyinyo Silverback Lodge: Five-star service that benefits local socioeconomic projects. **Mountain Gorilla View Lodge:** Prime location offering stunning Virunga vistas, plus live entertainment and budget-friendly pricing.

GET ROMANTIC

Watch a mountain sunset through massive picture windows while savoring drinks by the fireplace in your cozy room.

GREEN GLOBAL TRAVEL TIP

When you reserve your trekking guide, ask for Francois Bigirimana. He's the oldest ranger in the park, worked as a porter for Dian Fossey, and is every bit as entertaining as the mountain gorillas.

COUPLES ADVENTURES

Gorilla Trek Volcanoes Park ▲▲▲

Hikes to see the 10 mountain gorilla families range from moderate to difficult, and from one to three hours each way. Reaching a clearing in the dense forest and finding yourself surrounded by mamas, babies, and massive silverbacks is an experience you'll never forget.

Commune With Endangered Golden Monkeys ▲▲

Found only in the Virunga Mountains, these endangered Old World monkeys can be reached via an easy hike through gorgeous fields of pyrethrum flowers. Marvel at the social groups feasting on bamboo shoots and scampering through the treetops.

Iby'Iwacu Cultural Village ▲

Founded by a former game warden, this entertaining introduction to Rwanda's traditional cultures provides alternative employment opportunities for ex-poachers and their families. You'll get to be king/queen for a day, practice archery, grind grains, and participate in a mock wedding.

Hike to Dian Fossey's Grave ▲▲▲▲

Found at the site of her scientific base (called Karisoke for its location between Mount Karisimbi and Mount Visoke), Fossey's final resting place is noted by a simple marker and surrounded by the graves of her beloved gorillas. The arduous trek takes three to four hours, giving a greater appreciation for her trailblazing work.

⁜ Couples Advice

We believe that balance is what makes relationships last. Try to plan itineraries that appeal to your disparate interests in equal measure, with active adventures offset by pampering and cultural immersion. Bret is wilder and likes to explore nature, while Mary loves a little luxury and R & R. In the end, the diversity of activities makes our travels—and us, as people—more well rounded.

A young mountain gorilla at the lush Mount Sabyinyo

TO EXPLORE MORE ON THIS CONTINENT, CHECK OUT:

» Islands: Zanzibar, Tanzania...p. 72

» On Safari: Samburu, Kenya...p. 94

POWER COUPLE: *Bret & Mary*

This American couple launched *GreenGlobal Travel.com* in 2010 to share their love of ecotourism adventures, inspire people to travel and live more sustainably, and encourage everyone to do their part to make the world a better place. They also freelance for such organizations as National Geographic, Marriott and Hilton Hotels, and a host of other outlets.

URUBAMBA VALLEY

Peru

The heartland of the Inca Empire, a cordillera of glacier-capped peaks, and Andean culture at its finest, the Sacred Valley is the feather in Peru's llama-wool cap.

Reaching Machu Picchu is on nearly every traveler's bucket list, though this fixation with the "Lost City of the Inca" often obscures the beauty beyond the 15th-century citadel. Fortresses, temples, and historic towns are peppered throughout the valley and connected by a vast network of trails. Build anticipation for Machu Picchu with a couple days acclimatizing in the UNESCO-noted city of Cusco, then begin a multiday hike on an alternative Inca trail. Most hikers will be on the stone-paved "Classic Inca Trail" with a few thousand companions, but you can follow ancient messenger paths and aqueducts, exploring little-known ruins and villages among the 20,000-foot peaks. Traditional Andean culture emerges with farmers hand-tilling quinoa fields, women spinning llama wool, and horses hauling the day's potato harvest. After your intimate journey through the Sacred Valley, Machu Picchu will be even more spectacular.

WHEN TO GO
Visit April–June or September–October to avoid the bulk of rain and tourists.

WHERE TO STAY
Andenes al Cielo: A colonial mansion a short walk from Cusco's Plaza de Armas. **Inkaterra Machu Picchu:** A National Geographic Unique Lodge of the World, built in Andean-village style above Aguas Calientes. **Andean Treks:** Guiding excellent multiday hikes to Machu Picchu since 1980, including the under-the-radar Cachicata (aka Moonstone) Trail.

GET ROMANTIC
Stroll outside bustling Aguas Calientes to the serene Mandor Gardens. Enjoy the waterfalls, butterflies, orchids, and birdlife, followed by an early dinner at Mama Angelica restaurant.

HONEYTREK TIP
Although it's possible to see some excellent sites without the Boleto Turistico, 16 of the area's greatest highlights require this ticket. Spring for it.

Inti Punku ruins before the 19,334-foot Mount Veronica

One of Andean Treks' incredible team of porters

COUPLES ADVENTURES

Moonstone to Sun Temple Trek ▲▲▲▲

Traveling for three days along the Inca messenger trails, you will discover forgotten temples, quarries, and aqueducts. Pass through authentic Andean villages in the shadow of glaciated peaks. The Cachicata Trail ends in Ollantaytambo, where the scenic train will lead you to Aguas Calientes, the gateway to Machu Picchu.

Ollantaytambo Citadel ▲

Anchored by one the Inca's most important fortresses and temples, this Andean town is full of history and charm. Wander about the 15th-century dwellings (among the oldest in South America), explore the cliffside citadel, and hike to the Pinkuylluna granaries for the best view of town.

Summit Huayna Picchu Peak ▲▲▲

The most exhilarating hike with the best views of Machu Picchu can be found with this 1,000-foot

ascent. Rock-carved stairs, ropes, and tunnels wind up the pointy mountain to the former domain of the high priest.

Salinas Salt Pans ▲▲

Covering a mountain in a patchwork of milky pools and crystallized walls, these salt pans have been in use since Inca times. Under the shade of wide-brimmed hats and traditional dress, locals extract the salt by hand and give a glimpse into a centuries-old tradition.

✣ Feast From the Land

We set up camp below the snow-dusted Urubamba range. When the sun set, the only light remaining was from the star-filled sky and earth oven. Lamb and vegetables from a local shepherd were roasting under the hot stones and wild grasses. The chill at 15,000 feet and aches from two days on the trail quickly faded with the taste of the most succulent dinner, fit for an Inca emperor.

A whirligig flower along the trail

TO EXPLORE MORE ON THIS CONTINENT, CHECK OUT:

» Lakes: Lake Titicaca, Bolivia & Peru...p. 52
» Rain Forests: Yasuní, Ecuador...p. 192

The Paine massif and its spiky Cuernos (horns)

TORRES DEL PAINE

Chile

SOUTH AMERICA

CHILE

Torres del Paine

At the tip of South America where ice fields meet subpolar forests, windblown steppe, and saw-tooth peaks, Patagonia is the continent's grand finale. The star of the Chilean side is undoubtedly the 700-square-mile Torres del Paine National Park and UNESCO Biosphere Reserve. Enter from Punta Arenas or Puerto Natales, and follow the tangled grasses of the Patagonia steppe, looking for long-lashed guanacos and soaring Andean condors, until you reach mountains that break the mold. As if sculpted by the hands of a giant, the Paine massif (mountain range) is squeezed and smashed into craggy peaks, raw valleys, and deep lakes. The Torres, three sheer granite monoliths tucked in the center of the cordillera, have all hikers fantasizing about their approach, be it the iconic W Trek along French Valley and Grey Glacier, the 80-mile Q circuit, or straight up the moraine to the Mirador Las Torres. Push yourself to hike higher, paddle harder, ride farther. Mountain terrain doesn't get much better than this.

WHEN TO GO
Brisk Patagonia's warmer months are November–April; be prepared for four seasons in a day.

WHERE TO STAY
EcoCamp: Luxurious geodesic domes with Torres views, excellent cuisine, and guiding services. **Hostería Pehoé:** A surprisingly well-priced B&B on an island, surrounded by Lake Pehoé and the Paine peaks.

GET ROMANTIC
Find a spot in the grassy pampas, lay down blankets, and find fantastical forms in the clouds—a spouting whale, fluffy pancakes, the Starship *Enterprise*. Torres del Paine's lenticular clouds offer the perfect opportunity to dream and cuddle.

HONEYTREK TIP
Give your trip itinerary a two-day buffer. Distances are vast, the weather is highly unpredictable, and the park is more beautiful than you can imagine.

The fortress of glacial ice on Grey Lake

COUPLES ADVENTURES

Kayak Grey Lake ▲▲▲
Paddle between blue icebergs toward Grey Glacier, a craggy two-mile-wide and 100-foot-high face of the Southern Patagonian Ice Field. Head back to the beach for a hot cocoa or continue down the Grey River rapids to Serrano Village.

The "O" Circuit ▲▲▲▲▲
Encompassing the famed W Trek, and continuing around the entire glaciated massif and dramatically ending with sunrise at the Torres, this less traveled route will take your breath away for eight days straight.

Trailblaze by Horseback ▲▲
Explore like the Chilean cowboys of yore with a sunset ride to Cerro Paine or gallop from estancia to estancia across Torres del Paine and Bernardo O'Higgins National Park. Going beyond the roads

and trails, a Criollo horse will bring you to rarely seen landscapes.

Shortcut to Las Torres ▲▲▲
If a multiday camping expedition isn't your bag, try the five-mile Mirador Trail to the base of the Torres. Zigzagging up the moraine and rock scrambling to a hidden glacial lake, the sheer, soaring peaks will satisfy your Paine dreams.

✛ A Toast to Maté

Every Patagonia hiker carries water, snacks, and a raincoat, but a true Chilean hiker? A full maté tea set. We sat in the sunlight peeking between the Torres while our guide Rafael pulled out his thermos, gourd cup, and bag of yerba maté. Once the leaves were packed and steeped, he spun the cup and offered us a sip through the metal straw (as is customary among friends in Chile and Argentina). Sharing the caffeine-charged liquid at the pinnacle of the Paine cordillera was the Patagonian equivalent to popping champagne.

Mike sipping maté at the Mirador Las Torres

TO EXPLORE MORE ON THIS CONTINENT, CHECK OUT:
» Deserts: Atacama Desert, Chile...p. 154
» Ice: Los Glaciares, Argentina...p. 174

Hiking the volcanic Tongariro Alpine Crossing, New Zealand

Unbelievable Day Hikes

Treks of a lifetime that will have you home before dinner

NEW ZEALAND

1. Tongariro Alpine Crossing

With river valleys, fiery red craters, twin emerald lakes, and the "Mount Doom" volcano featured in *The Lord of the Rings* movies, this 12-miler through New Zealand's oldest national park is worthy of a hiking Academy Award.

U.S.A.

2. Humuʻula–Mauna Kea Summit Trail

If measured from its base (at the floor of the Pacific) to its peak, this Hawaiian mountain is 33,474 feet, 13,796 of which is above sea level. Tackle 4,600 feet of this dormant volcano with a full-day hike. Extra motivation: One of the world's leading astronomical sites is at the summit.

NORWAY

3. Trolltunga

Translating to "troll's tongue," this cliff sticks out over Lake Ringedalsvatnet with nothing below it for some 3,600 feet. Trek seven miles, past lakes, fjords, and glacier-topped mountains and pose for an iconic adventure travel photo.

JAPAN

4. Subashiri Trail

Take the path less traveled up Mount Fuji, Japan's highest point and national symbol. Start the nine-mile trek in the evening, enjoying views of the forests, lakes, and Tokyo city lights. Reenergize with a bowl of *udon* noodles and a midnight nap at the seventh station. Then, summit for dawn over the Land of the Rising Sun.

NICARAGUA

5. Maderas Volcano

Twin volcanoes rise out of Lake Nicaragua, creating Ometepe Island and a premier hiking destination. Both are challenging, while Maderas volcano is the more diverse pick with coffee plantations, petroglyphs, cloud forests, and a swimmable crater lake on top.

ITALY

6. Puez-Odle Altopiano

The chiseled Dolomites have a bounty of hut-to-hut hiking, but if you only have a day, you can still experience some of the highest peaks in the Southern Limestone Alps. Take the 12-mile route to the Puez Refuge, where you will be served 360-degree views with a side of apple strudel.

SOUTH AFRICA

7. Sentinel Peak Hike

Follow the sheer Amphitheatre cliffs and climb Mont-Aux-Sources via chain ladders. Explore the flat-top peak and peer over Tugela Falls, one the world's tallest at 3,110 feet.

U.S.A.

8. Cascade Canyon Trail to Lake Solitude

The magnificence of the 480-square-mile Grand Teton National Park comes to a head in this 16-mile hike. Passing through pristine ecosystems, with species dating to prehistoric times, this trail passes gorgeous lakes, waterfalls, and views to the Cathedral Group.

EYGPT

9. Mount Sinai

Whatever your religious beliefs, everyone can appreciate this holy hike's history and beauty. Three hours before dawn, ascend from one of the world's longest running monasteries and up the Steps of Penitence (hand-carved by monks). At the peak, sit before the mosque and church for sunrise views over the desert of biblical proportions.

CANADA

10. Rockbound Lake

As Canada's oldest park, Banff has perfected the art of hiking trails, with Rockbound among its finest. The winding path through the Rockies brings you to the Castle Mountain headwall: cliffs wrapping around a teal lake with views across the park.

Uros Islands, Peru

Chapter Two

LAKES, RIVERS & FALLS

Freshwater is the source of life that has drawn people to lakes and rivers since the dawn of time. Everything gets a little easier when you've got plenty to drink, fresh fish, a cool spot to take a dip, and a boat to paddle into the sunset. Water relaxes us, but it just as easily offers thrills. It is no coincidence that places deemed "the adventure capital" (. . . of Ecuador . . . of Africa . . . of the world!) are often found alongside rivers or lakes. Canyoneering, tidal-bore surfing, jetboating, and river rafting require a rush of freshwater. Waterfalls have a romantic side as well, with mist that brings exotic flowers, rainbows, and love-struck couples. Even small falls set the mood, so when they are the scale of Iguazú and Victoria Falls, sparks will fly. Sail the islands of Lake Titicaca, sleep on a private sampan in the Mekong Delta, hike the 100 waterfalls of Nam Ou, and maybe even tap your fountain of youth.

A fraction of the falls at the thunderous Iguazú

IGUAZÚ FALLS
Argentina & Brazil

SOUTH
AMERICA
BRAZIL
ARGENTINA
☐ Iguazú
Falls

Not just a waterfall—275 individual cascades, stretching nearly two miles. Iguazú Falls is more than a sight to see; it's a destination to be explored. Sure, Angel Falls in Venezuela is taller and Victoria has a wider single fall, but Iguazú wins for complexity and elements of surprise. Spanning Brazil and Argentina, the falls are divided by the Devil's Throat: a 269-by-492-foot chasm devouring 50 percent of the river's volume. The force pulverizes the water into a fine mist that not only creates countless rainbows but also a unique microclimate for exotic flora and fauna: toucans, caimans, jaguars, and more than 2,000 plant species. Begin your visit on the Brazil side for the best overall vista of the falls. Explore their paths for a few hours, then rest up for a big day (or two) on the Argentina side, home to 80 percent of the falls. Wander the extensive rain forest trails, brave a wet and wild Zodiac ride, and revel in the largest waterfall system in the world.

⬚ WHEN TO GO
After the October–March rainy season, April–June is the sweet spot for abundant falls, flora, and sunshine.

⬚ WHERE TO STAY
Boutique Hotel de la Fonte: Affordable luxury in Puerto Iguazú, Argentina's closest town to the falls. **Sheraton Iguazú:** The only hotel within Argentina's national park is a bit dated but worth the price.

♡ GET ROMANTIC
Hike through the rain forest to Arrechea Waterfall. Your three-mile trek will be rewarded with a peaceful swimming hole far from crowds.

☑ HONEYTREK TIP
Stamp your ticket before you leave the park and your second day will be half price. Staying at the Sheraton? They'll cover days three and four.

A toco toucan along the trails of the Upper Circuit

COUPLES ADVENTURES

Hike the Full Circuit ▲▲
Savor your visit by avoiding the trams and exploring this rare rain forest. Take the Green Trail to the Lower Circuit; it weaves through eight different lookouts, each revealing something new. Meander your way to the Upper Circuit, noticing the river-ravaged bridges and countless orchids, and walk the rim for jaw-dropping views.

Zodiac to the Falls ▲▲▲▲
With approximately 3.4 million gallons of water falling each second, the Devil's Throat doesn't seem like a logical place for a pleasure cruise. Tell your sensible side to take a backseat—on a 30-person Zodiac as it zips around the white water of Isla San Martín and into the eye of Iguazú's storm. Getting absolutely drenched, you'll squeal, giggle, and never forget these 15 minutes.

Full Moon Walking Tour ▲▲
In Iguazú, rainbows can defy darkness. For five nights around each full moon, park rangers lead

✧ Brazil Border Crossing

How we wish there was a scenic footpath over the Iguazú River from Argentina to Brazil. But alas, there's a highway with border patrol and a $35 to $160 visa (depending on your nationality). If you have the means, it's worth traveling to Brazil's national park. Ways to cross the border for a day:

1. Apply for a Brazilian visa in your home country (about two weeks).
2. Get a visa from the Brazilian Embassy in Puerto Iguazú, Argentina (about two hours).
3. Take your chances. Taxis and buses are sometimes waved across without stops for visa checks. If your heart is set on seeing Foz do Iguaçu, spring for the visa.

Straddling the border of Brazil and Argentina

walks from the rain forest to the Devil's Throat. Watch the colors shimmer off the falls, and toast your first moonbow with a complimentary cocktail. Reserve your spot in advance; add dinner at La Selva Restaurant and you can stay an extra hour in the heart of the park.

TO EXPLORE MORE ON THIS CONTINENT, CHECK OUT:
» Dunes: Jericoacoara, Brazil...p. 150
» Ice: Los Glaciares, Argentina...p. 174

INLE LAKE
Myanmar

ASIA

Inle Lake

MYANMAR

Forget the vacation homes and water sports of typical lakes, Inle offers something far more intriguing—a trip into the past. For nearly 50 years, Myanmar (also known as Burma) was under a military dictatorship and virtually closed to tourism. Sheltered from modernization, the people of Inle carried on traditions that continue to this day, living in stilted bamboo homes, farming with the power of water buffalo, hand-weaving vibrant textiles, and canoeing in the truly unique and graceful Inle style (standing at the bow and rowing with one leg). The country opened up in 2011, and although this region is quickly becoming a coveted travel destination, its thousand-year-old rituals are blissfully slow to change. Nyaungshwe is Inle's main travel hub with the bus station, harbor, guesthouses, bike shops, and so on. Base camp here to explore the area on your own, or check into one of the countryside inns for lake views and concierge service. Bike along the vibrant canals, spend time in the floating villages (Myanmar people are among the friendliest in the world), and hire a local boat captain to navigate 45 square miles of waterways and soak up a fascinating culture.

WHEN TO GO
Visit October–February to avoid monsoon season and the hottest weather. For flowers in full bloom and the annual Phaung Daw Oo Pagoda Festival, go in October.

WHERE TO STAY
Pristine Lotus Spa: Chic lakeside suites and duplexes floating on the water.
Nawng Kham, The Little Inn: A simple, budget-friendly downtown guesthouse with inviting outdoor space.

GET ROMANTIC
Enjoy dinner and a surprisingly good wine tasting at Red Mountain Estate Vineyards. Just before sunset, stroll through the vines, then find a table at their open-air restaurant.

HONEYTREK TIP
Ask your boat captain to steer away from the standard tourist stops at the umbrella factory, silver shops, and "Jumping Cat Monastery" (don't ask). Spend more time at the Five-Day Market, Shwe Indein Pagoda, and enjoying the serenity of the lake.

A fisherman rowing in classic Inle style

The countless stupas of Shwe Indein Pagoda

COUPLES ADVENTURES

Private Boat Tour ▲
Hire a captain at the docks for a sunrise departure. Watch the mist rise off the lake and the ballet-like rowing of Inle's fisherman. Be sure to stop at Inn Paw Khon village to see some of Myanmar's best weavers and catch the end of the rotating Five-Day Market (watching the dynamic hill tribes pack up their boats was our favorite part), then slow-cruise until sunset.

Shwe Indein Pagoda ▲
High above the lake, more than 1,000 majestic stupas are packed onto one little hill. Hike around the dazzling collection of 14th- to 18th-century ruins and the adjacent temple-topped mountain. Try to time your visit with Indein's incredible weekly market for a half-day visit. If you're tight for time, combine Indein with your all-day lake tour (it's 45 minutes up the scenic creek so you'll have to persuade your captain).

Bike Along the Lake ▲▲
Exploring by bicycle opens a window into the daily life of the local residents. Pedaling southeast from Nyaungshwe reveals scenes of farmers hand-watering their cabbages, women doing road construction dressed in elegant *longyis,* and brewmasters stirring their sugarcane cauldrons. Ride about six miles until you reach the village of Maing Thauk (you'll see an exceptionally long footbridge). Stop for lunch at a floating café, and then catch a boat across the lake.

✥ Words of Wisdom

We've never met friendlier people than in Myanmar. Kids and grandmas alike will blow kisses as you pass by, strangers will invite you for tea, and proud locals will show you their town in exchange for nothing but company. Learning a bit of their language helps foster these connections. Here are few phrases to start you off:

Hello: *Min ga la ba.*
How are you?: *Nei kaung la?*
Fine, thank you: *Ne kaon ba de.*
What is your name?: *Na meh be lou kor d'le?*
Pleased to meet you: *Tway ya da wanta ba de.*
Your food is delicious: *Thate koun ta be.*
Thank you: *Kyei zu tin ba de.*

A market vendor giving Anne a *thanaka* makeover

TO EXPLORE MORE ON THIS CONTINENT, CHECK OUT:
» Architecture: Bagan, Myanmar...p. 106
» Rain Forests: Khao Sok, Thailand...p. 182

Volcano view from our bungalow at Bahía Zapatera, Nicaragua

Power of the Lake

Few make it to Lake Nicaragua's second biggest island. Once the spiritual home to the Chorotega Indians and private getaway for the Chamorro-Cordova political dynasty, Isla Zapatera seemed untouchable—until recently. Done with politics, Rafael Cordova decided to share this magical isle with travelers. He showed us the crater lagoon, hidden petroglyphs, and artifacts he found as a child. Swinging in the hammocks of Bahía Zapatera, we felt we'd discovered a secret national treasure.

Mount Calvario offers one of Copacabana's best views

LAKE TITICACA
Bolivia & Peru

The spiritual birthplace of the mighty Inca, Lake Titicaca is one of the largest lakes in South America and is often celebrated as the highest navigable body of water in the world. The Inca arrived in the 15th century, though indigenous cultures have thrived here for millennia. Both the Peruvian and Bolivian sides beg to be explored with hikes through the ruins, a homestay with an indigenous family, and a sailboat trip to secluded beaches. Puno, Peru, is the tourism hub, but we suggest basing camp in the quirky colonial town of Copacabana, Bolivia. Its energy radiates from the tiled-dome basilica (just wait until you see the daily Blessing of the Vehicles) and trickles down to the lakeshore with painted fishing boats, fresh ceviche stands, and Bolivian women out for a stroll in their bowler caps and petticoats. Get your bearings with a hike up Copacabana's Mount Calvario for views to the city, snow-kissed mountains, rugged isles, and the lake's endless expanse. After a day or two in town, head to the islands for an unforgettable cultural journey.

PERU □ BOLIVIA
Lake Titicaca
SOUTH AMERICA

⊠ WHEN TO GO
The warmest and driest season is May–September, with temperatures in the 60s by day and 20s by night. At 12,500 feet in elevation, an alpaca sweater is your friend.

🏨 WHERE TO STAY
Rosario Lago Titicaca: A contemporary hotel with dashes of Bolivian decor and plenty of Western amenities. **La Cúpula:** A 17-room B&B with whimsical architecture and a central location—for a steal.

♥ GET ROMANTIC
Embark on a half-day boat trip and relax on secluded beaches with Inka Sailing's charters. They'll pack the bottle of cava; you just drink in the scenery.

✅ HONEYTREK TIP
Immerse yourself in the indigenous cultures with an overnight homestay. Prepare for rustic accommodations and enjoy.

Rower moving between the Uros floating islands

Cars decked out with streamers, confetti, hats, and toys lined up before Our Lady of Copacabana Basilica. Drivers had come to ask the patron saint of Bolivia to bless their journeys along the treacherous mountain roads. A priest approached a minivan with holy water. He sprinkled some on the engine, all four sides of the vehicle, and the driver. Family members cheered, set off firecrackers, and sprayed the hood with Coca-Cola (everyman's champagne). The priest continued to the next car, one of dozens in the day's Bendición de Movilidades, and he'd return tomorrow for this uniquely Bolivian ritual.

An Andean priest blesses a minivan's future journeys

COUPLES ADVENTURES

Hike Isla del Sol ▲▲▲
Explore the 80-some ruins scattered across this sacred Inca island. Store your bags in Copacabana and pack just enough to overnight and picnic, then board the water taxi to Yumani. Hike south to north along the five-mile trail, passing traditional villages, pristine beaches, and sites like Puma Rock and the Temple of the Sun. Finish in Challapampa for a hearty meal, sound sleep, and the return ferry.

Cruise the Uros Floating Islands ▲
Built entirely out of totora reeds and rope, these islands were handmade by the Uros people as a means to escape Inca rule. They have retained their rare architectural traditions and proudly share them with visitors today. This multi-island boat trip, albeit touristy, is too picturesque to miss.

Overnight at Taquile Island ▲▲▲
Spend the night with the Taquileño people, an inviting community famous for their UNESCO-recognized textiles. Homestay accommodations are bare bones (don't expect electricity), though the experience provides a valuable look into their craft, cuisine, and day-to-day life. Hike pre-Inca ruin by day and stay up for incredible stargazing.

TO EXPLORE MORE ON THIS CONTINENT, CHECK OUT:

» **Mountains: Urubamba Valley, Peru...p. 38**
» **Supernatural: Department of Potosí, Bolivia...p. 220**

LIVINGSTONE
Zambia

AFRICA

ZAMBIA
Livingstone

Maybe it's the waterfall's relentless roar or its spray, which can be felt for miles, but everything is more exciting around Victoria Falls. Cutting between the countries of Zimbabwe and Zambia, the Zambezi River spans 5,604 feet and plummets 354 feet, creating one the world's largest falls and a jaw-dropping landscape with exotic wildlife, tropical flowers, and plunging gorges. It takes the name of the 19th-century Queen of England, though we prefer the local Tonga name, the "Smoke That Thunders." Unlike most falls where you see them in one shot, this one reveals itself a little more with each adventure—river rafting, microlight flights, cliff hikes, and a death-defying plunge in the Devil's Pool. Head upstream and the landscape changes from lush rain forest to woodland savanna with roaming elephants, giraffes, zebras, and an occasional lion—be it on a game drive in Mosi-oa-Tunya National Park or canoeing the upper river. End each day sipping a sundowner and tasting the flavors of Africa at a riverside restaurant or floating dining room. Livingstone may be wild, but it has no shortage of luxury.

WHEN TO GO
April–August is your best bet for enjoying gushing falls, abundant wildlife sightings, and pleasant temperatures.

WHERE TO STAY
Tongabezi Lodge: Part luxury ecolodge, part adventure outfitter, and entirely amazing. **The Royal Livingstone:** Classic colonial hotel and the closest to the edge of the falls.

GET ROMANTIC
Spring for private dining on a lantern-lit sampan boat. If you are at Tongabezi, an African choir can serenade you over dessert.

HONEYTREK TIP
Spend some time upriver to avoid the crowds and experience the serene side of the Zambezi. Island-hop by canoe and be sure to stock it with Mosi Lager, fishing rods, and binoculars for hippo sightings.

Victoria Falls spanning Zimbabwe (left) and Zambia (right)

An African elephant along our Zambezi canoe route

COUPLES ADVENTURES

Knife-Edge Bridge ▲
Walk the path parallel to the 5,604-foot-wide sheet of water. Put on your raincoat and giggle through the spray and rainbows at one of the Seven Natural Wonders of the World.

Take to the Sky ▲▲▲▲
Hang glider meets go-cart, a microlight aircraft can swoop you over the falls, providing the ultimate aerial perspective of both the Zambia and Zimbabwe sides (without an extra visa).

Livingstone Island ▲▲▲
Take a speedboat to the famed isle at the precipice of the falls. Hold hands as you wade through the water, getting as close to the edge as you dare, and feel the "Smoke That Thunders." *Tip:* Sign up for the last trip of the day to enjoy sunset views and cocktail service.

✦ Don't Look Before You Leap

We were strapped together for the Zambezi Gorge Swing, poised to plummet 155 feet, then swing like a pendulum at 100 miles an hour. We shuffled to the edge of the platform. "One, two . . ." our heels inched farther, ". . . three . . . JUMP!" I hesitated, but forgot that I was attached to Mike, who was falling fast. That half-second delay sent us careening sideways toward the bottom of the rocky riverbed. Screams poured out of us—mine a cry of certain death, Mike's of complete elation. As the swinging subsided, I couldn't help but squeal and giggle along with him. Locking eyes, overjoyed to have escaped the Reaper, we kissed uncontrollably. The gorge swing wasn't so bad after all.

Mike's microlight flight over Victoria Falls

Safari in Mosi-oa-Tunya National Park ▲▲
Take a game drive through the palm-speckled grassland for the opportunity to see elephant river crossings, warthog chases, grazing zebras, and leaping impalas. Self-drive the circular route, opt for an organized tour, or combine a drive with a walking safari among rhinos for extra-close encounters.

....

TO EXPLORE MORE ON THIS CONTINENT, CHECK OUT:
» **On Safari: South Luangwa, Zambia...p. 98**
» **Deserts: Namib Desert, Namibia...p. 152**

Gutenfels Castle towers over the village of Kaub am Rhein.

RHINE GORGE
Germany

BY AUDREY SCOTT & DANIEL NOLL

EUROPE

Rhine □ GERMANY
Gorge

The Rhine River has been a coveted trade route since the Roman Empire. Throughout the centuries, many towns and castles developed along its shores to manufacture goods and protect this vital thoroughfare. Although the region's role in trade has diminished, the medieval towns and vineyard villages are teeming with culture and adventure.

The Rhine Gorge (aka Upper Middle Rhine Valley) between Rüdesheim and Koblenz has been recognized as a UNESCO site for its historical, cultural, and geographical importance. Half-timbered homes line cobblestone streets, vineyard paths wind into the hills, and castles tower over both sides of the river, all begging to be explored. You'll be drawn to the charming central squares of villages like Bacharach and Oberwesel, though we also encourage you to get lost in the backstreets and alleys for a rich taste of local life. Rhine residents are proud of their towns, and especially their wines and traditional food, so be sure to ask for their recommendations and allow yourself time to savor the region.

⊠ WHEN TO GO
April–May and September–October will be warm enough and have fewer tourists. December is particularly festive.

🏨 WHERE TO STAY
Breuer Rüdesheimer Schloss: A family-run hotel in a renovated 15th-century building, between the medieval town and vineyards. **Hotel Im Schulhaus:** A schoolhouse converted into a boutique hotel by a former student.

💟 GET ROMANTIC
Pick up a bottle of Rheingau Riesling and head to the vineyard trails outside of Lorch. Find a hilltop bench and watch the sun set over the river valley.

🌐 UNCORNERED MARKET TIP
Don't overplan your days. On a map, the distances can look short, but the real joy of this region is to slowly explore by foot, bicycle, and boat.

COUPLES ADVENTURES

Cable Car in Rüdesheim am Rhein ▲▲
Soar above the vineyards and gaze across the picturesque valley. At the top, take a short walk to Niederwald Monument for a bit of history on the 19th-century unification of Germany. Return to town via the vineyard footpaths.

Bike the Rheinsteig Weg ▲▲▲
Pedal along the 200-mile network of paths through villages, vineyards, and farms. If cycling isn't your thing, these trails are also great for hiking. Explore until dusk and take a train, bus, or ferry back to your hotel.

Rheingau Wine Tasting ▲▲
The Romans planted the first vines in the Rheingau, and the area's been perfecting its Riesling and Pinot Noir ever since. To appreciate local varietals and terroir, stop by the *wein* stand in Rüdesheim's market square (March–October), where you can sample vintages from four local wineries. If it's chilly, head to Drossel Keller's tasting room, museum, and bottle shop.

Burg Stahleck Castle Wanderings ▲▲
To fully appreciate Bacharach, one of the most picturesque towns along the upper Rhine, follow the steep path behind the main church up to the 1,000-year-old castle. This storied structure is now an impressive hostel, so you can enter and enjoy a light bite with panoramic views.

✤ Couples Advice

Use the "my day, your day" system to divide up responsibilities of planning and daily decisions. When it is your day, you are responsible for logistics, maps, and making the final call, if doubt strikes. This approach not only divvies up duties that may be undesirable, but it ensures that insignificant decisions are addressed immediately and don't turn into big issues.

Rüdesheim's lively pedestrian street, Drosselgasse

TO EXPLORE MORE ON THIS CONTINENT, CHECK OUT:

» **Mountains: Lauterbrunnen Valley, Switzerland...p. 32**

» **Architecture: Ghent, Belgium...p. 116**

POWER COUPLE: *Dan & Audrey*

The husband-and-wife team behind the award-winning travel blog, *UncorneredMarket.com*, inspires people to follow their curiosity and create a story-filled life. They share a more human dimension, often challenging stereotypes and shifting perceptions. After traveling for 16 years together and visiting more than 90 countries, they are still going—and still married.

Mekong fishermen checking their nets at dawn

MEKONG DELTA
Vietnam

ASIA
VIETNAM
Mekong
Delta

Wooden canoes laden with produce cluster together; women in conical hats extend their petite frames to exchange exotic fruits. Palm trees and rice paddies blend into a verdant backdrop, and the river adds a delicate shimmer to the scene. Few places are as photogenic as the Mekong Delta, but a picture can hardly capture its energy. Dubbed the "Rice Bowl" of Vietnam, the delta grows one-third of the country's produce on one-tenth of its land. Fisheries raise three million tons of fish annually, and the region cultivates over 2,000 varieties of flowers. Locals are busy at work, so even if not always warm and cuddly, they are an awe-inspiring group. Flowing from the Himalaya into 18 rivers that splinter into thousands of canals, the Mekong is easy to reach from Ho Chi Minh City or Phnom Penh, but it's hard to know where to begin. Cần Thơ, the largest city with the most extensive floating market, is worth a visit, though the smaller villages will get you closer to the action. Spending time on the mighty river is the natural draw; just be sure to peek behind the shore's green curtain. Biking the narrow paths between rice paddies, motorbiking up a mountain, and hanging out in the numerous plazas are fascinating flip sides to river life. Not just picture perfect, the Mekong Delta is a world of many dimensions.

 WHEN TO GO

December–May offer clear skies, lush land, and calm waters. Visit January–March for incredible flowers.

 WHERE TO STAY

Nam Bộ Boutique Hotel: Cần Thơ's contemporary colonial accommodation with river views, an excellent restaurant, and central locale. **Oasis:** The best of modest Bến Tre with a pool and bikes available.

💚 **GET ROMANTIC**

Cruise the canals in your own floating hotel, accompanied by a captain, chef, maid, and barman, plus bikes and a rowboat for excursions. Over two days and three nights aboard the Song Xanh Sampan, you'll explore key Mekong destinations like Sa Đéc, Cần Thơ, and some of the lesser known tributaries.

 HONEYTREK TIP

Watch for scams, and bargain like mad. Plenty of people are looking to make a fast buck, inflating prices or giving self-serving information. Do your research, shop around, and don't take it personally.

Sea of watermelons at the Phong Dien Floating Market

COUPLES ADVENTURES

Phong Dien Floating Market & Surrounds ▲▲
Ditch the morning crowds of Cần Thơ's massive Cái Răng floating market and ask your captain to chart a course to Phong Điền. This is a far more visceral shopping experience, where you go boat to boat and smell the melons, rub elbows with the farmers, and taste samples galore. On the way back, meander through the charming canal communities, then see the megasize boats of Cái Răng.

Bike Bến Tre ▲▲▲
Get a feel for rural life with a half-day cycle. From town, cross the Bến Tre River and follow the narrow paths into the jungle, coconut plantations, and rice paddies. Go with a sense of adventure (there is always an available waterway and boat to bring you back to town), and you'll love this serene side of the Mekong.

Colonial Sa Đéc ▲
French colonial architecture, Buddhist temples, floating flower nurseries, plus a bustling riverside market—towns don't get more charming in the Mekong. Head to the ornate 19th-century mansion of Huỳnh Thủy Lê (setting for Marguerite Duras's book *The Lover*), the Thiên Hậu Pagoda, and smell the thousands of flower species grown in the "Garden of Southern Vietnam."

✧ Play It Up

We love volleyball (it's actually how we met), so whenever we see a game happening around the world, we try to join the action. In Bến Tre, just standing on the sideline with a smile, we got subbed in and made 12 new friends. Whatever your sport, use it as way to transcend language barriers and bond with locals.

Anne spikes for her pickup team in Bến Tre.

TO EXPLORE MORE ON THIS CONTINENT, CHECK OUT:

» Dunes: Mũi Né, Vietnam...p. 144
» Supernatural: Siem Reap, Cambodia...p. 232

NAM OU RIVER VALLEY

Laos

ASIA

Nam Ou □
River LAOS
Valley

As you swing in a hammock at sunset with a Beer-lao in hand, a colorful longtail boat coasts along the Nam Ou River through the karst mountains. You think to yourself, "Could the good life get any simpler?" Then you take a boat upstream from Nong Khiaw to Muang Ngoi Neua. Until 2013, this village didn't have a road to the outside world, and they are still dabbling with fixed electricity. But wait, it gets simpler. Continue a couple hours along the footpaths to the hill tribes, and little has changed in centuries. Homes are woven from bamboo, chickens and pigs roam freely, and the barter system is common currency. Spend the night with Laotian villagers, explore the chiseled mountains, and savor a region that transcends time. Although seemingly utopian on the surface, Laos has a complex history. Nong Khiaw's dramatic karst caves were used as shelters during the Vietnam and Secret Wars. The Muang Ngoi Neua countryside still turns up bombshells when farmers till the fields. Laos's beauty is also in its resilience.

WHEN TO GO
October–February offer lovely weather before the hot and rainy season of March–September.

WHERE TO STAY
Nong Kiau Riverside: The most luxurious bungalows in town (remember, it's a simple place). **Nicksa's:** Pleasant riverside lodging and dining in Muang Ngoi Neua, also serving as a great base camp for overnight village treks.

GET ROMANTIC
Try traditional Lao barbeque with a date night at Nong Khiaw's Q Bar. Sitting around a crackling tabletop grill, play chef with a selection of delicious meats and vegetables.

HONEYTREK TIP
Don't count on the availability of ATMs, electricity, or most modern conveniences. Come with extra cash, a headlamp, and an open mind.

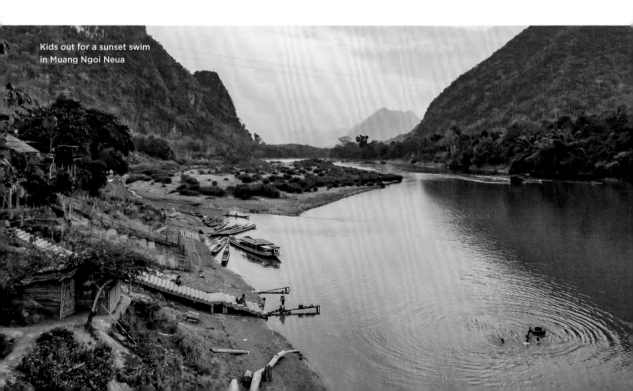

Kids out for a sunset swim in Muang Ngoi Neua

Among the 100 waterfalls on the Nong Khiaw trek

COUPLES ADVENTURES

Overnight in Huay Bo Village ▲▲▲
Hike two hours above Muang Ngoi Neua to immerse yourself in Laotian mountain culture. Stay at the village guesthouse and help harvest vegetables, fish with nets, and tinker with homespun river turbines (the main source of electricity). It's the real deal.

Phadeng Peak ▲▲
Hike to a panoramic vista of the Nam Ou River, sawtooth peaks, and traditional villages. After the two-hour climb above Nong Khiaw, soak up the scenery under the shade of a bamboo hut.

100 Waterfalls Hike ▲▲▲
Unlike most treks where the falls are at the end, this trail is blazed through a cascading river. With the help of Tiger Trail's guides, bamboo ladders, and an adventurous spirit, you'll rock scramble up a mile of waterfalls until you reach the most dramatic one for lunch and a dip. Return via a jungle trek and riverboat to Nong Khiaw.

Pha Tok Caves ▲▲▲
In the Vietnam and Secret Wars, Laos became the most heavily bombed country in history. (More bombs were dropped on this tiny nation than all of Europe combined during World War II.) Caves like Pha Tok served as air-raid shelters across the country. Visit these craggy limestone caverns for a lesson in history and geology.

✣ Timeless Travelers

On the floor of a wooden boat heading to Muang Ngoi Neua, we were crammed among young backpackers, villagers, and a French couple in their 60s. We were curious to know what led them to take such a rugged mode of transport. "We met backpacking in 1972," said Michele, "and have always loved a simple, local style of travel." They told us about their time hitchhiking across Thailand, camping with their kids in Europe, and their upcoming journey to northern India. At every phase of their lives, travel had been an essential element. And as his wife, Christiane, explained, "The more we travel together, the closer we become."

Boats line up at the docks of Muang Khua.

TO EXPLORE MORE ON THIS CONTINENT, CHECK OUT:
» Rain Forests: Khao Sok, Thailand...p. 182
» Supernatural: Siem Reap, Cambodia...p. 232

Kayaking the cliffs of the Apostle Islands, Wisconsin

Ultimate Freshwater Adventures

Find your rush in these extreme rivers, lakes, and waterfalls.

NEW ZEALAND

1. Tube Waitomo

Float through a network of natural limestone tunnels and grottoes, sliding down waterfalls and gazing up at a galaxy of glowworms. The bioluminescent algae create a dazzling effect, whether you are kicking back in an inner tube or rappelling the underground waterfalls.

U.S.A.

2. Kiteboard Columbia River Gorge

The lush chasm on the Washington and Oregon state border pulls wind from the Pacific coast up the gorge for some of the world's best kiteboarding conditions. The training schools in the area are top-notch, so even novices can catch some air.

NEW ZEALAND

3. Jetboat the Shotover

A true Kiwi invention, this jet propulsion boat maneuvers shallow waters at 50 miles an hour. Hop in and whiz down the scenic Shotover River, taking hairpin turns and 360-degree spins—coming within inches of the canyon walls and your nerve endings.

U.S.A.

4. Kayak the Apostle Islands

Lake Superior's glacial history, relentless waves, and subzero winters have sculpted the red sandstone islands into a kayaker's dream. Follow the curves of the dramatic coastline through this Wisconsin archipelago and into hidden sea caves.

ECUADOR

5. Canyoneer Cashuarco

Between the Andes and the Amazon, Baños de Agua Santa is the adventure capital of Ecuador, with canyoning at the top of its thrill list. Hike the jungle, zipline through a ravine, and cliff-dive into the river.

NORWAY

6. Parabungee in Voss

Begin by parasailing above a glacial lake, and once you're flying nearly 600 feet in the air, leap off the airborne platform and bungee jump to a new extreme. It's a double whammy for adrenaline junkies.

MALAWI

7. Snorkel Lake Malawi

Freshwater snorkeling isn't usually that exciting but Lake Malawi is a veritable aquarium, filled with some 600 species of cichlid fish in every conceivable color. Spend time below and above the water in this ecologically and culturally fascinating African lake.

NETHERLANDS

8. SUP the Amsterdam Canals

Though it sounds like an unlikely destination for water sports, the city's more than 150 canals offer the most adventurous way to explore the Dutch capital. Stand-up paddleboard under magnificent Renaissance bridges, past historic homes (including the Anne Frank House), and skim the surface of the 60-some miles of scenic waterways.

NEPAL

9. River Raft Sun Kosi River

Paddle Class V rapids crashing between the narrow gorges and forested canyons of the Himalaya. Follow the Sun Kosi toward the sacred Ganges, and marvel at the changing scenery as you go from the tallest mountains in the world to tropical jungles with chattering monkeys.

ICELAND

10. Ice Cave Jökulsárlón Lake

The deepest lake in Iceland is filled with icebergs and surrounded by a glacier, volcanoes, and black sand beaches. Spelunk the blue ice caves and stay up late for a chance to see the northern lights.

"At the beach, life is different. A day moves not from hour to hour but leaps from mood to moment. We go with the currents, plan around the tides, follow the sun."

—SANDY GINGRAS

Chapter Three

BEACHES & ISLANDS

Long stretches of white sand and turquoise sea are picturesque; however, we expect a little more from our beaches and islands. Sure, it's nice to kick back and relax to the soundtrack of crashing waves, but once we've taken a stroll along the water, read a magazine under an umbrella, and had that ceremonial piña colada, we crave more. We seek craggy coastlines, sandbars that emerge with the tide, and islands with more depth than a pretty perimeter. The best beaches don't just reveal themselves in a postcard. They want to be discovered with fins, boots, and boards, so when we do reach that perfect spit of sand, we feel it's been waiting just for us. We cannot always have the most scenic spots to ourselves, but if we have to share it, the people should enhance the experience, with a culture of explorers, spice traders, kings, artisans, and a history richer than the oldest resort. Challenge the notion of the perfect beach and discover your paradise.

Doors-off helicopter ride over the Nā Pali Coast

KAUA'I
U.S.A.

NORTH AMERICA

□ Kaua'i

UNITED STATES

A volcanic island rising from the seafloor, covered in tropical rain forest, cut with canyons, and surrounded by jagged cliffs—Kaua'i is more than just a pretty beach. Hawaii's "Garden Isle" has many dimensions and begs to be explored, from Hanalei Bay's luxury resorts to Kalalau Beach's hippie commune to Hanapepe's ancestral salt ponds. Fly into the island's hub of Lihue, rent a convertible, and cruise north through a place of cinematic beauty (you may recognize it from *Jurassic Park* and *Pirates of the Caribbean*). Sail along the sheer mountain coastline, take flight over the "Grand Canyon of the Pacific," and lace up your sneakers to hike the jaw-dropping Nā Pali Coast. This ancient isle is full of adventure, but don't worry, it also has some 50 white sand beaches and dozens of spoil-you-rotten resorts, for that vacation yin and yang. Whether your preferred mode of transit is a chopper or a pool chair with wheels, Kaua'i's got your joyride.

☒ WHEN TO GO
Dodge most of the tourists, rain, and price spikes in March–May and September–November. Pack your sunblock and umbrella.

▦ WHERE TO STAY
St. Regis Princeville: A Hanalei Bay location, chef Jean-Georges Vongerichten cuisine, and a 5,000-square-foot infinity pool are tough to beat. **Fern Grotto Inn:** Self-catering cottages with thoughtful amenities, including kayaks and bicycles, just north of Lihue.

♡ GET ROMANTIC
Take in sunset with a pineapple mojito at the Beach House, a South Shore restaurant with food as good as the views.

☑ HONEYTREK TIP
Renting a car is a must. Sure, there are cabs and bus tours, but you're going to want to pull over for countless photo stops, tempting trails, and cute towns.

A hand-carved sailing canoe pulls into Hanalei Bay.

COUPLES ADVENTURES

Sailing Canoe Excursion ▲▲

Explore Hanalei Bay in a 45-foot traditional sailing canoe, hand-carved by Hawaii native Trevor Cabell. Take his morning snorkel trip for calm waters and the best time to spot dolphins and turtles, or the afternoon History of Hanalei tour.

Helicopter the Island ▲▲

Just when you think Kaua'i couldn't get any prettier, you call in the chopper. Flying over Waimea (often called the Grand Canyon of the Pacific), hugging the curves of the Nā Pali Coast, and dipping into the crater of the Mount Waialeale volcano, a helicopter gives unrivaled access to the island's extreme landscape. Step up the adventure and fly "doors off" with Jack Harter Helicopters.

Hike the Kalalau Trail ▲▲▲

Only accessible by an 11-mile footpath, this section of Kaua'i's coast traverses five lush valleys and dramatic sea cliffs, and offers access to some of Hawaii's best beaches. Halfway there, most people hang a left at the river to see the waterfall, but shake the crowds and head toward the hippie

✣ Salt of the Earth and Sea

Pink salt glittered like crystals on the dining table, and it was as precious as it looked. The Kaua'i natives have harvested the Hanapepe salt patch for generations and are the only ones left in the archipelago practicing this ancient Hawaiian tradition. It's backbreaking work with no monetary compensation; as the ancestors dictated, Hanapepe salt can only be given away.

We slowly sprinkled the crystals over our mahimahi, and thought about the families working together in the red flats and how they were enhancing this meal. We thanked our local friend Kai for an incredible dinner, and he gifted us a small pouch of Hanapepe salt and said, "Welcome to Kaua'i."

Stacked surfboards, ready for a ride

commune (just don't be alarmed if you see a few topless hikers).

Surf Like a King ▲▲▲

Once a spiritual and artistic practice of Polynesian royalty, surfing is a quintessential Hawaiian experience. Take a lesson at the beginner-friendly Hanalei or Poipu Beach, or if you come during November through February's "big wave season," watch pros get barreled on the North Shore.

TO EXPLORE MORE ON THIS CONTINENT, CHECK OUT:

» **Mountains: Mount Rainier, U.S.A....p. 34**
» **History: Guanajuato, Mexico...p. 114**

NORTH ELEUTHERA
Bahamas

A little over a mile wide and 110 miles long, skinny Eleuthera boldly splits the teal Caribbean and deep blue Atlantic. Encircled by more than a hundred beaches, with pineapple fields in between, it's a pristine Caribbean island void of chain hotels, shopping malls, or even a stoplight. Deserted pink sand beaches and coral lagoons offer plenty of relaxation, while its lively neighbor Harbour Island is only a 10-minute water taxi away. This tiny isle was the former British capital of the Bahamas and boasts colorful clapboard houses and cobblestone streets, just wide enough for a golf cart (the primary mode of transit). Aristocrats, from the Duchess of Windsor to style queens like Diane von Furstenberg have spent ample time on Harbour Island, though unlike other star-studded beach destinations, Briland (its local name) is all charm and no pretension. The top-notch restaurants serve fish caught from hand-thrown nets, designer boutiques neighbor straw-hat stands, and although there are posh beach bars, the bottle shop is just as fun. North Eleuthera is a place of contrasts, surprises, delights, and in one word: paradise.

WHEN TO GO
December–April is peak season with shoulder months offering equally nice weather and an inviting locals scene.

WHERE TO STAY
The Cove: Between twin beach coves framed in coral cliffs, this resort is the star of North Eleuthera. **Coral Sands:** A historic and recently renovated boutique hotel on Harbour Island's three miles of pink sand beach.

GET ROMANTIC
Dine in an 18th-century summer home. Explore the Landing's chic plantation-style space, and sit on the terrace overlooking the sailboat-studded harbor for sunset and lobster with lemongrass risotto.

HONEYTREK TIP
There isn't any public transportation on Eleuthera, but with only one paved road and extremely friendly people, there is always someone heading your way. Yes, there are cabs, but try hitching a ride. The local encounters are priceless!

The path to James Point's pink sand beach

Golf cart cruising the main drag on Harbour Island

COUPLES ADVENTURES

Stand-Up Paddleboarding the Sea Cliffs ▲▲▲
Hop on a paddleboard, hug the coastline, and discover a slew of private beach coves and stunning rock formations. The Caribbean waters are serene so you can safely cover longer distances. The coastline north of Gregory Town (by Lenny Kravitz's house) is particularly gorgeous. Ask your hotel about boards or have them delivered by Eleuthera Beach Toy Rentals.

Dip Into the Queen's Baths ▲▲
The Atlantic wave action has carved the limestone cliffs and exposed a myriad of colors, textures, artistic formations, plus multiple swimming pools. Come at low tide and explore the rim of the deep cove, then rock scramble down and bask in the sun-heated baths.

Devil's Backbone Wrecks ▲▲▲
This jagged ridge of shallow coral reefs has been a shipwreck magnet for hundreds of years. That's bad for pirates, but incredible for snorkelers and divers looking to explore sunken relics. If you scuba, try Carnarvon, a 100-year-old lighthouse repair ship where you can swim through the boiler and spot eagle rays, turtles, and even hammerheads.

Snorkelers can head to the shallower Potato & Onion or the Train Wreck, a car that fell off a barge during the American Civil War.

History Tour by Golf Cart ▲
As the Bahamas' first capital, Harbour Island is where Bahamian history and style began. Hop in a souped-up golf cart with fifth-generation Brilander, Martin Grant, and explore the charming loyalist cottages, St. John's Anglican Church (it's bright pink), plus the best local haunts.

✦ Never a Dull Moment

"Where you headed?" shouted an old lady from her golf cart. When we said, "Downtown Spanish Wells," she replied, "You walked right past it!" Realizing there was little to do here, we decided to accept rides from anyone offering. Next pickup: Chain-smoking Richard and his lap dog, Peanut. So eager to give "new people" a lift, he nearly hit us. When we mentioned we were travel writers, he insisted we "review" his sister's B&B. She gave us a tour, then dropped us at the market to try Sheenah's pineapple cake. We spent the day looping the island, eating pastries, and chatting with colorful locals.

Wooden boat on Girls Bank, a bonefishing hot spot

TO EXPLORE MORE ON THIS CONTINENT, CHECK OUT:

» At Sea: Mesoamerican Barrier Reef, Belize...p. 126

» Road Trips: Western Cuba...p. 214

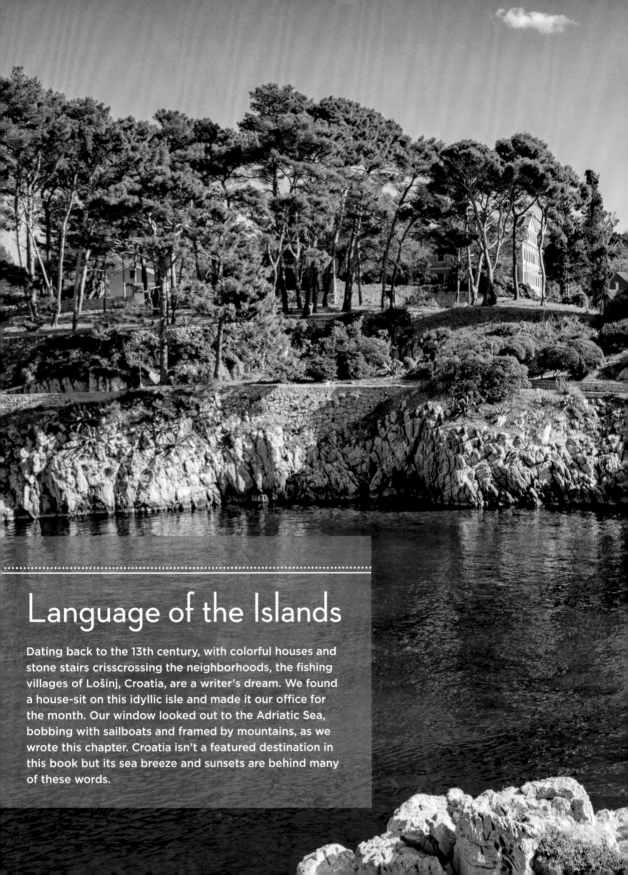

Language of the Islands

Dating back to the 13th century, with colorful houses and stone stairs crisscrossing the neighborhoods, the fishing villages of Lošinj, Croatia, are a writer's dream. We found a house-sit on this idyllic isle and made it our office for the month. Our window looked out to the Adriatic Sea, bobbing with sailboats and framed by mountains, as we wrote this chapter. Croatia isn't a featured destination in this book but its sea breeze and sunsets are behind many of these words.

The harbor and heart of Veli Lošinj, Croatia

ZANZIBAR
Tanzania

AFRICA

TANZANIA **Zanzibar**

The historic hub of the spice route and slave trade, this East African island has been shaped by the countless nationalities that have touched its shores. Sailors have been cruising the Zanzibar archipelago since 600 B.C., while Portuguese explorers, British colonialists, Arab merchants, Indian traders, and Omani sultans couldn't help but take up residence. Who wouldn't be lured by such a gorgeous place, with a lush landscape, fringed by sandy beaches and a bountiful sea? Though savvy travelers know Zanzibar's true beauty is in its mash-up of cultures and enigmatic charms. To this day there is no definitive map of historic Stone Town. The narrow streets seem to wind into knots and fray in every direction. The call to prayer echoes through the alleys, and women in colorful hijabs peek out from behind carved wooden doors. Once the sun sets, the smells of grilling seafood, the sounds of Swahili music, and the twinkling lights bring everyone to the waterfront night market. Explore the spice plantations behind the curries, sail in the wooden dhows of ancient traders, and stroll golden beaches made richer by a world of culture.

 WHEN TO GO

December–February offer perfect sun-bathing weather. June–October are still dry, a bit cooler, and coincide with the mainland's safari season.

 WHERE TO STAY

Baraza: This lavish Omani-style retreat on the eastern shore offers the best mix of blissed-out pampering and beachside adventure. **Zanzibar Coffee House:** Stone Town's favorite coffee shop has a stylish B&B in the adjoining 19th-century house.

GET ROMANTIC

On the panoramic rooftop of Emerson Spice Tea House, get cozy in a sea of colorful pillows, as you listen to live music and dine on Zanzibari delights.

 HONEYTREK TIP

Unless you're already in the Dar es Salaam airport, it takes longer to fly to the island than to travel the 22 miles by ferry. In addition to saving time and money, we like the boat for the coastal scenery and taste of local culture.

Biking the coral coast of Michanwi Pingwe peninsula

COUPLES ADVENTURES

Stone Town Walking Tour ▲
Wander the UNESCO World Heritage quarter with a local guide who can demystify the maze and bring more meaning to sites like the Omani old fort and slave market. Pointing out the prettiest carved wooden doors (the symbol of Zanzibar), local spice shops, and the best chapatis, he'll lead you to the island's treasures. On your own, be sure to visit the House of Wonders Museum and ultralocal Darajani Market.

Dhow Boat to the Sandbank ▲▲
Set sail on a traditional dhow toward Bawe Island. Hop out for snorkeling among the corals and tropical fish, then continue to the Sandbank, an otherworldly island that emerges with the changing tides. Enjoy a beach picnic, abundant birdlife, and comical ghost crabs.

Savor a Spice Plantation ▲
Learn how Zanzibari spices have flavored the country's history with a visit to one of the island's many farms. At an estate like Tangawizi, you can touch and taste fresh lemongrass, cardamom, lychee, jackfruit, and other exotic and aphrodisiac delights.

Bike to The Rock ▲▲
Take a day trip to the Michanwi Pingwe peninsula, bike the hard-packed beach, take a dip, and work up an appetite for The Rock. This tiny coral islet has just enough room for a gourmet kitchen, 12 tables, and one of the dreamiest restaurants along the Indian Ocean. Depending on the tide, wade, walk, or boat to an unforgettable seafood experience.

✣ Our Craziest Overland Journey

Google Maps said the coastal route from Ibo Island, Mozambique, to Zanzibar was not possible. But it was less than 500 miles straight up the coast; how hard could that be? So we sailed in dhow boats, hitchhiked on top of banana trucks, slept in mud huts, waded through rivers, rode in gin-smuggling pickups, and after 14 legs of transit and four days on the road, we made it. It was far from easy, but an unforgettable journey and one that showed us there is always a way.

Locals enjoying a melon at Darajani Market

TO EXPLORE MORE ON THIS CONTINENT, CHECK OUT:
» **Falls: Livingstone, Zambia...p. 54**
» **On Safari: Crater Highlands, Tanzania...p. 92**

RAILAY
Thailand

ASIA

Railay □ THAILAND

Only accessible by boat, the Railay peninsula has the feel of a far-flung island, but it's the thick jungle and sheer limestone cliffs that shelter this oasis from the mainland. Everyone loves a good karst mountain, dripping with stalactites and sculpted with caves, but no one more than a rock climber. Railay has more than 700 routes bolted into the crags, plus sea cliffs perfect for deepwater solo: free climbing over the ocean and high-diving down. Not just for adrenaline junkies, Railay has four Andaman Sea beaches to suit your style: Railay West (resortgoer), Railay East (flashpacker), Tonsai (devout climber), and Phra Nang (anyone seeking a "world's best beach"). Try them all; the journey to get there—swimming, hiking, rock scrambling, or beachcombing—is half the fun. Take a boat to the surrounding islands, night snorkel in the bioluminescent waters, and do what those in Railay do best—hang out and enjoy life.

WHEN TO GO
November–March are sunny but not too hot; monsoon season runs May–October.

WHERE TO STAY
Phutawan Resort: A serene and affordable retreat tucked into the cliffs of Railay East. **Rayavadee Resort:** This Small Luxury Hotel of the World has villas, private pools, butler service, and a restaurant inside a natural grotto.

GET ROMANTIC
Take a cooking class in Tew Lay Bar's beachfront kitchen. Dine on the fruits of your labor, then linger for sunset cocktails in their treehouse terraces.

HONEYTREK TIP
Pay attention to the tide schedule to maximize your time and experience. Plan your visit for Phra Nang Beach and the Lagoon Hike at high tide, and your walk to Tonsai at low tide.

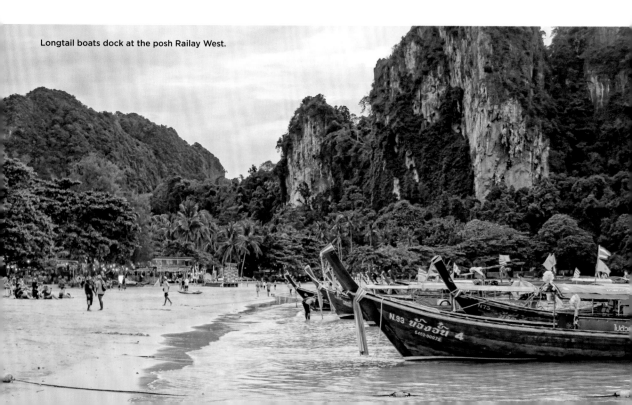

Longtail boats dock at the posh Railay West.

Climbing the karst stone formations of Tonsai

COUPLES ADVENTURES

Glow-in-the-Dark Snorkeling ▲▲
Take a late afternoon sail around the islands and stop at the disappearing sandbar for a sunset barbeque. When the fire dies down and the stars come out, it's time to find the darkest coves for an unforgettable snorkel. This region of the Andaman Sea is full of phosphorescent plankton, so when you swim through the water, it's like moving through a galaxy of stars.

Trek to Railay Viewpoint and Lagoon ▲▲▲▲
Halfway along the path to Phra Nang Beach, you'll see a steep, muddy, and gnarled slope; brave it for panoramic views over the peninsula. If that short but intense hike didn't faze you, continue through the jungle down the series of cliffs. At high tide, you'll find a sunken emerald lagoon.

Deepwater Solo Climbing ▲▲▲▲
Sail to the base of the craggy cliffs and swim toward the ultimate free climb. Pull yourself out of the water and Spiderman up the limestone face. Choose your handholds wisely—there are no ropes, and the sea is your safety net. While scaling the walls, be sure to stop on the ledges and take in the view. Just remember: The higher you climb, the higher the jump.

Backdoor Phra Nang ▲▲
Framed with drip-castle spires, this iconic beach draws its share of tourists and Thai fishermen (there's a shrine to a mythical sea goddess filled with colorful phallus offerings). To have a bit of paradise to yourself, walk to the end of the beach and through the canyon, where it opens up to a serene cove. Snorkel around the rock outcropping with swim-through arches, then back to Phra Nang Beach, taking in sweeping views the whole way.

❖ Traditions Old & New

We may have been spending Christmas in a Buddhist country, but we weren't going to skip our traditions! We decorated a banana tree with strings of popcorn, homemade seashell ornaments, and red and green Malay apples. We wrapped gifts in palm leaves and exchanged presents (coincidentally we both got each other swim goggles and Nutella). For our holiday feast we took a Thai cooking class. Panang curry will always taste a little bit like Christmas.

Decorating the Christmas (banana) tree

TO EXPLORE MORE ON THIS CONTINENT, CHECK OUT:

» Rivers: Mekong Delta, Vietnam...p. 58
» At Sea: Komodo, Indonesia...p. 132

Sunset at Ella's Place, laid-back bungalows in Salang

TIOMAN
Malaysia
BY VAUGHAN & LAUREN MANUEL MCSHANE

ASIA

Tioman □ MALAYSIA

When it comes to Southeast Asian beaches, Malaysia is still a lesser known wonderland. One of the 64 tiny islands making up the Seribuat Archipelago, Tioman is one of the largest at only 12 miles long. And after living in Malaysia for two years, we can say it's also one of the finest. Sculpted with beautiful bays and thick with tropical rain forest, the island has one main road, and boats are often the best way to reach its white sand beaches. As water sport lovers, we felt right at home on Tioman, with each bay offering different ways for us to commune with the ocean—be it stand-up paddleboarding, diving, snorkeling, swimming, or surfing. Although the island has gorgeous terrain, its true treasures lie beneath the surface of the 84°F water. Swim to offshore coral reefs where green turtles, butterfly fish, reef sharks, nudibranchs, and rays await. Just enough travelers visit Tioman to add to its funky laid-back vibe, but not so many as to overrun its unspoiled splendor. Come enjoy its magical marine life and wild beauty.

 WHEN TO GO

March–November are ideal. Many places close during monsoonal December–February, but surfers can still enjoy swells.

WHERE TO STAY

1511 Coconut Grove: Secluded, upscale beach huts in Juara. **Ella's Place:** Rustic cabins on Salang beach with hammocks and air-conditioning.

GET ROMANTIC

Pack a picnic and snorkeling gear, then sail to Coral Island or Monkey Bay for sunset. Both spots are often deserted with nothing but bone-white sand and a kaleidoscope of marine life below the surface.

 THE TRAVEL MANUEL TIP

The ferry schedule from Mersing changes with the tides, so check it before you go. Take out cash on the mainland or at the Tekek ferry terminal, the only place on the island with an ATM.

COUPLES ADVENTURES

Trek Pulau Tioman Reserve ▲▲▲

The inland rain forest is bursting with flora and fauna, like long-tailed macaques, Malayan colugo, and palm civets. Begin a trek from the Tekek mosque; it joins up with the 4x4 road, taking you through the jungle to Juara (our favorite beach).

Asah Waterfall ▲▲

Asah is known as the biggest waterfall on the island and around a 30-minute walk from Mukut Village. Enjoy a light trek in good walking shoes, or arrange a boat transfer and take in numerous bays along the way.

Shore Dive Salang ▲▲▲

Don your scuba gear, and walk right off the beach toward the vibrant Salang Wreck or Salang Jetty dive sites. Swim alongside the healthy reef with blacktip sharks, turtles, and colorful parrot fish. It's an excellent place for shore diving and getting PADI certified, but if you'd rather snorkel, just head left of the jetty for dynamic marine life.

Kayak the Bays ▲▲▲

Circumnavigate this densely forested isle by kayak. Pack plenty of water and sunblock, leave early in the morning, and venture to the various bays of ABC Beach, Tekek, Juara, and Salang. Take a breather on any of the beautiful beaches, and make sure you stop at the gorgeous cove of Monkey Bay.

❖ Couples Advice

Travel is always unpredictable, but that spontaneity can be quite romantic—like hopping on a motorbike and holding each other tight as you cruise a tropical island. When we arrive to a new beach destination, we always rent a scooter. It's the closest you'll get to nature while in transit. Being on the open road, with the freedom to explore wherever you please and duck into quiet nooks, naturally adds excitement. We once took our scooter over an island mountain pass, meant only for 4x4s, and we are definitely closer for the experience!

Scuba diving with a school of crescent-tail bigeye

TO EXPLORE MORE ON THIS CONTINENT, CHECK OUT:

» **Lakes: Inle Lake, Myanmar...p. 48**
» **Rain Forests: Khao Sok, Thailand...p. 182**

POWER COUPLE: *Lauren & Vaughan*

Meet the duo behind *TheTravelManuel.com*, voted Africa's Top Travel Blog for two years running. Lovers of water sports and outdoor adventure for couples and families (particularly with their adorable toddler), they will find any excuse to return to life on a tropical island, as long as there's Wi-Fi and espresso.

SAMANÁ
Dominican Republic

A lush peninsula on the northeast coast, awash with mountains, jungles, beaches, and islands, Samaná is somehow just under the tourist radar. The region has always marched to its own bongo drummer—from fiercely fending off invaders in the days of Columbus, to unique cultural celebrations like the three-month harvest festival, to their evangelical beliefs that still leave room for sultry salsa dancing. The residents are proud of the region's beauty and are making efforts to develop it slowly and sustainably. Santa Barbara de Samaná is the heart of the peninsula, so much so, that everyone just calls this town "Samaná." Dating back to 1756, the Spanish saw this protected bay, with its lush mountain backdrop, series of islets, and pocket beaches, as a good place to settle. You'll find several interesting colonial buildings (don't miss the corrugated iron church, La Chorcha), while the town's architectural signature is the dramatic footbridge that sweeps across the bay to the islands. Try ziplining, island hopping, bachata dancing, horseback riding, and a mix of luxury and local experiences to find the seductive rhythm of Samaná.

NORTH AMERICA
DOMINICAN REPUBLIC
Samaná

⊠ WHEN TO GO
February–May and October–November are the best months to beat the heat, crowds, and hurricanes.

⊡ WHERE TO STAY
Dominican Tree House Village: Thatch cabanas perched in the trees of El Valle are rustic cool with a community vibe and plenty of adventure offerings. **Sublime Samana:** A mix of self-catering beach villas and don't-lift-a-finger suites near the lively Las Terrenas.

♡ GET ROMANTIC
Escape to the beaches of Las Galeras and have sunset cocktails on El Cabito's cliffside terrace. Extend your blissed-out stay at their rustic chic hotel.

✓ HONEYTREK TIP
Time your Santo Domingo flight so you can catch the Monasterio de San Francisco Sunday concert series. A full stage is set up at the foot of the atmospheric 16th-century ruins, and the whole city seems to come out to shake a tail feather.

The tiny isle of Cayo Levantado, aka Bacardi Island

Ziplining through the lush El Valle

COUPLES ADVENTURES

Tandem Ziplining ▲▲▲
Set atop the highest mountain in the region, with 12 ziplines zigzagging through the canopy (some as high as 450 feet), Samaná Zipline is one of the most thrilling and scenic courses in the Caribbean. Strapped together, try flips, twirls, and upside-down kisses, while taking in incredible views of the valley, jungle, and beach.

Beach Day at El Valle ▲
A cove surrounded by mountains dotted with palm trees, rugged cliffs, golden sand, and an endearing locals scene, this is our favorite beach in Samaná. Stroll, swim, and grab a seat at the *palapa* bar to watch the fisherman pulling their boats ashore, boys throwing the baseball around, and waves crashing on the cliffs.

Horseback to El Limón Waterfall ▲▲
Hop on a *caballo* and trot through the streams, jungle, and mountains to the panoramic vista over the peninsula. Park your horse by the snack shack and

✤ Night at the Colmado

We followed the sounds of bongos, cowbells, and laughter to Colmado Anthony (*colmados* are the DR's typical open-air corner store, doubling as the neighborhood bar). We peered into this locals-only party with a smile, and a soon-to-be friend, Jaime, motioned us over. "Bienvenidos! Come have a glass of Mama Juana!" After a few sips of the herbal rum wine, we were swapping stories in Spanglish, attempting the merengue, and making plans to go to a baseball game the following day.

Sunday night concert series in Santo Domingo

join locals for a cerveza and game of dominos before your short hike down to El Limón, a 130-foot waterfall cascading into a spacious swimming hole, complete with grottoes.

Island-Hop Los Haitises National Park ▲▲
Sail across the bay until you are surrounded by dozens of karst islets and countless birds of prey. Slow-cruise around the isles, then follow the river system inland to the mangroves and caves. Cueva de la Linea is not only stunning with its spindly rock formations, but also fascinating with ancient pictographs from the Taíno natives.

TO EXPLORE MORE ON THIS CONTINENT, CHECK OUT:
» **On Safari: Tortuguero, Costa Rica...p. 100**
» **Rain Forests: St. Lucia...p. 190**

Maya ruins over the shores of Tulum, Mexico

Best-in-Class Beaches

Beautiful beaches come in all shapes and sizes. Find the one that suits your style.

AUSTRALIA

1. Colorful Sand: Rainbow Beach

Over 70 different colored sands make up the soaring cliffs of Queensland's Inskip Peninsula. These rich minerals have been evolving since the last ice age, and are as vibrant as ever. Teal sea and white sand before the rainbow cliffs add extra stunning contrast.

MEXICO

2. History: Ruinas de Tulum

White sand, turquoise water, and swaying palms would be enough reasons to visit Tulum, but pre-Columbian ruins towering over the beach take it to a whole new level. The Maya picked this site for its break in the reef, making it an ideal spot for ancient trading canoes and modern-day swimmers.

U.S.A.

3. Seashells: Sanibel

Most seashells roll right past Florida's beaches; however, Sanibel Island's south-facing shores are a veritable net for coquinas, conch whelks, and treasures hailing from across the Caribbean. Every tide brings new surprises and shellers from around the world to beachcomb Blind Pass to Lighthouse Park.

NEW ZEALAND

4. Natural Spa: Hot Water Beach

On either side of high tide, this geothermal beach becomes the grounds for a one-of-a-kind spa. Water (up to 147°F) filters up from underground fissures, so grab a shovel and dig yourself a hot tub.

ECUADOR

5. Wildlife: Española

The Galápagos archipelago is renowned for its diversity of wildlife, especially on Española Island. With more than a thousand giant tortoises, a waved albatross colony (the only one in the world), endemic lava lizards, and blue-footed boobies, it offers a truly wild day at the beach.

ITALY

6. Clothing Optional: Guvano Beach

A cove surrounded by steep cliffs and turquoise sea, only accessible via an old railway tunnel or boat, Guvano is not an easy place to reach, but that's what makes it perfect for nude bathers (and first-timers). No gawking passersbys to worry about, just people enjoying one of Cinque Terre's most au naturel beaches.

ST. MARTIN

7. Unlikely Attraction: Maho Beach

You'd think being directly under an airport flight path would deter people. Instead, the 747s, swooping less than 100 feet overhead, bring droves to scope the massive airliners, feel the powerful jet stream, and cheer in unison for this regularly scheduled thrill.

U.S.A.

8. Tidepooling: Moss Beach

Along the dramatic bluffs of California's Fitzgerald Marine Reserve, anemones, starfish, crabs, and sea urchins fill thousands of rock pools. Nearby harbor seal nurseries add a lively element to this couple-mile stretch of the Bay Area.

AUSTRALIA

9. Surfing: Bells Beach

Home to the Rip Curl Pro—the world's longest running surf competition—this Victoria state beach churns out consistently stellar waves. Large swells come from the Southern Ocean, hit this unique reef, and sculpt it to perfection.

SPAIN

10. Cliffs: Cathedrals Beach

With rock formations arcing like buttresses a hundred feet over the sea, this Galicia beach feels as grand as the Renaissance churches of Europe. The powerful Atlantic has eroded the cliffs into a series of walkways; come at low tide to explore them.

Masai Mara, Kenya

Chapter Four

ON SAFARI

No longer a tradition of hunting animals, safari has become a pastime of appreciating wildlife in their natural habitat. The only thing people shoot these days are cameras, and the trophies on the wall are stunning photographs. Following a dirt road through the golden savanna, yielding to wildebeest traffic, and off-roading to join a lion chase—this is our kind of game drive. By contrast, a walking safari brings a whole new dimension to the experience—listening for birdcalls, following paw tracks, and tasting plants used in native remedies. And Africa is not the only continent harboring large and exotic animals. The outback, the Arctic, tropical archipelagos, and nesting beaches around the world offer equally wild safaris. Walk with polar bears in Canada, kayak with penguins in the Galápagos, and cruise with saltwater crocs in Australia. No matter where you are when the sun sets, join the safari tradition of toasting to the beauty of nature with a sundowner on the rocks.

GALÁPAGOS

Galápagos Islands

ECUADOR
SOUTH AMERICA

Ecuador

Not just home to rare and unusual animals like the giant tortoise and blue-footed booby, the Galápagos Islands foster some 1,000 species that cannot be found anywhere else on Earth. The archipelago's isolation 600 miles off the coast of Ecuador and its long history without human inhabitants made it Darwin's lab for the theory of evolution. The islands' animals didn't develop a fear of people, and this ingrained naiveté invites some of the most engaging wildlife encounters. Playful sea lions swim up to snorkelers, penguins do laps around kayakers, and iguanas sunbathe next to your beach blanket. Although the wildlife knows no boundaries (you'll literally find sea lions sprawled on park benches and strutting the boardwalk), the islands are 97 percent national park and highly regulated, so humans cannot just roam as they please. Cruises are the most popular way to get around, while land-based trips allow you to dig deeper into the volcanic landscape and Galapageno culture. Spend the night on the mysterious Floreana Island, with its history of pirates, whalers, and disappearing baronesses. Hike the volcanoes and lava fields on Isabela. Scuba dive with hammerheads off San Cristóbal. And commune with giant tortoises as often as you can.

✈ WHEN TO GO

Wildlife sightings are incredible year-round—something is always migrating, mating, or hatching. For the calmest seas and clearest skies, visit February–April.

🏨 WHERE TO STAY

Finch Bay Eco Hotel: In the heart of the isles, this National Geographic Unique Lodge of the World is the ultimate base camp. **Active Adventures:** This highly experienced outfitter offers island-hopping trips with adventure-driven itineraries.

♥ GET ROMANTIC

Rarely visited by travelers yet beloved by sea lions, San Cristóbal's La Lobería beach is a unique place to lay out, relax, and watch these charismatic creatures play in the sand and waves.

✓ HONEYTREK TIP

The Galápagos doesn't have to cost a fortune. If you're on a tight budget, base yourself on Santa Cruz, where it's easy to arrange excursions and catch a ferry to other action-packed islands.

Galápagos sea lions shuffling about Punta Pitt beach

✥ Giant Tortoise Stats

1 Year: Survival time without food or water
11 Species: Remaining in the Galápagos
16 Hours: Nap time per day
152 Years: Age of oldest known tortoise
919 Pounds: Weight of Goliath, the largest male on record
15,000: Population of giant tortoises remaining (down from 100,000 in Darwin's day and the #1 reminder to protect this endangered species)

A giant tortoise grazing at Rancho El Manzanillo

COUPLES ADVENTURES

Scuba Dive Kicker Rock ▲▲▲
Rising some 500 feet out of the ocean, this boot-shaped island is split in two, creating a veritable fish highway. Over 2,500 marine species have been discovered in the Galápagos, and favorites like the scorpion fish, Pacific green sea turtles, and massive schools of whitetip reef sharks are regularly seen here. With excellent visibility, Kicker Rock is great for snorkelers and advanced divers looking for hammerheads.

Commune With Giant Tortoises ▲▲▲
Interesting encounters can be had at sprawling ranches like El Manzanillo and impressive breeding centers like Arnaldo Tupiza. To see giant tortoises in the wild, trek to Galapaguera Natural on San Cristóbal. Only accessibly by boat and a four-hour round-trip hike, the highlands are where you can find these centenarians among the Palo Santo trees and Galápagos milkweed, slowly on the move in their natural habitat.

Sierra Negra Volcano ▲▲▲
Hike through the tropical forest to the rim of the volcanic islands' largest caldera. Peer down the lush green walls, and watch mist roll over the black rock expanse. Keep trekking to Volcán Chico, through lava fields of fiery craters and fumaroles from a 1970s eruption. In an 11-mile trek, you'll experience a dozen stunning landscapes.

Kayak Tintoreras ▲▲
This group of islets clustered off Isabela is home to numerous wildlife colonies. As you paddle away from Embarcadero Beach, cheeky sea lions often follow along. Reach the craggy volcanic isles; rare birds, including the Galápagos penguins and blue-footed boobies, will be fishing, preening, and shaking their tail feathers. Keep an eye out for marine iguanas—this is the only place in the world you'll find them swimming.

TO EXPLORE MORE ON THIS CONTINENT, CHECK OUT:
» **Mountains: Urubamba Valley, Peru...p. 38**
» **Road Trips: Volcano Avenue, Ecuador...p. 212**

TOP END
Australia

◻ **Top End**

AUSTRALIA

A wild landscape and cultural identity so uniquely Australian, the outback has no rival. By definition, it's the vast, remote, and largely impassable interior of the country, though at the top of the Northern Territory, the rugged outback shows its softer side. Close to the Timor Sea, the monsoonal climate brings bird-rich wetlands, lotus-filled lagoons, rivers rushing between sandstone cliffs, and even rain forests. It's where Australia's Aboriginal culture thrives, with 40,000 years of tradition carrying on through spirited music, art, and storytelling. The original custodians of the land, the Wulna and Yolngu people, will guide you through the UNESCO World Heritage site of Kakadu and a plethora of national parks for a deeper cultural context. People from over 50 countries make up the population of Darwin (the Northern Territory capital and gateway to the parks), and strong Aboriginal influences give this tropical metropolis its own rhythm and flair. If you're looking for the massive saltwater crocodiles and notoriously venomous snakes of the outback, don't worry, you'll find them here, too—though the beauty and culture of the Top End is what will leave a lasting mark.

WHEN TO GO
April–September bring sunshine and unfettered access to the park. Although a bit rainy, January–February offer lush landscapes and spectacular lightening shows.

WHERE TO STAY
Adventure Tours: This fun-loving outfitter runs multiday Top End trips with comfy camps around the national parks. **Wildman Wilderness Lodge:** Sumptuous cabins and safari tents and plenty of outback excursions from the Mary River Wetlands.

GET ROMANTIC
Take a quick hike alongside the 200-foot cascade of Gunlom Falls, and reach its natural infinity pools. Hop in and feel the current's gentle massage as you take in stunning views over Kakadu.

HONEYTREK TIP
Catch Darwin's Mindil Beach Sunset Market on Thursdays and Sundays. Try outback delicacies like crocodile or kangaroo steaks, and stay late for a didgeridoo jam session at this locals' hot spot.

Crocodile River along the Aboriginal Arnhem Land

Wallabies are a common sight in the Top End.

COUPLES ADVENTURES

Croc Spotting in Corroboree Billabong ▲▲
The Mary River Wetlands are a haven for rare migratory birds, pythons, and saltwater crocodiles—particularly in Corroboree. Cruise through the billabong, covered in pink lotus flowers, and keep an eye out for crocs as large as 23 feet long and 2,600 pounds.

Ubirr's Ancient Rock Art ▲
In a country with the longest continuously practiced artistic traditions, Ubirr has some of the finest preserved rock paintings. Browse the Aboriginal art on a guided walk around this beloved section of Kakadu National Park. Look for symbols of creation, hunting, play, and law, in rich reds and yellows, then climb the sandstone cliff shelters for sunset over the Nardab Floodplain.

Litchfield Termite Mounds ▲
Sculptural towers with tunnels, arches, chimneys, and nursery chambers are the beautiful product of millions of busy termites. Head to Litchfield National Park to see a veritable city of magnetic termite mounds and the nearby cathedral mounds reaching as high as 17 feet.

Dig Into Katherine Gorge ▲▲
Enter the sandstone country of Nitmiluk National Park and explore the 13 stunning gorges by hiking trail, canoe, river cruise, or helicopter. Seeing the swift river flow between the sheer red rock walls is impressive from any vantage point, especially with stealthy freshwater crocs on the shore and rock wallabies bouncing along the cliffs.

✦ Killer Knowledge

Australia is notorious for its deadly animals, and although sharks and crocs can kill you, honeybees still cause more deaths than both combined. That said, it's always good to know a dangerous animal when you see one (for bragging rights, if nothing else).

Eastern brown snake: This slender serpent's bite stops blood from clotting.

Sydney funnel-web spider: Its venom is more potent than cyanide.

Giant centipedes: All those legs are stingers.

Saltwater crocodiles: The largest living reptile has a bite six times stronger than a great white.

A fearsome saltwater crocodile patrols the banks.

TO EXPLORE MORE ON THIS CONTINENT, CHECK OUT:

» At Sea: Tasman District, New Zealand...p. 124

» Rain Forests: Daintree, Australia...p. 180

A Sabi Sand sunset and an inspiration for G&Ts

KRUGER
South Africa

AFRICA

□ **Kruger**

SOUTH
AFRICA

Safari destinations, filled with lions, elephants, rhinos, and other aggressive animals, rarely let tourists drive around on their own. Kruger National Park, on the other hand, has such incredible roads, rangers, and overall infrastructure that even two urbanites in a 2WD rental can safely take a game drive. Paved roads don't only make for a smooth cruise around the park, but also attract animals by minimizing dust on nearby trees for hungry giraffes and creating a sun-heated siesta spot for lions, baboons, and buffalo. You'll be astonished how many of Kruger's 800 animal species you can see without leaving your car. Though if you trek along the animal paths with a ranger, spend the night in a bird hide shelter, and off-road with safari experts in the Sabi Sand Game Reserve, you'll see why this is one of Africa's most impressive parks. Kruger not only boasts the "big five" (rhino, elephant, African buffalo, lion, and leopard) but also more large mammals than virtually any other park on the continent. Combine the rare opportunity of a DIY game drive with a classic luxury safari camp for the best of both worlds.

WHEN TO GO
The dry season (June–October) thins the bushveld vegetation for clearer game sightings, plus these winter months bring cooler temperatures and fewer mosquitoes.

WHERE TO STAY
Earth Lodge: Sculpted into the hills of the Sabi Sabi Game Reserve, this ecolodge offers crème de la crème accommodations and safari excursions. **Mvuradona Safari Lodge:** At the foot of Kruger National Park and Lionspruit Game Reserve, it's a steal for couples wanting a self-drive safari and a romantic retreat.

GET ROMANTIC
Climb up a centuries-old leadwood tree to your open-air bedroom in Chalkley Treehouse. A flowing canopy bed and lounge area with views over Lion Sands Game Reserve make this a true love nest.

HONEYTREK TIP
If you plan on seeing more than one national park in South Africa, get the SANParks Wild Card to save on entrance fees.

Our safari guide yielding to elephant traffic

COUPLES ADVENTURES

Sweni Wilderness Trek ▲▲▲
Walk with a ranger along the animal paths and Sweni River, where herds of wildebeest, zebra, and buffalo come to drink and lions hunt. Spending three nights in the park's remote huts and waking up to sounds of honking hippos and laughing hyenas is one of Kruger's most intimate safari experiences. Book this small-group trek well in advance with SANParks.

Classic Big Five Safari in Sabi Sand ▲▲
Seeing the big five is never a guarantee, but within the Sabi Sand Game Reserve, your odds will never be better. Without fences or national park restrictions, your luxury lodge's highly trained guides can off-road, drive into the night, and get to the heart of the action.

Mananga Adventure Trail ▲▲▲
Rent a 4x4 and head to one of the most secluded and wildlife-rich areas you can reach without a guide. Only six cars a day are allowed to traverse the 30-mile dirt track, to minimize impact on the pristine savanna and maximize intimate encounters with zebra, wildebeest, buffalos, even cheetahs and lions. *Note:* Bookings are only accepted the night before or same day at Satara Rest Camp.

Shipandani Overnight Hide ▲▲
From a camouflaged cabin on the Tsendze River, watch green-backed herons, diederik cuckoos, lilac-breasted rollers, and more of the park's estimated 517 bird species swoop over the water. Spending 24 hours in this scenic and discreet spot gives you an unrivaled look into a day in the (wild)life of Kruger National Park. Pack your binoculars, telephoto lens, and picnic for a world-class birding adventure.

✤ Food Fight

The CB radio mumbled a message in Afrikaans, prompting our safari guide to make a swift U-turn. As we arrived to the scene, a leopard was gnawing on a kudu flopped over a tree branch. With each bite, his 200-pound dinner would slide lower. When he tried to remedy the tenuous placement, the carcass slipped from his jaws, plummeting toward a pack of hyenas waiting below. In one instant the leopard and hyenas launched for the meat, setting the scene for a bloody clash, though somehow the cat nabbed it first and shot back up the tree to savor his meal.

A lioness and her two curious cubs

TO EXPLORE MORE ON THIS CONTINENT, CHECK OUT:

» **Deserts: Namib Desert, Namibia...p. 152**
» **Road Trips: Western Cape, South Africa...p. 200**

Lilac-breasted roller perched in Sabi Sand, South Africa

Lovebird

Driving through the South African bush, our safari guide hit the brakes. Did he see a lion? A rhino? Nope, a tiny bird. The lilac-breasted roller, or Gewone troupant, is a symbol of fidelity in the Afrikaner culture, he told us. Traditionally, men would ask for a woman's hand in marriage by proposing with one of its vibrant feathers. "Troupant" is an evolution of their word *trouband,* the wedding band, and a sighting still makes locals' hearts flutter.

CRATER HIGHLANDS
Tanzania

AFRICA Crater Highlands

TANZANIA

The wildebeest migration, Maasai warriors, the cradle of mankind, and one of the world's largest volcanic calderas—East Africa's highlights shine bright in the Crater Highlands. Adjacent to the plains of the Serengeti, the Ngorongoro Crater harbors some 25,000 large animals (including the big five) within the walls of an extinct volcano. The crater is northern Tanzania's big draw, but the diverse wildlife spreads across the region's mist forests, mountains, shifting dunes, gorges, and saline lakes. Arrive when the wildebeest birth over 300,000 calves and move as a pack of two million with predators hot on their heels. You'll feel Ngorongoro Conservation Area's raw power strike you to the core. As if the wildlife wasn't enough, the area's human history dates back 3.6 million years, with hominid footprint excavations to prove it. The nomadic Maasai, draped in crimson textiles and layers of beads, continue to herd their sheep and cattle as they have for centuries. It's a timeless safari destination, and that's just the beginning.

WHEN TO GO
June–September is the coolest and driest season. Catch the great wildebeest migration January–April. February offers best odds to see the calving frenzy.

WHERE TO STAY
Nomad's Serengeti Safari Camp: A mobile operation dedicated to following the herds, setting up their luxury camp wherever the action unfolds. **Ndutu Safari Lodge:** A perfectly positioned (and priced) option for the migration with 34 stone cottages, all facing the bountiful Lake Ndutu.

GET ROMANTIC
Pack your sundowner kit and head to the Ngorongoro Crater rim. Sip Amarula over ice as you watch the wildlife below and the sun slip behind the volcano walls.

HONEYTREK TIP
The Ngorongoro Crater is one of Africa's most regulated and fee-heavy parks. Reserve in advance and find a local and more affordable safari guide in Karatu town.

Dozens of zebra grazing the Ngorongoro Crater floor

Maasai warriors stand before a traditional house.

COUPLES ADVENTURES

Safari on the Crater Floor ▲▲
Descend 2,000 feet into the Ngorongoro Crater, through the mist forests to the expanse of grasslands and lagoons. Safari's element of surprise is half the fun, though for specific sightings, Lake Magadi is full of flamingos, Lerai Forest harbors massive elephants, and the endangered black rhino is often seen near the Lemala ascent road. Have a picnic at Ngoitokitok Spring to dine with hippos.

Meet Your Ancestors at Olduvai Gorge ▲
Preserved in the volcanic rock and excavated by legendary archaeologist Mary Leakey, a trail of multiple footprints reveals links to our hominid ancestors. Take a tour at the ongoing Laetoli excavation site, and visit the Olduvai Gorge Museum for informative exhibits, lectures, and casts of the ancient prints.

Wildlife-Watch Lake Ndutu ▲
Head to this action-packed spot on the wildebeest migration route, favored by conservationist Jane Goodall and leading wildlife filmmakers. The water

✤ Flying Feathers

Our safari guide stopped the car before a pair of ostriches. (Even though they are the world's largest bird, this wasn't exactly the big game we were looking for in Africa.) "Just wait," he said. The male ostrich crouched down, spread his wings, and started to sway side to side, swirling his neck in an apparently sexy fashion. The female coyly looked on, evaluating his dance moves. She sat down in approval and he giddily skipped her way. The sparks and feathers went flying. For more interesting courtship rituals, turn to page 103.

Wildebeest, the star of the great migration

source, covered woodlands, and grass plains bring the herbivores and carnivores in droves. Giraffe, striped hyena, elephant, cheetah, and lion populations keep things interesting along this scenic 40-square-mile lake.

Hike Empakaai Crater ▲▲▲
Take in the view of the Ol Doinyo Lengai volcano, Lake Natron, and Mount Kilimanjaro from the crater rim. Walk through the forest, keeping an eye out for buffalo, hyena, and elephant, then descend to the salt lake, where thousands of flamingos line the shore. This strenuous three- to five-hour hike rewards with some of the best vistas in Tanzania.

TO EXPLORE MORE ON THIS CONTINENT, CHECK OUT:
- » **Mountains: Virunga Mountains, Rwanda...p. 36**
- » **Islands: Zanzibar, Tanzania...p. 72**

A Grant's gazelle sparring session in Shaba Reserve

SAMBURU

Kenya

AFRICA

Samburu □ KENYA

Three of northern Kenya's greatest wildlife reserves (Shaba, Buffalo Springs, and Samburu) are connected by rivers, mountains, and golden grasses, creating a landscape so beautiful it rivals the wildlife. The Ewaso Nyiro River cuts through the arid expanse, leaving lush banks of fanning doum palms and riverine forests. The water brings reticulated giraffes, Masai lions, and the rare Grevy's zebra out for a drink. Tucked into the Great Rift Valley, the area has remained largely untouched by tourism or development, allowing the nomadic cultures of the Borana, Samburu, Meru, and Turkana people to carry on their traditions. You might see them swaddled in vibrant textiles, collecting salt on the shores of a crater lake, or passing on stories through song. A place of cinematic beauty and intense encounters, Samburu was a film location for *Out of Africa* and *Born Free.* What might normally be an average safari sighting, like vultures picking at a skeleton or sparring Grant's gazelles, always elevates to a Darwinian drama.

WHEN TO GO

The dry seasons of December–March and June–October are ideal for Samburu safaris and sunshine.

WHERE TO STAY

Elephant Bedroom Camp: Luxury tents in a lush riverside setting with extensive safari offerings. **Saruni Samburu:** An ultrachic lodge built into a mountaintop, complete with a spa, photographic hide, and open-air rooms with sweeping views.

GET ROMANTIC

Ask your lodge about a bush breakfast. Whether a riverside omelet station or a simple picnic, dining among the acacias and singing birds is a sublime experience.

HONEYTREK TIP

Central Kenya holds many more safari gems, like Aberdare and Meru National Parks. If you have extra time, add Mount Kenya and the Masai Mara to the south.

A luxe safari tent at the historic Joy's Camp

COUPLES ADVENTURES

Spot the Samburu Big Five ▲▲
Elephants, rhinos, buffalos, leopards, and lions can be found around numerous African parks, but Samburu has its own exclusive big five: the long-necked gerenuk, reticulated giraffe, Grevy's zebra, beisa oryx, and Somali ostrich. Game drive the park with a local guide and the endemic animals will reveal themselves.

Overnight at Joy's Camp ▲
See the region through the eyes of renowned conservationist and author of *Born Free,* Joy Adamson. Spend the night at the site of her former home in the exquisite Shaba Reserve, decorated with the keepsakes from her life raising and releasing Penny the leopard. This luxurious tented camp is a piece of safari history.

Magado Crater in Living Color ▲
Culturally and geologically astounding, saline pools in shades of yellow, red, and green have been hand-harvested by the Meru people for thousands of years. Walk around the salt-encrusted pools, meet the miners, and photograph a truly colorful scene.

✥ Our Wildest Encounter

We marveled at a cheetah gracefully moving across the savanna, searching for a higher vantage point. She approached our safari vehicle with great speed, and our excitement faded to fear. With a pounce, the cheetah landed on the rim of our open roof. Our hearts were lodged in our throats, as she kneaded her paws on the hot metal. Not wanting to scare her, but needing to capture this unfathomable moment, I reached for my camera. Just after I started filming, as if on cue, the cat walked inches from Anne's head, and leaped down the hood. We took our first breath in what seemed like an eternity. (To watch the video, see *www.HoneyTrek.com/Cheetah*.)

Our best and riskiest photo op

Black Rhino Tracking ▲▲▲
In efforts to protect and restore this critically endangered species, the Sera Community Conservancy has reserved more than 133,000 acres for black rhinoceroses to roam free. Spend a few days tracking these majestic creatures (back in their natural Kenyan habitat after 30 years) and support the first community-based rhino sanctuary in Africa.

....

TO EXPLORE MORE ON THIS CONTINENT, CHECK OUT:
» **Mountains: Virunga Mountains, Rwanda...p. 36**
» **Falls: Livingstone, Zambia...p. 54**

A polar bear family moves across the icy Hudson Bay.

CHURCHILL
Canada

BY **DALENE & PETE HECK**

There is something that stirs deep inside your soul when you lock eyes with a polar bear. An unmistakable rush of contemplation of the world: about our place, our effect on each other, and the interconnectedness of all living beings. And few places are better than Churchill, the self-proclaimed "polar bear capital of the world," to experience such an intimate exchange between human and beast. Accessible only by plane or train, this tiny Manitoba town sits on the west shore of Hudson Bay. During late fall, polar bears outnumber residents as they converge near the water's icy edge, waiting for it to freeze over so they can begin their hunt for seals. Come summer, the bears retreat into the boreal forests, and tens of thousands of beluga whales fill the water. During our multiday tour on an elevated "tundra buggy," we navigated rocky paths to encounter bears and other elusive wildlife, like the snowy owl and arctic fox. However, the ivory predators that crossed our path (45 in total!) stole the show.

CANADA □Churchill
NORTH
AMERICA

 WHEN TO GO

October–November offer the best window for polar bear encounters. June–August's warm weather offers tons of outdoor activities, including beluga whale–watching, and still a chance to spot a few polar bears.

 WHERE TO STAY

Frontiers North Adventures: A solid outfitter with lodging options in town and on tundra buggies. **Seal River Heritage Lodge:** Deep in polar bear territory, this rustic chic lodge pairs with Churchill Wild expeditions.

 GET ROMANTIC

Few experiences are more romantic than smooching under the aurora borealis. Head away from town lights for the most vibrant night sky.

🌐 **HECKTIC TRAVELS TIP**

Don't forget that you'll be visiting one of Canada's northernmost destinations. Bundle up and wear layers.

COUPLES ADVENTURES

Dogsledding ▲▲▲
Learn the ropes and history of Canadian sledding from a race pro, then meet your husky team who wants nothing more than to run, run, run! The experience of mushing through the tundra is as cultural as it is a rush.

Chopper Tour ▲▲
Peer over historic forts, boreal forests, expansive waterways, and an array of wildlife on a helicopter tour. In the fall, polar bears are easier to spot than you might think, as their ivory fur pops against winter's stark white snow. Summer offers beautiful views of the flowing waterways and whale-watching opportunities.

Polar Bear Walking Safari ▲▲▲▲
Walk among giants, as they hunt for food, care for their young, and test the ice along Hudson Bay. Tours are available with highly experienced guides, who will safely get you as close as possible to these powerful carnivores in their natural habitat.

Snorkel With Whales ▲▲▲
When the ice pack breaks up in summer, over 40,000 belugas migrate into the Churchill River to feed, socialize, and breed. Swim among these friendly white whales, listening for their unique whistles and watching their graceful moves. Snorkeling offers an intimate and intense wildlife experience. Kayaking is also a thrilling option.

✧ Couples Advice

This may seem like counterintuitive guidance for traveling pairs, but our best piece of advice is to plan some time apart. It's not often that couples spend 24/7 together, but suddenly, whether on a vacation or journey around the globe, you find yourself sharing every waking moment in each other's presence. Remember, it's okay to have some alone time and do one or two solo activities. This way you can fulfill your own personal interests and have fun stories to share at the end of the day. The time apart may even spark up a little romance.

A beluga whale surfaces in the Churchill River.

TO EXPLORE MORE ON THIS CONTINENT, CHECK OUT:
» **Mountains: Mount Rainier, U.S.A....p. 34**
» **Ice: Western Greenland...p. 170**

POWER COUPLE: *Dalene & Pete*

The Hecks have been traveling nonstop since 2009. This intrepid Canadian couple chronicles their journey at *HeckticTravels.com* and has received many accolades along the way, including being named National Geographic Travelers of the Year in 2014. They are also the co-founders of Hecktic Media Inc., a successful and entirely virtual business that keeps them on the road.

SOUTH LUANGWA
Zambia

AFRICA

ZAMBIA — South Luangwa

Said to be one of the last and greatest unspoiled swaths of wilderness, the end of the Great Rift Valley sees few people—except the savviest of safarigoers. The lush expanse of woodlands, plains, and oxbow lagoons along the powerful Luangwa River attract a remarkably diverse and dense wildlife population. Among a handful of major rivers that has never been dammed, it can rise, flood into lagoons, change course, and irrigate the plains for an emerald expanse. During the rainy season, roads become waterways and boats are the primary way to navigate South Luangwa National Park. Safari opportunities abound all year, it just depends on your timing and preferred mode of transit—powerboat, 4x4, or foot. Set out on a game drive to watch leopards on the hunt and endemic Thornicroft's giraffes graze the treetops. Take to the water and commune with the hippos and crocs, or embark on a multiday bush walk. South Luangwa is said to be the birthplace of the African walking safari and where the switch to photographic safari took hold in Zambia.

WHEN TO GO
Dry season (April–October) is a great time to wildlife-watch. The November–March rains transform the arid terrain to a lush jungle, poised for river safaris.

WHERE TO STAY
Nsefu Camp: A historic and intimate riverside retreat by Robin Pope Safaris. **Mfuwe Lodge:** The sophisticated flagship of the Bushcamp Company, an outfitter with six properties walking distance apart.

GET ROMANTIC
Overlooking a hippo-filled lagoon, follow their lead and enjoy a Luangwa spring mud exfoliation. Continue with the Bush Spa's deep cleanse, cucumber wrap, and massage treatment.

HONEYTREK TIP
Instead of a bush plane straight into the park, take the slow road from Mfuwe Airport. Even on the outskirts, you'll likely have wildlife sightings and fascinating local encounters.

Our safari vehicle breaks for a bush breakfast.

Thornicroft's giraffes boast heart-shaped spots.

COUPLES ADVENTURES

Emerald Season Boat Safaris ▲▲
Slow-cruise the flooded ebony groves and spot an abundance of crocodiles, hippos, and elephants. Dock on the lush banks for a picnic and take an afternoon bush walk before heading to the next stop on your lodge-to-lodge river safari.

Bush Walk ▲▲▲
Connect with Mother Nature on a one- to five-day walking safari, a pastime that's said to have originated in South Luangwa. Follow paw tracks, identify birdcalls, smell medicinal plants, and see what crosses your path. Odds are you'll spot a few of the park's estimated 14,000 elephants and 400 bird species.

Get Local in Kawaza Village ▲▲
Take part in traditional Zambian life: harvesting vegetables, grinding maize, drawing water from a well, and sharing a traditional meal with the Kunda people. Go for the day or spend the night in their mud-and-thatch homes to take your immersion one step further. No gimmicks: This is an authentic community and award-winning project that benefits local people.

Photographic Workshop ▲▲
Safari offers a once-in-a-lifetime opportunity to photograph big game in the wild. Embark on a multiday safari with a local wildlife expert and professional photographer who can teach you the optimal field techniques, camera settings, artful compositions, and ways to bring your subjects to life. Savvy guides will bring you to the most scenic spots at all the right times.

❖ The Next Generation of Safari

Our safari guide's 10-year-old son had a penchant for hunting birds with a slingshot. When the boy giddily displayed a lilac-breasted roller, his dad spoke careful words: "Son, you are not only taking a life; you are hurting Daddy's job. Let's try a new game." He gave his son an old field guide and marked the species that frequented their neighborhood. "Every time you see a new bird, circle it in the book, and I'll give you a treat." Our guide was proud to say that his son hasn't killed an animal since and wants to be a wildlife guide when he grows up.

Southern carmine bee-eaters sitting peacefully

TO EXPLORE MORE ON THIS CONTINENT, CHECK OUT:

» Falls: Livingstone, Zambia...p. 54

» Road Trips: Western Cape, South Africa...p. 200

The Tortuguero River, between the beach and rain forest

TORTUGUERO
Costa Rica

NORTH
AMERICA

COSTA
Tortuguero RICA

One of the largest sea turtle colonies in the world, Tortuguero translates to the "land of turtles." Starting in March, the 2,000-pound leatherbacks lumber onto the beach, followed by the hawksbill, loggerhead, and green turtles, coming to nest by the tens of thousands. Once the babies hatch and disperse, so do the majority of visitors; however, the area's other 800-some species of wildlife are here year-round. This corner of northeast Costa Rica encompasses 11 different habitats (rain forests, rivers, mangroves, lagoons, beaches, and so on), creating a stunning array of landscapes and incredible biodiversity. Anytime you're outside, you're basically on a bird-watching adventure, with macaws, toucans, kingfishers, and oropendolas swooping overhead. Massive green iguanas stroll the grounds of your hotel, and spider monkeys swing from the trees outside your room. Take your exploring to the next level with a kayak safari through the network of canals, a night walk in the jungle, or a zipline through the canopy. No matter which season you arrive, you'll see why Tortuguero is aptly dubbed the "Amazon of Costa Rica."

WHEN TO GO
March–May bring fewer tourists, less rain, and the world's largest turtles. There will always be some rain (about 20 feet annually) and abundant wildlife.

WHERE TO STAY
Tortuga Lodge: A delightful riverside retreat with rustic chic rooms, lush grounds, hiking trails, and guided excursions. **Aracari Garden:** A great base and budget option for independent travelers in Tortuguero village.

GET ROMANTIC
Before your walk under the stars with nesting sea turtles, build excitement for the evening with a private boat ride and dinner on the riverbanks (available through Tortuga Lodge).

HONEYTREK TIP
To enter the nesting beach at night, you'll need a guide, but during the day you can go solo (despite what some locals say). Just stay along the vegetation and mind where you step.

A green sea turtle hatchling crawls to sea.

COUPLES ADVENTURES

Jungle Trek by Day and Night ▲▲

Put on some wellies and romp around the lowland Caribbean rain forest, teeming with more than 400 species of trees and over 2,000 species of plants. Take the park's two-mile Gavilan Trail to spy capuchin and howler monkeys, or perhaps a three-toed sloth taking a snooze. Go for a guided night hike to see nocturnal curiosities like red-eyed tree frogs and praying mantis.

Volunteer With Sea Turtles ▲▲▲▲

The Sea Turtle Conservancy, the world's first and arguably most accomplished organization of its kind, offers one- to three-week volunteer programs from March to October. Survey the beaches as massive leatherbacks lay 80 to 100 eggs each or collect data on newborn green turtles, all while assisting in research that protects the four species that call Tortuguero home.

Kayak the Canals ▲▲

Paddle silently through the national park's extensive network of canals and lush lagoons, keeping your eyes and ears peeled for wildlife, like river turtles, speckled caiman, otters, and even the elusive West Indian manatee. Along the banks, water-loving birds like great blue herons, kingfishers, and egrets won't be hard to spot.

Bird-Watch ▲

Take a nature walk or boat ride with an ornithologist and you'll see dozens of Tortuguero's more than 300 bird species. With powerful monoscopes and heightened senses, your guide will help you identify keel-billed toucans, crested eagles, and slaty-tailed trogons like a pro.

✦ Welcome to the Jungle

As we walked toward our room at Tortuga Lodge, admiring the palms and flame-hued heliconia along the path, we nearly tripped on a four-foot-long green iguana. We excitedly waved over a staff member, though to our amazement she was only mildly enthused by our sighting. "They're amazing," she said, "and everywhere." Each of our strolls from that point on had an iguana sighting—by reception, on the patio, in a tree, or on the lawn tearing into a freshly fallen mango. After our fifth sighting we stopped alerting strangers, but the harmony between humans and animals in Tortuguero never ceased to amaze.

Wild iguana lounging by the pool at Tortuga Lodge

TO EXPLORE MORE ON THIS CONTINENT, CHECK OUT:

» At Sea: Mesoamerican Barrier Reef, Belize...p. 126

» Rain Forests: Monteverde, Costa Rica...p. 186

Smitten Adélie penguins move in for the cuddle.

Wildlife Courtship Rituals

Quirky, adorable, and astounding strategies to get the girl and keep the love alive.

BOWERBIRD
1. The Decorator

A lady bowerbird has a discerning eye for style, and she judges her mate on his decorating skills. The male works tirelessly to build an elaborate nest, adorned with flowers, berries, and any vibrant accents (especially in her favorite color, blue). He even artfully landscapes a path, showing the way to his love nest.

SEAHORSE
2. The Disco Duo

Holding tails, swimming snout to snout, and giddily changing colors, seahorses are among the most affectionate pairs. This courtship goes on for days and continues through the male's pregnancy (you read that right, he carries over 1,000 babies to term).

ADÉLIE PENGUIN
3. The Rock Hound

This Antarctic species makes a nest out of rocks, beginning with a courtship stone. Appealing to the females' maternal senses, a male will scour the beaches for the prettiest pebble he can find and give it to her as a proposal. If she feels it's her lucky rock, it will be his lucky day.

NURSERY WEB SPIDER
4. The Gift Giver

Like bringing a girl a box of chocolates tied with bow, the male spider wraps a treat in his finest silk to show he's interested. Players bundle up whatever they can find, but those who prepare a heartfelt (and tasty) offering will receive love in return.

GALÁPAGOS WAVED ALBATROSS
5. Fred & Ginger

When mating albatrosses reunite after much of the year apart, they can barely contain their excitement and have to dance it out. Like a choreographed routine, they swirl their bills, clack their beaks, point their heads to the sky, and let out sounds akin to *Woohoo!*

JAPANESE PUFFER FISH
6. The Artist

These males might not have showy colors, but they've got the artistic skills and patience of a Tibetan monk. Similar to a sand mandala, he arranges the grains into an intricate geometric design (even embellishing it with shells), all the while building a safe and attractive haven for his future mate to lay her eggs.

RED-CAPPED MANAKIN
7. The Moonwalker

This unassuming little bird begins his courtship process by finding a smooth branch and making it his dance floor. He waits patiently and when he sees a looker, he channels his inner Michael Jackson—effortlessly gliding back and forth, striking poses, and flapping his wings so fast they hum a little tune.

PRAIRIE VOLE
8. Old Faithful

Rodents have never been as cute as prairie voles going steady. The male wouldn't dream of leaving his female, and shuns the floozies that try to woo him away. Looking out for one another, they cuddle for warmth and regularly preen each other to keep up their good looks. And when it comes time for kids, it's shared child rearing all the way.

PEACOCK
9. The Hypnotizer

This brilliant pheasant flaunts his long train in iridescent blues, greens, and golds, as a little tease. When he finds a lady he's interested in, he'll fan his eyelike plumes into a towering dome, and shimmy for a hypnotic spectacular.

BONOBO
10. Lover, Not a Fighter

These kinky primates don't just court one another for the sake of procreation; they mate as a means of greeting, solving disputes, having fun, and showing their appreciation for one another. For bonobos, there is no honeymoon phase; it's a life of love.

Shwedagon Pagoda,
Myanmar

> *"Architecture is the very mirror of life. You only have to cast your eyes on buildings to feel the presence of the past, the spirit of a place; they are the reflection of society."*
>
> —I. M. PEI

Chapter Five

HISTORY & ARCHITECTURE

Gazing upon a thousand-year-old temple, with its chipping facade and fading frescoes, your imagination stirs. You dream of kings praying in silk robes, chants echoing, and incense swirling around the space. Just when you think you've entered a museum, a woman leaves a flower at Buddha's feet. Great architecture is full of life, made to celebrate prosperity, unity, and craftsmanship. Even as civilizations change, most rulers know better than to destroy a beautiful building. Instead they build upon it, adding personal touches. As time passes, what began as a tenth-century temple has become an enduring cultural icon. We love sites that preserve history through use, not velvet ropes. In Sintra, the courtyard of the National Palace is the town square. Cappadocia uses its Roman cave dwellings as hotels. China, after the destructive Cultural Revolution, now holds all things ancient close to the heart. Discover places where history comes alive.

BAGAN
Myanmar

ASIA
MYANMAR
Bagan

magine 2,000 ancient Buddhist temples hugging a river and dotting the plains for 26 square miles. Now, imagine 10,000 filling that same space. From the 10th to 13th centuries, the Pagan Kingdom (the first power to unify the country) went on a building spree of epic proportions. Golden stupas, brilliant frescoes, and floor-to-ceiling Buddhas were constructed in celebration of Myanmar's first capital.

Over time, invasions, earthquakes, and the harsh climate have claimed nearly 80 percent of the monuments—but you would never know by looking at the incredible density of stunning temples. Bagan is on the UNESCO World Heritage Tentative List for its imperfect restorations and scrappy approach to maintenance, though, in some ways, that adds to the appeal. It's not just the thousands of temples that make it so special, but the families that tend the grounds, the cows that graze between them, and the peace found when sitting atop a secluded pagoda with the one you love.

WHEN TO GO
Bagan gets its share of heat and rain. November–February are ideal, especially around a full moon.

WHERE TO STAY
The Hotel @ Tharabar Gate: Among the area's most luxurious resorts, located along the ancient city walls. **Bagan Thande:** A great vibe and value for a riverfront location within the archaeological zone.

GET ROMANTIC
Shake the sunset crowds at Shwesandaw Pagoda and bike along the river to a more secluded temple. Ask nicely and groundskeepers may let you have the roof to yourselves.

HONEYTREK TIP
Take the train from Yangon or ferry from Mandalay, and trade a bit of comfort and speed for priceless local encounters and a classic Myanmar experience.

Thousands of ancient temples cover the Bagan plains.

Old and new Buddhas often fill the temple niches.

COUPLES ADVENTURES

Northeast Corridor by Carriage ▲
Spend time at Ananda, among the oldest, holiest, and most ornate temples in Bagan. From here, catch a traditional horse cart toward the massive golden stupa of Shwezigon Pagoda and Gubyauk-gyi Temple with some of the best preserved frescoes. After these essential stops, ask your driver for his favorite off-the-track temples and local eats.

Bike Beyond the Walls ▲▲▲
Within the old walls of Tharabar Gate, you'll naturally gravitate toward the tallest pagoda of Thatby-innyu and the gleaming Bupaya, but the best of the kingdom is off the main maps. Get lost, climb ruins, chat with monks, and pay homage to forgotten temples. To cover more ground, rent an e-bike.

Balloon Bagan ▲▲
It's virtually impossible to see all 2,000 temples, but a hot air balloon is your best chance. Floating over a sea of tiered pagodas cloaked in morning mist helps you grasp the magnitude of the archaeological zone and ambitious dreams of the Pagan kings. Even if flying is not for you, pack a sunrise picnic and watch them fill the sky.

Scale Mount Popa ▲▲▲
Set on a sheer volcanic peak, Popa Taungkalat Monastery is one of the nation's most sacred and photogenic sites. Home of the Great Nats, the 37 animists spirits fused into Myanmar Buddhism, this must-see mountain is lined with shrines, exuberant devotees, and cheeky monkeys. Wake up to hike Mount Popa crater, through lush valleys to the ultimate views of the monastery in the sky.

✥ Granny, Get Your Slingshot

While admiring the artwork of Thabeik Hmauk temple, we heard a burst of laughter outside. It was three generations of groundskeepers taking slingshot practice. When the grandpa saw our huge smiles, he waved us over for a turn. I pulled back the giant rubber band, and my rock pitifully fell to the floor. When the second attempt to hit the tin can went awry, Granny came on the scene. She gave me a nod, as if to say, "Take notes." Lining up her target with a wrinkly squint, she stretched the band to its max and, "Ping!" In unison, we all burst into cheers and laughter—the universal language.

Anne's slingshot lesson at Thabeik Hmauk temple

TO EXPLORE MORE ON THIS CONTINENT, CHECK OUT:
» Mountains: Emeishan, China...p. 28
» Lakes: Inle Lake, Myanmar...p. 48

Hot air balloons float over the Love Valley at sunrise.

CAPPADOCIA
Turkey

Cappadocia
TURKEY *A S I A*

Blanketed in volcanic tuff, Cappadocia has been slowly eroding into magnificent rock towers (called fairy chimneys), ruffled valleys, castle-like cliffs, and one the most otherworldly landscapes. As if its geological beauty weren't enough to fascinate, these lava formations have been hand-carved into thousands of houses, inhabited by the Hittites, Romans, Ottomans, and present-day Anatolians. The conical rock homes with wonky windows and doorways are Cappadocia's signature, though that's just scratching the surface.

Stuck between warring Persian and Greek rivals and on the fringe of the Byzantine Empire, Cappadocia was often a battleground, driving locals to build in the peace of the subterranean. Follow the rough-hewn tunnels and go deep into dozens of underground cities. Explore fifth-century rock monasteries where Christians practiced in secrecy. Then discover the luxury side of cave dwelling, at one of the five-star hotels and restaurants in the cliffs. Cappadocia has long been a place of refuge, and continues to be the perfect escape for adventurers and romantics alike.

 WHEN TO GO

Cappadocia can get quite hot and cold, even in the same day. April–June is a pleasant time, as is September–October, with even more cultural festivals.

 WHERE TO STAY

Museum Hotel: The only Relais & Châteaux property in all of Turkey and Castle Hill's finest cave accommodations. **Kelebek:** From basic rooms to suites, this Göreme hillside hotel offers the must-have cave experience for all budgets.

GET ROMANTIC

Glide over the volcanic valleys and ancient dwellings in a hot air balloon. Touchdown and toast with a champagne breakfast. Not just romantic, it's also the best way to grasp the complex landscape.

HONEYTREK TIP

Sprawling Cappadocia has mind-boggling layers of history. A knowledgeable guide with transportation, like the pros at Matiana Travel, will be invaluable.

Volcanic tuff carved into dwellings on Castle Hill

COUPLES ADVENTURES

Kaymakli Subterranean City ▲▲
Deep below the Earth's surface, nearly 100 tunnels connect an ancient world where an estimated 3,500 people once lived. Mind your head and tuck in the belly as you move from one tiny room to the next, seeing where wine was pressed and copper was crafted. Although a portion of the underground city is a museum, locals still use some caves as cellars and stables.

Hike From Love to Rose Valley ▲▲
Start in Love Valley, descending the white walls into a psychedelic Eden. Meander through the garden of wild fruits and discover geological masterpieces around every bend—from solid waves of lava flow to mushroom-tipped towers. Stop in the Byzantine rock village of Çavuşin and loop back through the equally beautiful Rose Valley.

Göreme Open-Air Museum ▲
UNESCO has acknowledged this site as one of the world's best examples of post-iconoclastic Byzantine art. Even if religious paintings aren't your thing, the maze of cliff-carved monasteries will ignite your inner Indiana Jones. Climb into tenth-century cave

✥ Cappadocia Time Line

There is a long and winding history of civilizations in Cappadocia. Let these approximate dates be your benchmark:

1700–1200 B.C.: Hittite Empire

1200–700 B.C.: Neo-Hittite and Tabal Kingdom

500–300 B.C.: Persian Empire

300 B.C.–A.D. 17: Kingdom of Cappadocia

17–1071: Roman State to Byzantine Empire

1071–1400: Seljuq Turks

1400–1922: Ottoman Empire

1922–present: Turkish Republic

Byzantine art at the Dark Church at Göreme Open-Air Museum

churches, peer into the craggy refectories where thousands of monks once dined, and don't miss Tokali Church for the most significant paintings.

Beyond Uçhisar Castle ▲▲
This fortress-like mountain was carved by villagers to escape enemies storming the plains. Wander the multilevel network of rock shelters, then head down Castle Hill to explore the abandoned conical cave dwellings. Climb up hand-sculpted stairs and hang out in ancient penthouses.

TO EXPLORE MORE IN THIS REGION, CHECK OUT:

» **At Sea: Cyclades Islands, Greece...p. 134**

» **Supernatural: Pamukkale, Turkey...p. 224**

Hopperstad stave church in Sogn og Fjordane, Norway

The Perfect Pair

In the face of termites, fires, winds, and 900 years of unforgiving winters, Hopperstad has endured. Just inland from Norway's largest fjord, this stave church often goes unnoticed, though it's among the oldest still standing. Few wooden masterpieces can compare, though its neighboring oak tree comes close. We sat beneath its umbrella of red leaves, and looked up at the scalloped shingles and carved Norse motifs. Like kindred spirits, one wild and one refined, they complemented each other perfectly.

FENGHUANG
China

ASIA
□ Fenghuang

An emerald river pours from lush mountains. Ming dynasty bridges arch over the waters. Stilted houses perch along the shore. Wooden canoes are propelled by bamboo poles, and hill tribe women wash their clothes on the riverbanks. This 1,200-year-old Hunan city is picture-perfect and acclaimed as one of the most beautiful towns in China. Fenghuang (translating to "phoenix town") is wildly popular among the Chinese, but somehow the droves of giddy and proud nationals don't make it feel mobbed, but rather a supremely happy place. By day, the temples, historic homes, and ancestral halls invite you in; by night, lights illuminate the swallow-tailed roofs, stone archways, and pagodas with a rainbow of reflections shimmering off the water. Everyone is out enjoying the riverside cafés, strolling with their sweetheart and reveling in the festive ambiance. The town will easily dazzle for two days, while nearby destinations, like the Southern Great Wall and the Wulingyuan forest of rock spires (p. 234), will keep you busy for an adventure-packed week in Hunan Province.

WHEN TO GO
March–May and September–November offer the most temperate weather in this subtropical climate. If you are averse to crowds, pack your coat and visit in serene December–January.

WHERE TO STAY
Phoenix Melody Inn: The most upscale, traditional riverside hotel. **Fengxiang Jiangbianlou Inn:** Basic, cheery rooms with balconies. Both have friendly English-speaking staff (rarer than you'd think).

GET ROMANTIC
Just before sunset, walk northwest of the river along Nanhua Road to the hilltop park. Pack a few Tsingtaos and dumplings, and watch the ancient structures of old town light up one by one.

HONEYTREK TIP
To see people reveling in their own country's beauty is a cultural experience—feed off their enthusiasm. If you need a little space, walk along the water's edge. The photo ops are better here anyway.

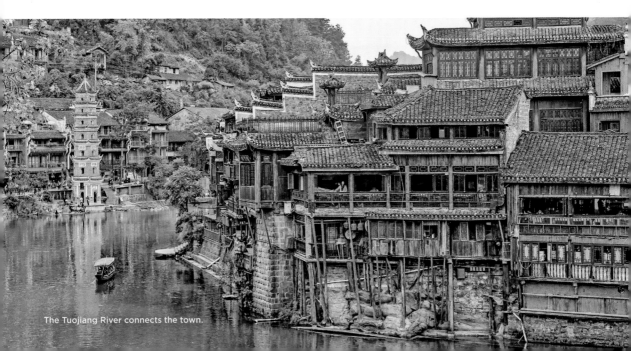
The Tuojiang River connects the town.

Hunan-style food stalls line the street each night.

COUPLES ADVENTURES

Through-Ticket Treasures ▲
A ticket is needed to enter the old town; it's good for two days and grants entrance into 10 sites, including historic homes, fortresses, temples, and vista points. East Gate Tower, Yang Family Ancestral Hall, Shen Congwen's home, and Chongde Hall offer the best mix, especially when paired with wandering the narrow flagstone streets.

Bamboo Boat Ride ▲
Hands down, the most popular activity in town, and rightly so, this ride offers a unique perspective on Fenghuang, showing the underside of bridges, the weathered stilts of the *diaojiaolou* (Chinese for "house with hanging feet"), and fishermen dipping their nets alongside you; plus, you get to ride a little rapid.

Huang Si Qiao Castle ▲
Head 15 miles out of town to see one of China's best preserved stone castles. Built in the seventh century from bluestone boulders, and held together with steamed sticky rice and calcium carbonate, this mountain fortress is the real deal.

The Southern Great Wall ▲▲
Another great wall of China, this structure passes 118 miles through Fenghuang's mountains and valleys with over 800 military structures. This 16th-century work has largely been rebuilt, but it's still impressive for its scale and opportunities to explore.

✛ Costume Photo Shoot

After watching the Chinese tourists get all gussied up in traditional Miao dress and being approached by countless photo hucksters, we finally broke down and had our own kitschy costume session. I'm not sure who was more entertained—us or the swarm of Chinese tourists giggling at the sight of these two *gweilos* in full garb. If you can't beat 'em, join 'em.

A photo peddler turned buddy

TO EXPLORE MORE ON THIS CONTINENT, CHECK OUT:

» **Mountains: Annapurna Sanctuary, Nepal...p. 24**

» **Supernatural: Wulingyuan, China...p. 234**

Glorious monuments surround Plaza de la Paz.

GUANAJUATO
Mexico

NORTH
AMERICA
MEXICO □ Guanajuato

A narrow valley lined with colorful houses, connected by winding stairwells, tunnels, and alleyways, Guanajuato is a maze of treasures. Rounding a bend can lead to a pocket plaza, colonial casas, or the ultimate tamale. Ambling downhill, you reach Plaza de la Paz and a boulevard wide enough for architects to spread their wings. Both the Aztec and Spanish were drawn here for the mountains full of silver and gold. During the 16th to 19th centuries (when Guanajuato accounted for two-thirds of the world's silver production), the colonialists spared no expense. Opulent churches, ornate theaters, and metropolis-like mines have collectively put it on the UNESCO map, while the University of Guanajuato and the international Cervantino arts festival keep it young and lively. Music fills the streets, from mariachi bands to *callejoneadas,* a tradition where musicians in 17th-century costumes serenade passersby. Open your heart to Guanajuato and you'll most certainly fall in love.

WHEN TO GO
The mountain locale keeps it from getting too hot or rainy. Come any time or try to catch October's Festival Cervantino.

WHERE TO STAY
Villa María Cristina: A 19th-century townhouse on an elegant boulevard, earning its Relais & Châteaux stripes. **Alonso 10:** An eight-room historic hotel with contemporary suites in the heart of town.

GET ROMANTIC
Sneak a lucky kiss on Callejon del Beso. Legend has it, forbidden lovers lived across the street, but with balconies so close, their lips could still meet.

HONEYTREK TIP
Start your city exploration at the mountaintop monument of El Pipíla. It offers the best view of Guanajuato, and gives insight on how this labyrinth comes together.

Mexican baroque architecture within the basilica

COUPLES ADVENTURES

The Mining World of La Valenciana ▲▲
Trace Guanajuato's wealth back to the silver vein running through the village of La Valenciana. Walk 200 feet deep into the San Ramón Mine and visit the museum at San Cayetano, where generations of miners give tours. See how the dirty work paid off with a visit to the 18th-century Valenciana Church, considered by UNESCO to be one of the best examples of baroque architecture in Latin America.

Diego Rivera's House ▲
Mexico's famed muralist and husband to Frida Kahlo was born in old town Guanajuato. Tour his childhood home, with its 19th-century furnishings and keepsakes, and the adjacent museum with over 100 original Rivera works—from studies for his murals to the cubist paintings influenced by his time with Picasso.

Insider Street Food ▲
Follow the foodies from Mexico Street Food Tours to the best carts, bakeries, and markets behind this dynamic cuisine. Nibble your way through the bustling Hidalgo Market to hidden kitchens with

✤ Couchsurfing Karma

We knew it would be tough to navigate the Mexico City megalopolis on our own, so we reached out to Rodrigo and Maria José on Couchsurfing, a website that pairs open-minded travelers with local hosts offering a free place to stay. "Bienvenidos!" Ro and Majo exclaimed with a hug. Newlyweds, architects, and proud citizens, they wanted to show us the best of their city. They took us to a street festival, their favorite museums, a local mescal bar, and even threw a little party in our honor. Not even a paid tour guide would do all that, and they did it for nothing but the love of cultural exchange. We cannot wait to show them our hometown someday.

The sharing economy often leads to friendships.

grandmas making enchiladas mineras, and street carts flipping crispy gorditas. Top off the day with a Mexican coffee and horchata ice cream.

Juarez Theater Performance ▲
Catch a concert, play, or ballet at this grand theater, virtually unaltered since its opening day in 1903. Even without a show, it's worth taking a tour of this neo-classical masterpiece and peering into the 902-seat space to see the architectural detail in every square inch—from gilded fretwork to embroidered swags.

TO EXPLORE MORE ON THIS CONTINENT, CHECK OUT:
» **Deserts: Durango, Mexico...p. 148**
» **Road Trips: The Southwest, U.S.A....p. 206**

GHENT
Belgium

BY KRISTIN HENNING & TOM BARTEL

EUROPE

Ghent □ BELGIUM

A break in the clouds inspires residents to pause by the water and soak up the sun. Scenic river bends, picturesque bridges, bicycles, a university, and lovely architecture define this youthful city, which has the historic air of nearby Bruges without the hordes of tourists. In the Middle Ages, Ghent's busy port and flourishing textile industry made it the second largest city in northern Europe. Since then, it has balanced commerce with craftsmanship, wielded both secular and religious power, and mixed traditional and pop cultures. Today, the city center is known for a triple treat: St. Bavo's Abbey, St. Nicholas' Church, and the UNESCO-noted belfry of the town square.

Along the Lys River, rows of Flemish-style buildings with steep roofs, stepped facades, and articulated brick-work are artfully mirrored in the canal. Locals and visitors are drawn to the riverfront paths of Graslei and Korenlei to enjoy the airy views. The largest car-free zone in Belgium, the historic center is especially inviting to enthusiastic pedestrians like us. And when we want to take a seat, it is happily in front of a bowl of steaming moules frites, the perfect side dish to a day in Ghent.

WHEN TO GO

April–August are recommended for best weather, with a July bonus: the annual Jazz Festival. We lean toward autumn and October's Film Fest.

WHERE TO STAY

Ghent River Hotel: Within two historic buildings—a Renaissance house and a cotton factory—this is the only downtown hotel accessible by water. **Ghent Marriott:** This four-star hotel, perfectly located on the river, offers an upscale blend of new and old.

GET ROMANTIC

As lights flicker in the water, a late-night walk along the river is a sure bet. Wake up to meet the early morning colors before a breakfast of authentic Belgian waffles.

TRAVEL PAST 50 TIP

Read *The Monuments Men* (or watch the movie) and double your appreciation of the Van Eyck painting "The Adoration of the Mystic Lamb." This St. Bavo altarpiece is one of Europe's most coveted works of art.

Lively restaurants around the Graslei medieval port

COUPLES ADVENTURES

Bike to Your Heart's Content ▲▲▲
Get to know Ghent's bike-friendly culture. Try shorter rides along the city's greenways, follow the Chateau Route along the Scheldt River, tour the 34-mile Lys Region route for great countryside views, or even bike the cross-country cycling trails to Belgium's other major cities.

Paddle the Canals ▲▲
Rent a canoe to experience Ghent as early traders might have seen it. River canals, the original city thoroughfares, provide impressive views of the medieval center. Plenty of guided inland waterway excursions are available.

Sample Local Beers ▲
Belgian beer culture goes back to Roman times, and as Christianity rolled in, so did better brews. Today's certified Trappist beers (like Chimay) are still produced by monks. Around town, pubs offer flights for sampling, serving each style in its proper-shaped glass. Visit Huyghe Brewery to see where the famous Delirium ales are brewed.

Stroll Graffiti Street ▲
The alleyway of Werregarenstraat features everything from local art giants to unsung practitioners. Adding to the intrigue, this free-form art display is always evolving. For a town laden with history, a street like this demonstrates Ghent's willingness to remain bright, vibrant, and open to change.

✦ Couples Advice

Traveling often means living in tight quarters. After a career working together—being around each other all the time—we've developed some handy ways to avoid getting on each other's nerves. First, respect each other's privacy and need for quiet time. Serious conversations can wait until both are in the mood to discuss. Second, go off on your own every now and then. Alone, we move at our own pace, observe distinct things, and stop for different reasons than when we're together. Finally, listen. Listen carefully and even an old story becomes new.

Flemish architecture along the canals

TO EXPLORE MORE ON THIS CONTINENT, CHECK OUT:
» **Rivers: Rhine Gorge, Germany...p. 56**
» **Road Trips: North Coast, Ireland & Northern Ireland...p. 208**

POWER COUPLE: *Kris & Tom*

Since choosing to exchange their homestead for a traveling life in 2010, Kris and Tom have found themselves at home in over 60 countries on six continents. They gravitate toward cultural and historic centers, national parks, long treks, and tasty food. Former publishers from Minneapolis, they find half the fun of traveling is sharing their stories and photos on their blog, *TravelPast50.com*.

SINTRA
Portugal

EUROPE

□ **Sintra**
PORTUGAL

Set high in the mountains, just 20 miles from Lisbon with cool temperatures and views to the ocean, Sintra has always been in fashion. From the Moors to medieval royalty to the European jet set, people have flocked to this seductive locale for a millennium. Each group left its stylistic mark, turning this town into a veritable Architecture 101. Start at the tenth-century Moorish Castle, snaking along a mountain spine. It's straight out of a storybook with landscaping like an enchanted forest—partly because King Ferdinand II embellished it to echo his adjacent palace. His whimsical sensibilities were largely the foundation for the Romantic style that spread across Europe in the late 19th century. Sintra became the place for the elite to flex their creative muscles with grand summer homes in a canon of international styles and boundless imagination. Hike to the Pena Palace and see architectural fantasies played out in a rainbow of colors. E-bike through the hills, past dozens of Romantic-era mansions blending global motifs. Embrace the romance in the air with a carriage ride, a glass of port, and a night in your own palace.

✈ WHEN TO GO
Avoid the heat and summer crowds with an April–June or September–October visit.

▦ WHERE TO STAY
Tivoli Palácio de Seteais: A true 18th-century palace, converted into a five-star hotel with lavish details fit for royalty. **Sintra Bliss House:** A contemporary and comfortable hotel in the heart of town with a fabulous breakfast buffet.

♥ GET ROMANTIC
Dine where the locals go on date night. Sit on the patio or under the stone arches of Tacho Real, enjoying traditional dishes like bacalhau à brás and listening to Portuguese guitar.

☑ HONEYTREK TIP
Sintra is a major day-trip destination from Lisbon, particularly in summer. Stay for a few days and enjoy the quiet of the mornings and magical evenings while the tour buses are away.

The eccentric Pena Palace overlooking Sintra

Azenhas do Mar village perched on the sea cliffs

COUPLES ADVENTURES

Architecture Crash Course ▲
Sintra's National Palace stands as one of the country's best preserved examples of medieval style: Gothic, Mudéjar, and Manueline. Spend time in King Dinis's 14th-century chapel, and get dizzy on its geometric detail. Look up at the ceilings in King João's wing, and find hand-painted caravels and mermaids. Keep an eye out for the Manueline hallmarks of twisted ropes and anchors.

E-bike the Countryside to Seaside ▲▲▲
Follow the savvy guides from Park E Bike through the rocky countryside. Stop at the serene 16th-century Convent of the Capuchos, pass the Colares vineyards, and head down to the beaches of Azenhas do Mar. Have an early dinner at the cliffside restaurant by the same name, before zipping back up the mountain—without breaking a sweat.

Hike to the Palaces ▲▲
Rather than take a rickshaw, follow the 45-minute Lapa Trail up the forest path. Reach Pena Park with its 500-plus species of hand-selected trees. Tour King Ferdinand's fully furnished and over-the-top Pena Palace, then continue your walk to the Moorish

✥ Love and Faith in Sintra

An Airbnb listing of a 16th-century villa, once a retreat for monks with its original stone chapel and herb garden, inspired our family friends Natasha and Tyler to wed in Portugal. They had never been to the country together and most guests hadn't even heard of Sintra, but suddenly 60 of us were flying across the Atlantic. Nerves about the unknown had been building within the group for months, but the moment Sintra's palaces came into sight, we all knew this story would end with happily ever after.

Quinta de São Thiago wedding, sealed with a kiss

Castle. Explore the winding embattlements, enjoying views of the city and sea, before taking the Santa Maria Trail back to town.

Gardens of Quinta da Regaleira ▲
Created by a wealthy Brazilian returning to his Portuguese roots, this early 20th-century conceptual garden and mansion is replete with symbolism. Descend the spiral staircase into the Iniciatic Well, hop from stone to stone in the grotto, stroll down the Promenade of the Gods, and peer into the chapel laden with Masonic references.

TO EXPLORE MORE ON THIS CONTINENT, CHECK OUT:

» At Sea: Cyclades Islands, Greece...p. 134
» Snow: Tromsø, Norway...p. 168

Historic Festivals

Where worldwide traditions began and local celebrations thrive, these places know how to party.

ITALY
1. Putignano Carnival

One of Italy's longest running *carnevales,* Puglia is a trendsetter for this worldwide event. Parading with 50-foot-high floats, it's reminiscent of Rio but wonderfully quaint, with papier-mâché figures and kids tossing confetti. Get sexy for the costume balls and eat extra gelato before Lent reins you in.

INDIA
2. Braj Holi

Go where this Hindu celebration of color, love, and springtime began—in Lord Krishna's hometown. The spirited villages of Mathura and Vrindavan stretch the festival to 40 days, with playful powder fights and processions between ancient temples.

UZBEKISTAN
3. Navruz

For over 2,500 years, the Persian calendar's New Year's Day (March 21) has been celebrated across West and Central Asia, though Bukhara's Seyil festivities are among the most entertaining. Bonfires, wrestling, horse races, plays, and good tidings are spread across the city for a week.

SCOTLAND
4. Ceres Highland Games

Ever since Robert the Bruce gave the nod in 1314, Ceres village has been hosting this competition of strength, rhythm, and grace. Watch kilted Scots compete in the caber toss, sheaf pitch, and tug-of-war, interspersed with Highland dancing and competitive bagpiping.

CHINA
5. Gedong Mask Festival

Before a 400-year-old Tibetan monastery, fanciful dancers in painted masks and an orchestra of monks perform dramatic Buddhist allegories. The Naxi people (and virtually no Westerners) are in attendance for this Benzilan village spectacular.

SPAIN
6. Festival of San Fermín

Don your best whites and red handkerchief, and get ready to run (or at least party) through the streets of Pamplona. More than just the Running of the Bulls, there are some 400 other events. Folkloric music, street theater, fireworks, and parades spread across nine days of revelry.

ARGENTINA
7. Pachamama Festival

Digging holes in the ground and filling them with food, coca leaves, and chicha liquor, the Andean people feed Mother Earth each August. A deeply spiritual and beautiful series of ceremonies, this harvest ritual is best witnessed by taking the "train to the clouds" to San Antonio de los Cobres.

THAILAND
8. Lanna Songkran

Every April, Thailand takes to the streets with Super Soakers and water balloons for the world's wettest New Year's celebration. Chiang Mai balances the silliness and holiness of this holiday with rituals like cleansing Buddhas, building sand sculptures, and Lanna-style dancing.

MEXICO
9. Purépecha Day of the Dead

Celebrate those who've passed with parades, serenades, and *ofrendas* of their favorite foods. This fusion of pagan and Catholic holidays is at its most traditional on Janitzio Island, home of the pre-Columbian Purépecha people. Watch the procession of candlelit boats, where fishermen twirl their butterfly nets to lure spirits to the grand fiesta.

MYANMAR
10. Phaung Daw Oo Pagoda Festival

Standing on slender boats and rowing with their legs, hundreds of graceful boatmen parade a magnificent golden shrine around Inle Lake. When the three-week procession arrives to Nyaungshwe, join the vibrant hill tribes people to welcome the holy float and watch the leg-rowing championships.

Quirimbas Archipelago, Mozambique

Chapter Six

AT SEA

Considering 71 percent of the Earth is covered by ocean, we should really spend more time at sea. It's soothing, adventurous, mysterious . . . the ultimate escape. Life mellows when you've got the sound of the waves, the warmth of the sun, and an endless horizon before you. Though stare at it long enough and curiosity reels you in.

Sailing revolutionized travel. Not deterred by rugged terrain or beholden to roads, boats can skirt the impassable. Once explorers sailed around the globe, the world was no longer flat, but a circle that connected us all.

Set sail toward a beach without footprints and watch for playful sea lions and soaring pelicans. Meet cultures where time is still told by the tides. Dive below the surface into a coral garden with a flurry of fish. Submerge to the depths where hammerheads patrol ancient shipwrecks. Surface and find a pair of deck chairs to watch the sunset over a sea of possibilities.

Sandfly Bay and the teal waters of Abel Tasman National Park

TASMAN DISTRICT
New Zealand

AUSTRALIA

NEW ZEALAND
Tasman District

Turquoise waters, golden beaches, and verdant palm trees—you'd think Abel Tasman National Park was somewhere in the Caribbean. The Dutch explorer spied this section of the South Island coastline in 1642, but it was virtually untouched until the mid-1800s. Fur seals, blue penguins, and manta rays had the run of the place, and with the help of New Zealand's progressive parks system, they still do. The 37-mile coastal trail along the granite headlands, lush forests, and sandy coves classifies as one of the country's nine Great Walks, though the ability to combine tramping with kayaking, biking, and boating sets it apart. Water taxis run from trailhead to trailhead, and outfitters help connect sections of the track with paddling excursions and overnight stops in historic lodges. Venture outside the bounds of the park and you'll find some of New Zealand's finest vineyards, biggest sand dunes, and most artistic Kiwis.

☒ WHEN TO GO
Visit the country's sunniest region year-round. Consider May–August for temperatures in the 50s, calm seas, more animals, and fewer people.

▦ WHERE TO STAY
Abel Tasman Lodge: A modern, well-priced B&B at the park's gateway of Marahau.
Wilsons Abel Tasman: An outfitter offering excellent adventures, many overnighting at their historic homes within the park.

♡ GET ROMANTIC
Charter a private boat with Gourmet Sailing. Cruise the scenic coastline, then hop out for a swim or hike while they prepare a multi-course lunch.

☑ HONEYTREK TIP
Download the Project Janszoon app for the park's maps, history, tides, flora, and fauna. It's like having a visitor center in your pocket.

New Zealand fur seals basking on the coastline

COUPLES ADVENTURES

Kayak Torrent & Bark Bays ▲▲▲
Paddle between these bays with a spin around Pinnacle Island's playful fur seal colony. Transition from the sea to the river with a paddle up Bark Bay Inlet, among waterfalls and flowering kānuka trees.

Hiking Pitt Head and Beyond ▲▲
As you walk from the Anchorage landing, through beech forest with its symphony of native birds and multiple coastal viewpoints, the trail reaches the dazzling turquoise and gold Te Pukatea Bay. Return for an easy 1.5-hour loop, or continue 3 hours along the last leg of the Great Walk to Marahau.

The Great Taste Trio ▲▲▲▲
Indulge in all the region's delights with a multi-day bike ride along Tasman's Great Taste Trail, through wineries, orchards, artsy enclaves, and plenty of coastline. Say farewell to the Gentle Cycling Company and meet the Wilsons Abel Tasman crew to continue your five-day journey

✤ Super Duck

As we kayaked up Bark Bay Inlet, our guide Whitey shouted, "Blue duck! A blue duck!!!" It looked like a reasonably cute bird to us, but judging by the excitement in his voice, a sighting like this was something to behold. Blue ducks ride the rapids like pro paddlers, swirling around rocks, popping out of white water, and fishing along the way. This was the first Abel Tasman sighting in over a decade. Our photograph even made the local newspaper.

A victorious eight-mile paddle to Split Apple Rock

combining hiking and kayaking between their luxury in-park lodges.

Farewell Spit ▲▲
A skinny sand spit jutting 15 miles into the sea has long been a magnet for shipwrecks, beached whales, and bird colonies. Take a 4WD dune bus from Collingwood to the 19th-century lighthouse, slide down massive sand dunes, observe up to 90 species of birds, and learn about this wetland's unusual history.

TO EXPLORE MORE ON THIS CONTINENT, CHECK OUT:

» On Safari: Top End, Australia...p. 86
» Supernatural: Rotorua, New Zealand...p. 228

MESOAMERICAN BARRIER REEF
Belize

NORTH AMERICA

Mesoamerican
Barrier Reef

BELIZE

Running 600 miles through the Caribbean Ocean from Mexico to Honduras, the Mesoamerican Barrier Reef System is the second largest in the world, with Belize's corridor among the best and brightest attractions. Sheltered from the sea's pounding surf and wind, the clear waters are the perfect playground for sailors, snorkelers, and sun worshippers. The Great Blue Hole and Shark Ray Alley are pilgrimage sites for divers, though you don't need a scuba certification to access the best of the vibrant reef. Coral gardens and many of the estimated 500 species of fish thrive mere feet below the surface. Watching nurse sharks peek out from a cave, clownfish flutter between the tentacles of an anemone, and eagle rays flap their massive wings, you can feel like Jacques Cousteau with just a snorkel. Sail by the 450 atolls, troll your handline for dinner, sip rum punch, and find your white sand beach.

WHEN TO GO
Besides stormy July–September, sunshine awaits. Divers will love December–May's top-notch visibility (up to 130 feet).

WHERE TO STAY
Colinda Cabanas: Cheery beachside B&B on Caye Caulker with complimentary bikes and kayaks. **Maya Beach Hotel:** Oceanfront getaway in Placencia, ideally situated for marine and land-based adventures.

GET ROMANTIC
Join the Caye Caulker ritual of sunset, reggae, and cocktails at the Split. The chill vibe is intoxicating.

HONEYTREK TIP
Bring your own mask and snorkel. In return for a little luggage space, they will inspire numerous underwater adventures.

Sailing toward our island camp with Raggamuffin Tours

Caye Caulker's accommodations and island vibe

COUPLES ADVENTURES

Liveaboard Scuba Trip ▲▲▲

Calling all divers: This may be the holy grail of liveaboards. Spending three to seven days between Turneffe Island and Lighthouse Reef Atolls holds endless opportunities for world-class wall, drift, and coral garden diving, including the Great Blue Hole, Elbow, and Front Porch.

Saltwater Fly-Fishing the Flats ▲▲

Forget deep-sea fishing trips; the shallow turquoise waters are where to find the feisty fish and palm-swayed scenery. Learn the art of casting for the elusive bonefish, permit, and tarpon in world-class destinations like Ambergris, Turneffe, or Rendezvous Cayes.

Castaway Sailing ▲▲▲

From the Rasta isle of Caye Caulker, join the pros at Raggamuffin Tours for three days of sailing the remote reef and camping (or glamping) on pristine isles. Snorkel the coral, spearfish for ceviche, build bonfires, and drink rum like sailors. Riding the wind to Dangriga, you'll experience the best way to travel south.

Snorkel With Whale Sharks ▲▲

From the serene beach town of Placencia, sail east to Gladden Spit, a spawning ground for snapper and grouper. This fish buffet brings massive whale sharks close to the surface from March to June. If you are lucky, you can swim alongside these 40,000-pound filter feeders and feel like a shrimp.

✥ Fish or Peanut Butter?

Our sailboat cast off from Caye Caulker into the labyrinth of atolls. During the briefing for our three-day journey, the captain held up a fishing rod and a gallon-size tub of peanut butter, and said, "The menu is up to you guys." After countless hours without a bite on the lines, the first mate grabbed his speargun and asked if I wanted to help catch some dinner. We dove in and swam after a school of barracuda. He was fearless and I was building up courage, as we came within feet of the razor-toothed beasts. We returned to the boat with something better than grape jelly, and felt like culinary heroes.

Freshly caught barracuda for Belizean stew

TO EXPLORE MORE ON THIS CONTINENT, CHECK OUT:

» On Safari: Tortuguero, Costa Rica...p. 100
» History: Guanajuato, Mexico...p. 114

Pot of Gold

"Look!" our kayak guide exclaimed, "A Milford blue cloud!" Clear skies are so rare in Fiordland, New Zealand, that cheeky locals have coined a meteorological term for a break in the clouds. Channeling that positive Kiwi attitude, we paddled through a rain shower, deeper into the dramatic fjord. The blue cloud was getting bigger, and a faint rainbow was growing brighter. Then a second rainbow emerged like a halo around us for something far better than sunshine.

Our sea safari's Bangka boat and island lodging

NORTHERN PALAWAN

Philippines

ASIA

PHILIPPINES
Northern Palawan

Unroll your map of the Philippines' 7,641 tropical islands and hone in on the archipelagos splitting the Sulu and South China Seas—now you've found paradise. Start in the Calamians, with their black limestone mountains, turquoise lakes, and sunken battleships. Although most continue by plane to the consistently voted "world's best beach" of El Nido, you'll slow-cruise it, Filipino style, exploring remote islands on a catamaran Bangka boat. Snorkeling and kayaking your way through the pristine waters of the Linapacan Strait, you'll sleep on white sand beaches that rarely see a footprint. Grilling freshly caught clams in adobo spices over a bonfire and under the stars, you'll seriously contemplate the castaway lifestyle. Reaching the Bacuit Archipelago and its luxury resorts, you return to your senses after a massage and cocktail. You smile, knowing you've made it.

WHEN TO GO
October–May bring clear conditions for sailing. Divers, shoot for April–May.

WHERE TO STAY
The Birdhouse: Safari-style tents decorated to perfection, overlooking El Nido's Marimegmeg Beach. **La Natura Resort:** Serene bungalows with a pool and tour offerings, near the adventure hub of Coron.

GET ROMANTIC
At the far end of El Nido's Las Cabanas Beach, treasure hunt for gorgeous seashells, then pop into the resort for sunset cocktails with a perfect island view.

HONEYTREK TIP
El Nido's boat operators have strategically broken up the best islands into separate trips. See your ideal beaches in one shot with a private tour. Worth it.

Kayangan Lake tucked within the peaks of Coron Island

COUPLES ADVENTURES

Archipelago-Hop From Calamians to Bacuit ▲▲▲
Tao Philippines has crafted an exclusive five-day journey between Coron Town and El Nido, setting up boutique camps on deserted islands and among traditional fishing villages. Stopping at secret snorkel spots and powder-sand beaches while fishing for dinner en route is the ultimate way to experience remote Palawan.

World War II Wreck Diving ▲▲▲▲
In 1944, a U.S. air raid sank a fleet of Japanese warships hiding in the coves of Coron Bay. Advanced divers can swim through the wheelhouses and corridors of *Olympia Maru,* the *Irako,* and more, while snorkelers can easily spy the *Lusong* and *East Tangat* gunboats in shallower waters.

Swim Coron's Translucent Lakes ▲
Black karst mountains envelope the turquoise waters of Kayangan, one of the Philippines' clearest lakes. You can see every detail of the underwater cliffs, creating optical illusions akin to the artwork of M. C. Escher. Explore the surrealist landscape with some inverted underwater rock climbing, then hike over to its gorgeous sister lake, Barracuda.

SUP the Bacuit Archipelago ▲▲
While most El Nido tourists will be sardined in a boat, you'll be freely exploring the azure waters on a stand-up paddleboard. Breaking away from the A-B-C-D tours, your guide will zip you to the most scenic coves, timed for maximum tranquility and adventure.

✛ Renegade Island Hopping

We flew to Busuanga to join Tao Philippines' popular tour across the archipelagos, but it was booked full. Determined to make the five-day island-hop, even though everyone said there was no other way, we went to the docks and sweet-talked a Bangka captain. With a kayak, snorkel gear, fishing line, and a bottle of rum, we charted our own waters, guided by little more than a gut feeling. Stopping whenever we saw a reef or deserted isle that called our name, we explored at will and without limitations. We reached El Nido feeling like Captain Cook or a merry band of pirates with secret treasures, forever ours.

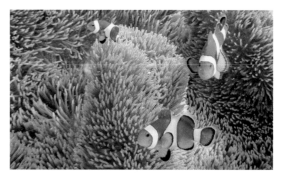
Clownfish flitting around the anemones

TO EXPLORE MORE ON THIS CONTINENT, CHECK OUT:

» **Mountains: Cordillera Central, Philippines...p. 26**
» **Dunes: Mũi Né, Vietnam...p. 144**

KOMODO
Indonesia

ASIA

INDONESIA
Komodo □

The cool currents of the Indian Ocean collide with the warm waters of the Pacific, creating the perfect storm for a profusion of marine life. Komodo National Park was created to protect the only habitat of the world's largest lizard, but the ecosystem below the islands was found to be just as important. In the heart of the Coral Triangle (a region with 76 percent of all known coral species in just 1.6 percent of the world's oceanic area), Komodo's 29 islands and countless reefs are at the pinnacle of its biodiversity. Sharks, manta rays, sea turtles, dolphins—these crowd-pleasers are here, of course. But it's the weird and wonderful that keep divers coming back. Pygmy seahorses, dugongs, clown frogfish, and nudibranchs—these vibrant creatures mesmerize, especially when their habitats are equally exhilarating. Ride the roller-coaster current, encircle a pinnacle, scour the muck, snake through a coral cave. Then surface within a ring of rippled mountains and pink sand beaches.

⊠ WHEN TO GO
Post-monsoon April–June make for lush mountains and calm seas with high visibility. Avoid turbulent January–February.

⊞ WHERE TO STAY
Bayview Gardens: Chic, secluded rooms with spectacular views over Labuan Bajo (the park's gateway town). **Dive Komodo:** Established liveaboard outfitter, with solid staff, equipment, and accommodations.

♡ GET ROMANTIC
Escape to the honeymoon-worthy Seraya Kecil, a mile-long isle with one sexy hotel. Wake up to panoramic views and swim along Seraya's untouched reef.

☑ HONEYTREK TIP
Komodo's currents bring incredible marine life but also pose dangers. Choose an operator with high safety standards, and only take on water activities within your capabilities.

Hiking the rolling hills above Horseshoe Bay

Wall diving the Coral Triangle

COUPLES ADVENTURES

Liveaboard Scuba Diving ▲▲▲

Sail into the jaw-dropping archipelago for three or more days, giving yourself time to explore the slew of dive sites, pristine island mountains, and hidden beaches. Put Castle Rock, Batu Bolong, the Cauldron (below), Manta Alley, and the Golden Passage at the top of your wish list.

Dive the Cauldron ▲▲▲▲

Descend 75 feet into a craggy trench, enveloped in a rainbow of soft and hard corals, then merge onto the fish superhighway. No swimming required, the powerful current will pull you alongside schools of giant trevally, neon sweetlips, and blacktip sharks. Set your reef hook and watch the sea world fly by.

Trek With Dragons ▲▲

Although Komodo Island is known for its dragons, Rinca has a denser population and better terrain

✤ Five Reasons to Liveaboard

Multiple days at sea with back-to-back scuba dives can seem intimidating (and pricey). Here's why it's worth diving in:

1. **Remote Access:** Many of the best sites cannot be reached in a day trip.
2. **Night & Sunrise Dives:** Not all fish work the 9-to-5.
3. **Next Certification:** Level up while you dive with on-site classes and training.
4. **Built-in Sailing Trip:** Explore far-flung islands between dives.
5. **Camaraderie:** Bond with people who share your deep blue passion.

Scuba gear poised for a night dive

to view them. The two-hour trek to the watering hole affords sweeping island views and the best chances to see these nine-foot-long lizards in the wild.

Summit Padar Island ▲▲

A volcanic isle sculpted with sharp peaks, four arcing bays, and sandy beaches in three colors, Padar is the national park's supermodel isle. Hike up for views of the impossibly beautiful terrain, then down to one of the world's few pink sand beaches.

TO EXPLORE MORE ON THIS CONTINENT, CHECK OUT:

» **Rivers: Mekong Delta, Vietnam...p. 58**

» **Supernatural: Central Flores, Indonesia...p. 222**

CYCLADES ISLANDS

Greece

BY ELAYNA CARAUSU & RILEY WHITELUM

EUROPE

GREECE Cyclades

Our sailing journey around the world began in this historic archipelago, and even after 30,000 nautical miles and setting nostalgia aside, we can still say the Cyclades top the nautical charts. The Greek Isles have been sailed for millennia, and when you are surrounded by such history with dashes of mythology, it's a deeper kind of travel. Standing on Delos, the birthplace of Apollo, or exploring Andros, a civilization thriving since the ninth century B.C., gives every step a little more gravity. The Cyclades are veritable icons of Aegean style, with white- and blue-domed buildings, reminiscent of a frothy sea and cloudless sky. We'll admit, this irresistible beauty comes with its share of tourists, but that's why you are bringing your own boat! Whether you're a captain or swabbie, the Cyclades is perfect for sailors of all levels. Sunshine, calm anchorages, short distances, and plenty of islands that never see a ferry make it easy to get away. Hop out for a snorkel, cast a line for dinner, and rock yourself to sleep.

WHEN TO GO

Meet Meltemi, a northerly wind, carrying you along at an average of 15 knots from June–September—perfect conditions.

WHERE TO STAY

AthensWas Hotel: Steps from the Temple of Olympian Zeus, a chic and serene city retreat to bookend your sea voyage. **Sunsail:** An international outfitter offering charter, flotilla, or skippered Cyclades trips from Athens.

GET ROMANTIC

Anchor in Kythnos for pure relaxation. An island this pristine will connect you with nature, as you swim in the cool waters and stargaze on deck.

SAILING LA VAGABONDE TIP

Prepare for your journey by spending time at your local yacht club. There are often sailing events to meet other yachties who are more than happy to share their knowledge. Make friends, jump on board, and get a feel for the open water!

COUPLES ADVENTURES

Overview in Poros ▲

Cruise into the protected anchorage on the south-west side of the island and marvel at the ruins of the 19th-century Russian naval base. Anchor your boat, row your dinghy to land, and hitch a ride to the clock tower for a 360-degree view of Poros Island and mainland Greece.

Get Wild in Ios ▲▲▲

Bask in the fun and sea at this party island (where Elayna lived and we met). Start your day scuba diving the Ios wreck, and return for sunset happy hour, live music, and ocean views at Harmony Mexican Bar. Continue to Mylopotas Beach and barhop until sunrise.

Fresh Fish Amorgos ▲▲

Infrequently serviced by ferry, Amorgos has kept its small town vibe. Walk the quay to any of the sea-food restaurants serving Greek delicacies like *kala-marakia gemista* (stuffed squid). Many locals will take you spearfishing for free, in exchange for a bit of your catch. You will see them in action on the shore, so don't be shy and go introduce yourself.

Be Charmed in Paros ▲

Dock near the old fishing boats in the Naousa marina, and get lost in the magical Old Port, considered to be one of the prettiest villages in the Cyclades. Wander the winding alleyways and listen for *lavouto* jam sessions. Relax on Kolymbithres or Monastiri, our favorite beaches on this golden sand isle.

✦ Couples Advice

Once on board, there are always a few important jobs and responsibilities that need to be addressed. To avoid any drama, designate each of your roles. (Elayna does all the provisioning, cooking, navigating, and deckhand work, while Riley checks the weather, adjusts the sails, and makes the big calls.) Being at sea is an absolute breath of fresh air, but it can get quite hairy at times. It is important to work together, make each other laugh, and always keep positive for smooth sailing.

Delos, among Greece's key archaeological sites

TO EXPLORE MORE IN THIS REGION, CHECK OUT:

» History: Cappadocia, Turkey...p. 108
» Road Trips: Central Georgia...p. 210

POWER COUPLE: *Riley & Elayna*

This Australian couple has been sailing around the world nonstop since 2014 on the 43-foot monohull *La Vagabonde*. Crossing the Mediterranean, Atlantic, Caribbean, and Pacific Oceans, they have sailed 30,000 nautical miles and counting. Sailing and videography are their full-time jobs as they capture their journey on YouTube and at *Sailing -LaVagabonde.com*.

NORWEGIAN FJORDS
Norway

Norwegian
Fjords   NORWAY
E U R O P E

Seven hundred years before Columbus's first voyage, the Vikings were exploring far-off lands, with little more than stars and birds to guide them. Sailing is just what you do when you grow up with over 15,000 miles of coastline and 1,100 fjords—and Norway does it well. The journey from the medieval capital of Bergen to the Russian border is said to be the most beautiful sea voyage in the world, and we cannot argue. The Atlantic Ocean flows between glaciated mountains and along fishing villages without roads to the outside world. Weathered men in knit caps tend racks of codfish drying in the sun. They stand before their brightly colored houses, painted to defy the months when the sun doesn't shine. Sail deeper into the Arctic Circle and watch the northern lights grow stronger with coronas bursting into pink, green, and purple fireworks. Come in the summer months and forge ahead to the Svalbard Archipelago to see polar bears patrol the ice sheets and to hike glaciers under the midnight sun. With Viking roots, Norway doesn't cruise—it explores.

WHEN TO GO

November and March hit the sweet spot for both northern lights and ample daylight. May–August bring around-the-clock hiking and an open passage to frozen Svalbard.

WHERE TO STAY

Hurtigruten: The national ferry doubles as an expedition ship with year-round departures, and numerous embarkation ports and price points. **G Adventures:** This expedition outfitter offers one- or two-week all-inclusive trips with an active focus.

GET ROMANTIC

Build excitement for your sea voyage with a funicular ride up Bergen's Mount Fløyen for incredible views of the charming medieval city and fjords. Stay for an espresso at Fløien restaurant or enjoy the folk concerts in summer.

HONEYTREK TIP

Whether you come during the dark days or sunny nights, you'll likely need some sleep aids. Eye masks, melatonin, and tea are your friends.

The seaside village of Urke within the Hjørundfjord

The medieval buildings of the Bergen wharf

COUPLES ADVENTURES

Hjørundfjord and Norway's Narrowest Valley ▲
Follow the road tucked between steep alpine summits, past storybook stone houses, to a dazzling viewpoint of Lyngstøl Lake, the mountain pass, and the ocean beyond. On your return, stop at the 19th-century Hotel Union Øye (a favorite hideaway of European royals) for reindeer stew and a wander around the whimsical rooms.

Zodiac the Lofoten Archipelago ▲▲
Cross the Arctic Circle and reach the Lofoten Wall, with mountains as high as 3,300 feet shooting up from the sea. Zip between the granite-peak islands and white sand beaches, keeping an eye out for Atlantic puffins and sea eagles, then stroll the fishing villages lost in time.

North Cape Cliffs ▲
Reach 71° 10' 21" N, and dock at Honningsvåg, just some 1,300 miles shy of the North Pole. Observe a quarter million seabirds nested in the cliffs, including many endemic high Arctic species. Watch the fantastic documentary at the North Cape Museum, and snap a photo beside the massive globe at the top of the world.

Svalbard Arctic Wildlife-Watch ▲▲▲
Go where walruses, seals, reindeer, arctic foxes, and polar bears rule the frozen tundra. Sweep the archipelago's icebergs and glaciers like explorer Roald Amundsen for wildlife sightings you cannot get anywhere else.

✧ The Locals' Route

A team of high school wrestlers boarded our cruise ship, not for a bonding experience or spring break, but commuting to a match. The 125-year-old Hurtigruten is the only public transit connecting the fjords of Norway's far north—and that made us love it even more. Our voyage from Bergen to Kirkenes wasn't just an exercise in tourism, but a mission to deliver the mail, pick up fish, and bring families home at the end of the day. Stopping in 34 charming port towns, many well off the tourist track, we had a window into real life in the fjords.

A fellow Hurtigruten ship passing in the twilight

TO EXPLORE MORE ON THIS CONTINENT, CHECK OUT:

» Snow: Tromsø, Norway...p. 168
» Road Trips: North Coast, Ireland & Northern Ireland...p. 208

Communing with manta rays at the German Channel, Palau

Must-Dive Sites

Discover the biggest fish, brightest coral, and wildest wrecks across the seven seas.

MALAYSIA
1. Barracuda Point

Surrounded by 1,900-foot-deep canyons, Sipadan attracts its share of big fish, with Barracuda Point at its vortex. In addition to swarming hammerheads and leopard sharks, hundreds of razor-toothed barracuda circle in a hypnotic formation.

AUSTRALIA
2. S.S. *Yongala*

One of the world's top wreck dives alongside the world's largest reef . . . what more could you ask for? The 358-foot ship has been on the seafloor since 1911, giving it ample time to grow a proper coral garden and attract mantas, octopuses, bull sharks, and storms of fish.

SOUTH AFRICA
3. Sardine Run

Every May through July, billions of sardines travel north from the cold seas off South Africa's Cape Point to KwaZulu-Natal. As if this quantity of a single species wasn't impressive enough, thousands of birds, dolphins, sharks, and whales belly up for the bottomless buffet.

COSTA RICA
4. Bajo Alcyone

A volcanic island 340 miles off the coast, Cocos Island offers a string of about 20 pristine sites— from vertical walls to drift dives. The highlight of a liveaboard is undoubtedly Bajo Alcyone, with its veritable Sharknado of scalloped hammerheads, whitetips, and blacktips, plus its mobula ray cleaning station.

JAMAICA
5. Port Royal

This Sin City for early European explorers and pirates was forcibly moved to the bottom of Kingston's seafloor. Struck by an earthquake-tsunami combo in 1692, the city's grand architecture, taverns, and tall ships are now covered in coral and begging for exploration.

CANADA
6. Bylot Island

Closer to Greenland than Toronto, this Canadian Arctic dive site is only accessible by snowmobile and Inuit sled. Dive between the floes and iceberg underbellies, keeping an eye peeled for narwhals, seals, polar bears, and walruses. Not just an exhilarating cold-water dive, it's an Arctic safari, above and below the water.

PALAU
7. Ngemelis Island

People come to Palau for its estimated 1,300 species of reef fish and 500 species of coral, and to dive this massive pelagic playground. Blue Corner and German Channel are two of the world's most famous dive sites, boasting 13 species of sharks and high visibility you'll have to see to believe.

ITALY
8. Neptune's Grotto

The Alghero sea caves' freshwater origins give it glorious stalagmite formations and supersize fish. Protected from predators, conger eels and lobsters grow twice their normal size; plus, this grotto is spacious enough that you can dabble in top-notch cave diving without a special certification.

EGYPT
9. S.S. *Thistlegorm*

The Red Sea is blessed with top-notch visibility, 80°F bathwater, hundreds of miles of vibrant coral, and a wreck that may take the cake. This British transport ship was sunk during World War II, spilling army tanks, locomotives, motorbikes, rifles, and heaps of spare parts for planes and cars.

ECUADOR
10. Cousin's Rock

Playing to the best of both worlds, this volcanic formation nurtures macrowonders like colorful nudibranchs and Galápagos seahorses in its coral, while its depths bring the big fish in droves. To top it off, curious sea lions often greet you on your safety stop.

Namib Desert, Namibia

*"There is a desert I long to be walking,
a wide emptiness: peace beyond
any understanding of it."*

—RUMI

Chapter Seven

DESERTS
& DUNES

Deserts own the extremes. And those who brave the hot sun, freezing nights, and eternal dry spell are rewarded with utter beauty. It's a self-selecting place, only for the hearty and optimistic. A dried-up lake? It's a sea of shimmering salt crystals. A flowerless field? A cactus paradise. Relentless wind? A landscape that's always evolving. Walk along a dune, slide down its slopes, and come back to find a clean slate in the morning. There's no building on sand. Mother Nature made it off-limits for developers and reserved it for adventurers. Those who adore the desert sun but not the intense heat have an oasis in the high altitude of the Andes and Sierra Madres. Those who love the Sahara-like landscape but prefer the refreshing respite of the sea are in luck. The beaches of Brazil and Vietnam have the best of both worlds. Ride a dune, hike a canyon, or catch a wave and a shooting star. You're the intrepid pair the desert is waiting for.

Balanced Rock, a beloved formation in Arches National Park

MOAB
U.S.A.

NORTH AMERICA

Moab □ UNITED STATES

Like a wild child who's run away from overbearing parents, Moab lives free at the eastern edge of Utah. It's the kind of place you visit and leave with dreams of starting a bike shop, brewery, jewelry studio, or anything that lets you wake up to blue skies and red cliffs. Often dubbed the adventure capital of the Southwest, it makes rock climbing, off-roading, mountain biking, and BASE jumping all too tempting. Epic parks—Arches, Canyonlands, and Dead Horse Point State Park—plus, the mighty Colorado River are all in its backyard. The little city of Moab first boomed in the 1950s, when uranium was discovered in the hills. Those days are long gone, but their old mining roads are now legendary for 4x4 and biking trails, especially with its grippy "slickrock" sandstone. After a day of kicking up dust, head to town for a microbrew and live band, or a desert safari camp for dinner under the stars. In Moab, you do what you please.

⊠ WHEN TO GO
With approximately 250 days of sunshine a year, you'll have plenty of blue skies. April–May and September–October have ideal temperatures (70s–80s).

⊞ WHERE TO STAY
Moab Under Canvas: Sophisticated safari-style tents and tepees at the scenic juncture of Arches and Canyonlands. **Hauer Ranch:** Near the Colorado River with views to Fisher Towers, this horse ranch has two spectacular self-catering houses.

♡ GET ROMANTIC
Try a wine tasting at Castle Creek, Utah's largest winery. Sit on the riverside deck with a glass of their award-winning Petroglyph White and Monument Red.

☑ HONEYTREK TIP
Beware of heat stroke. Hydrate (about a gallon daily), wear light-colored clothes (no tank tops), don a wide-brim cap, take breaks, and use sunscreen religiously.

Mountain-biking trails zigzag through the desert.

COUPLES ADVENTURES

Off-Road Hell's Revenge ▲▲▲

Hop in a 4x4 and traverse the sandstone domes and slickrock fins on this legendary 6.5-mile trail. Steep climbs and descents roller-coaster through Abyss Canyon and past striking vistas of the La Sal Mountains and Colorado River. Stop to check out the fossilized dinosaur footprints, and take lots of hard-core selfies.

Fly Over Canyonlands & Arches National Parks ▲

Grasp the magnitude of the valleys, peaks, and plateaus of the two national parks with an hour in the air. Flying low in a Cessna, look into the Maze, the Island in the Sky, the confluence of the Colorado and Green Rivers, and spot rock formations you'd never see from land.

Mountain Bike Dead Horse Point Loop ▲▲▲

If you've got the skills, bike the legendary Slickrock Trail. For the rest of us, the entry-level Dead Horse

Our first major road trip together took us to six national parks from Vegas to Moab. Camping in Bryce Canyon, bouldering to picnics spots in Capitol Reef, and following dirt lanes toward endless red rock panoramas, we reached Moab after 10 days of adventure and yearned for more. We became forever smitten with Utah and road trips into the Wild West.

Claret cup cactus match Moab's red sandstone.

Point route is the best in Moab for exhilarating terrain and phenomenal views. Work your way up the mesa, ride the rim, and flow down groomed trails for 14 miles (or less with bail-out options).

Hike the Devil's Garden ▲▲

This section of Arches National Park contains the largest concentration of significant natural arches in the country and arguably the world. Begin between two sandstone fins and reach the 306-foot-long Landscape Arch. Admire the desert views framed in Partition Arch, and countless other wonders on this 7.5-mile loop.

TO EXPLORE MORE ON THIS CONTINENT, CHECK OUT:

» History: Guanajuato, Mexico...p. 114
» Road Trips: The Southwest, U.S.A....p. 206

MŨI NÉ
Vietnam

ASIA

VIETNAM — Mũi Né

Mũi Né is a dynamic but often misunderstood destination—starting with its name. It has become interchangeable with a strip of package resorts located in the neighboring Hàm Tiến, but the true Mũi Né is four miles east. It's a palm-fringed fishing village with a harbor of circular bamboo boats (a quirky design, originally created to evade a French colonial levy), and some of the best seafood in southern Vietnam. Head inland and you'll find massive red and white sand dunes, reminiscent of the Sahara, but sparkling with lagoons of lotus flowers. The dunes create a microclimate that defies Vietnam's monsoon season with only half the rainfall of its surrounding cities and consistent cross-onshore winds—a kiteboarder's dream. The 200 days of 12-plus knots draw most of the tourists to Rang Beach, but what they don't realize is the breeze blows just as well on the prettier stretches of Bình Thuận Province, like Kê Gà with its 19th-century lighthouse, white sand, and dramatic rock formations. Buck the package tours and hotels, hop on a motorbike, explore between the dunes, and find Mũi Né's inner lotus.

WHEN TO GO

October–March offer ideal wind and sunshine. *Note:* Most kiteboarding operations close April–September.

WHERE TO STAY

Source Kiteboarding & Lodge: A laid-back beach hotel with airy rooms, a sweeping rooftop terrace, and a solid kiteboarding school on Malibu Beach. **Princess D'Ân Nam Resort & Spa:** A member of the Small Luxury Hotels of the World, with Indochine-chic villas on the secluded Kê Gà beach and fantastic excursions.

GET ROMANTIC

Watch the sun set over the Red Dunes. The fire-hued sand is even more dramatic when the twilight casts shadows on every ripple. Rent a sled for extra thrills.

HONEYTREK TIP

The dunes can be windy, which means sand is whipping about. Wear lightweight pants and sunglasses, and bring a waterproof camera or case to keep the grains out.

Sand sledders take on the White Dunes at sunset.

The unique and curious boat styles at Mũi Né harbor

COUPLES ADVENTURES

Explore the White Sand Dunes ▲▲
Walk the ridges and leap down the slopes at this desert by the sea. Continue to Lotus Lake for the contrast of a flowering oasis against the mountains of sand. If you're feeling adventurous, try the quad bikes (just negotiate and agree on the details beforehand).

Take a Kiteboarding Lesson ▲▲▲
Learn the ropes from a five-star school like Windchimes at the west end of Hàm Tiến, or Source Kiteboarding on Malibu Beach (also great for intermediates). Already a pro? Enjoy the gorgeous Kê Gà, especially left of the lighthouse.

Frolic the Fairy Spring ▲
A stream has carved through a hard-packed dune, revealing colorful layers of sand, limestone, and clay. Meander the shallow waters between lush green banks and drip-castle formations for a half hour, until you reach the waterfall.

Get Local at the Mũi Né Fish Market ▲
From dawn until around 10 a.m., fishermen come ashore with their boatloads of rock cod, yellowtail, and a cornucopia of other fish. Their family members sift, weigh, and haul away the catches in baskets suspended from bamboo poles. It's a beautiful blur of conical hats, colorful boats, and resilient people.

✣ Little Moscow

With the communist connection, Russians can enter visa-free and via cheap flights, so Hàm Tiến (the resort strip west of Mũi Né) has become their party playground. When we saw more menus written in Cyrillic than Vietnamese characters, we knew we had to get out of Moscow Dodge. We took off on a motorbike, followed the dune-lined roads, and found the real meaning of Mũi Né.

Kiteboarders flock to Hàm Tiến Beach.

TO EXPLORE MORE ON THIS CONTINENT, CHECK OUT:

» Mountains: Cordillera Central, Philippines...p. 26

» Rivers: Nam Ou River Valley, Laos...p. 60

Frolicking down Sunset Dune in Jericoacoara, Brazil

Sand Slide

From the top of a 100-foot dune in the center of town, we watched the sun slip behind the sea. When the glow extinguished, the crowd let out whistles and cheers, then the drums of the capoeira circle began, ushering us back to town. We clasped hands and leaped over the edge. Our bodies moved like a runaway train as the sand avalanche and gravity propelled us forward. Laughter and squeals didn't help our grace or sense of balance, but made it the best way down.

DURANGO
Mexico

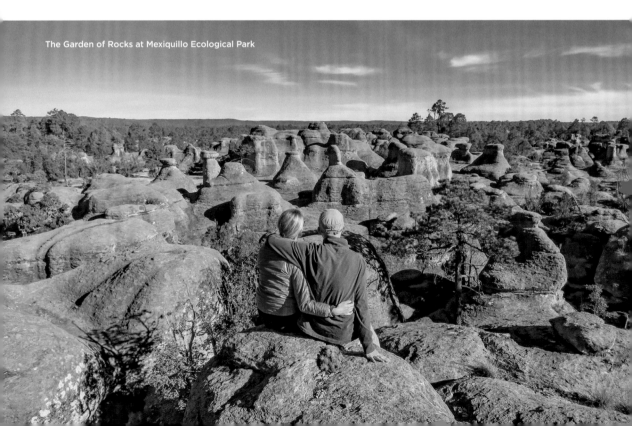

NORTH
AMERICA

Durango
MEXICO

Where the Chihuahua Desert and Sierra Madre Mountains meet, Durango is one of Mexico's most isolated and mysterious states. Hiking the 10,000-foot peaks, wandering the awe-inspiring Dunas de la Soledad, and exploring the UNESCO World Heritage site of Mapimí, you wonder why more travelers haven't heard of this place. Still, its illusive reputation is well deserved, with spots like the 16th-century ghost town of Ojuela and the Zone of Silence, where airwaves allegedly flatline. Get to know Durango with a few days in its pristine Spanish colonial capital. Ride the revolutionary trails of Pancho Villa on horseback. Learn about its surprisingly robust film history (this big-sky desert has starred in over 150 movies), and drive the estimated 2,000 curves along the legendary Devil's Backbone. Find out why Durango is the real Wild West.

WHEN TO GO
High elevation quells the desert heat. October–May are sunniest; expect cool nights.

WHERE TO STAY
Hostal Mexiquillo: A simple family-run guesthouse with fantastic guiding services, adjacent to the Mexiquillo Ecological Park. **Hotel Gobernador:** One of Durango City's finest hotels and restaurants.

GET ROMANTIC
Hike to the Mexiquillo fireman's lookout (ask the locals). Carefully climb the 50-foot ladder to your private cabin in the sky. Savor sunset views with a mescal toast.

HONEYTREK TIP
There are often travel warnings for Durango, but we've spent months in the region and never felt unsafe. To be cautious, don't drive after dark or stay out too late.

The Garden of Rocks at Mexiquillo Ecological Park

The colonial streets of Durango City

COUPLES ADVENTURES

Road-Trip the Devil's Backbone ▲▲

Drive down Mexico's engineering wonder of Route 40D, a road with 61 tunnels and 115 bridges, including one of the highest cable-stayed bridges in the world, at 1,322 feet. Return to Durango on the original Route 40, a veritable corkscrew up the Sierra Madres culminating at the foreboding cliffs of the Devil's Backbone.

Boulder the Garden of Rocks ▲▲

Igneous rocks stack like gorditas in the Mexiquillo Ecological Park. This lunar labyrinth is waiting to be explored, climbed, and photographed. Boulder in the morning, then continue to the dramatic waterfall and ghost train tunnels in the coniferous forest.

Hollywood's Wild West ▲

That classic Western showdown on the dusty streets, between the saloon and the sheriff's office— this is where it happened. Explore the 1960s sets, graced by the likes of John Wayne, Clint Eastwood,

and others, now reclaimed as the very entertaining amusement park: Paseo del Viejo Oeste.

Mysterious Mapimí ▲▲

The UNESCO Biosphere Reserve and its colonial towns will fascinate for days. Walk the 1,000-foot suspension bridge into Ojuela's maze of mines, see if your compass spins out in the Mapimí Zone of Silence, slide down the Dunas de la Soledad, and sleep in one of Mexico's esteemed Pueblos Magicos.

✧ Locals' Tip

On a whim, we applied to house-sit in Mazatlán, Mexico, and within two weeks we had the keys to a beach house and 20 new local friends. Immersing ourselves into the community, we heard about the epic drive to the neighboring state of Durango and off we went, up the Devil's Backbone. We'll admit, we wouldn't have otherwise thought to visit the state of Durango, but now it's our turn to pass on the secret.

Hugging the curves of the Devil's Backbone

TO EXPLORE MORE ON THIS CONTINENT, CHECK OUT:

» Beaches: Samaná, Dominican Republic...p. 78
» Rain Forests: Monteverde, Costa Rica...p. 186

Lagoons nestle between the dunes of Jeri.

JERICOACOARA
Brazil

Jericoacoara
BRAZIL

SOUTH
AMERICA

Fourteen miles from the nearest paved road, a sandy track winds between mountainous dunes to the Atlantic Ocean. Then, like an oasis, the little beach town of Jericoacoara appears. Rastafari, surfers, artists, and savvy travelers amble down the sand streets, lined with organic cafés and caipirinha stands. The sky is speckled with sails pulling kitesurfers across the waves. As dusk approaches, hundreds of people migrate up the 100-foot sand dune in the heart of town. When the sun drops below the horizon, everyone cheers, then skips, rolls, or sandboards down toward the music. Torches are lit, drums are beating, and the capoeira circle is growing larger. Long legs swoop and slash through air in this martial art ballet. The rustic *barraca* bars are muddling lime, sugar, cachaça, and passion fruit juice. The streets twinkle with lanterns, and the smell of sizzling seafood summons you to dinner. Soon the tables will be pushed aside and the *forró* dancing will spark up. You begin to move in unfamiliar ways—something has come over you. It's Jericoacoara.

WHEN TO GO
July–January bring sunshine and enough breeze for kiteboarding or windsurfing. For fewer crowds, avoid December–February.

WHERE TO STAY
La Villa Jericoacoara: A blend of Brazilian and European influences, this is a luxurious option with dune views. **Baoba:** A charming and classic Jeri *pousada* (guesthouse) just off the main street.

GET ROMANTIC
On a Wednesday or Saturday, have a late dinner at Dona Amélia. As midnight approaches, the lantern-lit space transforms into the town's best forró dance party. Watch the sultry moves for a few dances, then give them a whirl.

HONEYTREK TIP
Pack a flashlight. Jeri's romantic ambiance and traditional ways don't allow for streetlights. You're also going to need it for your sunrise hike (read on).

Caipirinha, the sunset cocktail of choice

COUPLES ADVENTURES

Catch Sunrise & Sunset Over the Ocean ▲▲
An hour before dawn, hike to the Pedra Furada, the magnificent stone arch in the surf and veritable symbol of Jericoacoara. After a day of adventure, join the Jeri ritual of climbing Sunset Dune for one of Brazil's only ocean *pores do sol* (sunsets). You may even see the "green flash" phenomenon.

Take a Capoeira Lesson ▲▲
A Brazilian martial art, created by African slaves to disguise their fight training with music and dance, is still practiced daily on the beaches of Jeri. After watching the masters gracefully spar at the sunset sessions, you'll want to learn a few acrobatic moves in the morning classes.

Surf the Sand and Wind ▲▲▲
Dabble in Jeri's two biggest board sports: windsurfing and *skibunda* (slang for "sandboarding"). Start your day with windsurf lessons at one of the IKO-certified schools and finish with a ride down Sunset Dune. You can rent boards by the hour on the main street.

Dune Buggy to Nova Tatajuba ▲▲
Explore sand mountains, blue lagoons, and fishing villages on a private dune buggy tour. Cover more terrain on the Nova Tatajuba route, climbing colossal dunes and fording rivers on your way to the hammock-lined oasis of Torta Lagoon.

⁜ Riding Jeri Style

We strolled over to the beach stables for a horseback ride. We hopped on our horse, expecting the "guide" to do the same. Instead he handed us a branch, gave Quicksilver a slap on the butt, and *hi ho!* We galloped into the sunset for a classic Jeri tour.

Jeri's iconic rock arch: Pedra Furada

TO EXPLORE MORE ON THIS CONTINENT, CHECK OUT:

» **Falls: Iguazú Falls, Argentina & Brazil...p. 46**

» **Rain Forests: Manaus, Brazil...p. 194**

NAMIB DESERT
Namibia

BY LINA & DAVID STOCK

AFRICA

Namib
Desert
NAMIBIA

One of the oldest deserts, the Namib stretches inland from the Atlantic Ocean, covering the entire coast of Namibia and spilling into Angola and South Africa. Having endured arid conditions for roughly 55 to 80 million years, it contains some of the world's driest regions. Owing to its antiquity and unique environment, it is home to some 25 species of endemic reptiles, plus iconic African wildlife like zebra and gemsbok. The stark beauty had us feeling like we'd touched down on another planet. The sheer size of the dunes and contrast of colors had us eager to experience them from every angle, with adventure activities from sandboarding to skydiving. Although most of the desert is inaccessible, there are several must-see attractions found in the Namib-Naukluft National Park. The most famous is the Sossusvlei area, with towering orange sand dunes surrounding stark white salt pans. Access to the park is by gravel roads or a light aircraft from Windhoek. The adventure begins even before you arrive.

WHEN TO GO
The only time to avoid the Namib Desert is December–February, when temperatures can climb over 120°F.

WHERE TO STAY
Sossusvlei Lodge: Luxury safari tents in Sesriem (the gateway to Namib adventure) are the ultimate in desert accommodations. **Namib Desert Lodge:** A step above the rustic camping experience, with a restaurant, pool, and private bungalows.

GET ROMANTIC
Take in sunset from the top of Dune 45, the most iconic in Namib and standing more than 500 feet tall. Watch the sun melt into the desert sand.

DIVERGENT TRAVELERS TIP
Stay up late stargazing, and climb at least one of the dunes. The views will be well worth your efforts.

Climbing Dune 45 in the early morning fog of Sossusvlei

COUPLES ADVENTURES

Hike to Deadvlei ▲▲
Feel the sand move beneath your feet as you hike toward the most famous salt pan in the Namib Desert: Deadvlei. Reach the white expanse, backed by orange dunes and dotted with 900-year-old petrified camel thorn trees. Go early in the morning and you'll have the photogenic scene to yourselves.

Skydive Over the Sea & Sand ▲▲▲▲
Jump from a plane at 10,000 feet for an unforgettable perspective of the Namib. Taking to the sky is the only way to see how the desert meets the Atlantic Ocean; plus, you'll join a select group of adrenaline junkies.

Safari Through Sossusvlei ▲
Hop into a 4x4 and go crashing through the sand while seeking out some of the biggest dunes on the planet. Early morning safaris offer the opportunity to watch game (picture the silhouette of a long-horned gemsbok against the sand) before exploring the area on foot.

Sandboard the Dunes ▲▲▲
Similar to snowboarding, sandboarding gives you a chance to race down the mountainous terrain. Alter Action Sandboarding pioneered the sport on the Namibian coast and staked claim to a 330-foot star dune with six different faces, catering to beginner and advanced riders. Be daring and try a jump; the sand is forgiving.

⚜ Couples Advice

Embrace that not all things are going to be romantic when traveling. There will be situations where you're sweaty, tired, and hungry. The last thing you want to do is get cuddly, and that's okay. Make light of it, and admit how you're feeling in the moment. You'll be surprised how that clears the air for both of you and makes the situation more tolerable. Lastly, don't dwell on it, and remember you're only one shower or meal away from feeling fabulous again.

Petrified trees stand strong in the Deadvlei salt pan.

TO EXPLORE MORE ON THIS CONTINENT, CHECK OUT:

» **Islands: Zanzibar, Tanzania...p. 72**
» **On Safari: Kruger, South Africa...p. 88**

POWER COUPLE: *Lina & David*

These high school sweethearts from Wisconsin ditched the American dream to travel the world. Some of their greatest adventures involve camping for 119 days from Cape Town to Cairo, hiking on the Great Wall of China, and sea kayaking safaris in the Philippines. Find the Stocks' award-winning photography, videos, and travel advice on *DivergentTravelers.com*.

ATACAMA DESERT

Chile

SOUTH AMERICA

Atacama Desert

CHILE

Sheltered between the 17,000-foot peaks of the Andes and the Chilean Coastal Range, the Atacama averages less than an inch of rain a year. It's the driest desert in the world, with some areas never recording a single drop or visible sign of life. This would seem like an inhospitable place, but pleasures are in its harsh extremes. The ancient lakes have dried into massive salt flats, shimmering with crystals and sky blue puddles. Volcanic geysers shoot plumes of steam 70 feet high, and their mineral-rich water adds to a kaleidoscopic crust. Life is far from Pleasantville, but that's never stopped anyone—from the second-century civilizations to the current-day astronomers, thrill seekers, and spa-goers that grace San Pedro de Atacama. The town's adobe and stick-roof buildings appear endearingly primitive, though behind those earthen walls are boutique hotels, mountain bike shops, and pisco sour bars buzzing with life. No matter what you're measuring—rain, ambiance, or adventures—Atacama is off the charts.

✈ WHEN TO GO

The climate is stable, typically 70s by day and 40s by night. Avoid the full moon for optimal stargazing.

▦ WHERE TO STAY

Awasi: A Relais & Châteaux lodge with an adventure focus, exceptional cuisine, and private guiding services. **Terrantai:** A 200-year-old colonial home updated with Andean and contemporary detail; centrally located and comparatively well priced.

♡ GET ROMANTIC

Tierra Atacama resort pairs excursions with spa sessions. Hike Moon Valley and return to a Reiki and crystal massage. Explore El Tatio Geysers in the chilly morning air, followed by a hot stone rubdown.

☑ HONEYTREK TIP

By far one the best adventures in South America is the 4x4 journey from the Atacama to Bolivia's Uyuni Salt Flats (p. 221). Book it in San Pedro.

Steam billowing from El Tatio geyser field

COUPLES ADVENTURES

Horseback Ride Moon Valley to Death Valley ▲▲▲
Trot through the lunar labyrinth of red caverns, cliffs, and tunnels, listening for the sound of crackling salt. Reach the ledge of the cordillera for lunch, then gallop through the sand dunes of Death Valley. It's the most intimate way to explore these two popular places.

Sunrise at El Tatio Geysers ▲
While San Pedro is still dark and cool, drive to the largest geothermal field in the Southern Hemisphere. Watch a hundred puffy white fumaroles billow from the crusty earth, until the sun's warmth scatters the steam. Wander around the shallow pools, admiring the rainbow of geometric formations.

Atacama Salt Flats & Lagoons ▲▲
Within the 1,158-square-mile Los Flamencos National Reserve, the earth shatters into a mosaic of crystallized tiles and pools. Go to Laguna Chaxa to see four species of flamingos strut the shallow waters. End with sunset at Laguna Salada, with its floating plates of salt and rosy reflections of the Andes.

✢ Be a Buoy

Atacama's Cejar Lagoon has a salinity rivaling the Dead Sea. It's so buoyant, it's virtually impossible to swim, but a hysterical exercise to try. Limbs float uncontrollably with every stroke, and belly laughs won't help your progress. Give up doing laps; lean back as if in a chaise, meditating on the view of the volcanoes and complimentary salt exfoliation.

Kicking back in salty Cejar Lagoon

Stargaze With an Astronomer ▲
With zero percent humidity and virtually no light pollution, the Atacama is home to the world's clearest skies. Take a Sky Tour with Celestial Explorations, one of South America's largest public observatories, and peer through their high-powered telescopes to see hidden stars, galaxies, and realms of the universe.

TO EXPLORE MORE ON THIS CONTINENT, CHECK OUT:

» **Mountains: Torres del Paine, Chile...p. 40**

» **Supernatural: Department of Potosí, Bolivia...p. 220**

Hot air balloon over the ancient Thebes Temple, Egypt

Desert & Dune Adventures

Sandboard, dune bash, and explore stunning landscapes only an arid oasis could offer.

MEXICO

1. Ride the Chihuahua Rails

More akin to a roller coaster than a train, the Chihuahua al Pacifico (El Chepe) hugs the curves and cliffs of Copper Canyon—one of the deepest in the world. This supremely scenic 12- to 18-hour ride stops in Tarahumara Indian villages and a hiking wonderland.

EGYPT

2. Hot Air Balloon the Valley of the Kings

Float over the lush Nile Delta and dip below the desert rim into the royal necropolis, dating back to 16th century B.C. See the sprawling temples of Karnak and Luxor. Marvel at the aerial view of elaborate pharaoh tombs.

JORDAN

3. Hike to Petra

This 50-mile trek, along the historic crossroads of Arabia, Egypt, and Syria-Phoenicia, is the ultimate way to reach this world-famous caravan city. Wander the narrow red canyons and marvel at the rock-carved facades with a richer context and appreciation for their history.

MOROCCO

4. Camel Trek the Sahara

Atop the desert's most traditional mode of transport, follow the ancient caravan routes past coral dunes, volcanic mountains, and crumbling casbahs. Make stops to roam the souks and Berber villages for a proper Saharan experience.

U.S.A.

5. Sandboard Coastal Dunes

The Oregon Dunes National Recreation Area has 40 miles of sand dunes, making one big playground. Strap on a sandboard and ride to the ocean and lagoons at Honeyman, or hit the jumps and grind the rails at Sand Master, among the original sandboard parks.

BOLIVIA

6. Sleep in the Salt Hotel

Spend the night in the middle of the largest salt flat on Earth. Luna Salada Hotel is made almost entirely of the white stuff (walls, floors, beds, desks, the works). Best yet, sleeping in the architectural marvel gives you quality time in the Salar de Uyuni, a surreal expanse of crystallized desert.

U.S.A.

7. Witness a Speed Record

The smooth track of Utah's Bonneville Salt Flats has seen the speed records broken since the advent of cars. Don't miss the annual Speed Week for your chance to see hot rods, belly tankers, and streamliners top 600 miles an hour on this natural drag strip.

MONGOLIA

8. Hunt for Dinosaur Eggs in the Gobi

Explore Bayanzag, a paleontology mecca where 140 new species of dinosaurs and the first dino eggs were discovered. The little-visited Flaming Cliffs still turn up 80-million-year-old fossils, so walk with a keen eye around this stunning section of the southern Gobi.

PERU

9. Fly Over the Nasca Lines

The way to truly see the ancient geoglyphs of the Nasca Desert is by aircraft. Identify the massive hummingbird, lizard, whale, and a dozen other animals etched in the earth. Then, continue to the more recently discovered Palpa lines, with their equally fascinating human depictions.

UNITED ARAB EMIRATES

10. Dune Bashing

Renegade driving through the dunes is a favorite pastime across the deserts, though Dubai's car culture does it best. Hop in a Hummer or Land Cruiser to slide, spin, bounce, and blaze a trail through the Arabian Desert.

"Snow falling soundlessly in the middle of the night will always fill my heart with sweet clarity."

—NOVALA TAKEMOTO

Chapter Eight

SNOW & ICE

f you can handle freezing temperatures, so much more of the year and world will open up to you. Put on the right gear and a snowy forest looks ideal for a hike, a glacier invites a climb, and an iceberg-filled lake inspires a kayak session. Cold is just a frame of mind, and those who don't overcome that icy mental block will miss auroras dancing across the sky, the thunderous calving of a glacier, or a penguin nibbling on their camera strap. Frosty places hold precious secrets and share them with the hardy. Sami reindeer herders, Antarctic scientists, and Vermont maple tappers understand the beauty of winter and how to tame it with a blazing fire, woolly blankets, hot toddies, and cuddles at the end of the day. Though you don't always need frigid weather to enjoy the ice. Some glacial destinations are even better in summer when sunshine and spas cut the chill. Find a cool getaway. It will bring you closer in more ways than one.

Anne paddling through the brash ice of Pleneau Bay

ANTARCTIC PENINSULA
Antarctica

Antarctic Peninsula

ANTARCTICA

The coldest, driest, and windiest continent is as close to utopia as it gets. Not owned or exploited by any nation, Antarctica is shared by 53 countries for scientific advancement and the common good of humanity. Mother Nature runs this show, and with the ocean, wind, and wild animals on her side, she's crafted one of the most stunning places on Earth. About 600 miles from the tip of South America, with one of the world's most dangerous seas in between, the voyage to Antarctica is reserved for the intrepid. After two days on the Drake Passage, with 25-foot swells and virtually no sign of life, a pod of humpback whales appear. You follow them toward icebergs with penguins waddling along the ridges. The gleaming white continent comes into focus—and this is just the beginning. From here, you'll Zodiac cruise to gentoo penguin colonies, kayak through glacier-fringed archipelagos, and walk in the footsteps of polar explorers.

 WHEN TO GO

November–March is expedition season. November–December allow for snow sports. January is warmest (34°F average) and baby penguin season. February brings whales.

WHERE TO STAY

Quark Expeditions: Among the most adventurous, fun-loving, and affordable fleets. **One Ocean:** A luxurious ship with an adventure and environmental focus. *Note:* Most trips are 8 to 11 days, departing from Ushuaia, Argentina, or Punta Arenas, Chile.

GET ROMANTIC

Few make it this far. Head to the top deck and celebrate with a champagne toast to love, glaciers, and penguins.

HONEYTREK TIP

Don't pay full price. Sign up for expedition newsletters to track flash sales. November and March trips tend to be cheaper. Find last-minute deals in Ushuaia.

Fur seals playing on the shores of Deception Island

COUPLES ADVENTURES

Kayak Safari ▲▲▲
For the most intimate way to explore Antarctica, book the paddling package. Having a tandem kayak for the week, you'll have the extra space and freedom to enjoy the serenity of the white continent. As you quietly paddle around islands and bergs, penguins cross your path and curious seals swim alongside you.

Take the Polar Plunge ▲▲▲▲
Jumping into the frosty sea is an Antarctic rite of passage. Standing at the edge of the gangplank in your swimsuit and looking out to a frosty landscape, you will have doubts. Jump anyway. The 30°F water will reinvigorate the senses and give you bragging rights for life.

SUP Around Icebergs ▲▲▲▲
In a sheltered bay, slip your stand-up paddleboard into the icy waters and find your balance. Maneuver between blue icebergs in jagged formations (while trying not to take your second polar plunge). Hug

✣ Landing on our Seventh Continent

We swung our legs out of the Zodiac and set foot on the land that extends to the South Pole. We practically ran up the steep mountain, enjoying every slippery step and bits of hail that pelted our faces. We reached a rocky outcropping above the glacier-lined Neko Harbour, and it felt like our four years of honeymooning were culminating at this one moment. This called for champagne. We popped the cork, and the wind sent sparkling wine into the air and up our noses. Giggling from the tickly bubbles, utter joy, and complete awe, we drank in the milestone moment.

Holding the flag of Antarctica with pride

the islands for wildlife sightings and revel in the fantastical reflections.

Come Face-to-Face With Penguins ▲▲
Stopping at multiple colonies, you'll see gentoos, chinstraps, and Adélies waddle, slide, splash, and generally be adorable. Although you should never approach a penguin, if you kneel down and stay still, curious chicks will often come right up to you. Keep your fingers crossed for anchorage at the lively Aitcho Islands or the historic Port Charcot.

....

TO EXPLORE MORE ON THIS CONTINENT, CHECK OUT:
» **Mountains: Torres del Paine, Chile...p. 40**
» **Falls: Iguazú Falls, Argentina & Brazil...p. 46**

WESTLAND
New Zealand

From the tallest peaks of the Southern Alps, miles of glaciers flow down to a temperate rain forest and golden beach. Such diversity of terrain seems impossible within one national park, but Westland Tai Poutini has it in spades. Driving along the South Island's West Coast, a valley of ice appears through the podocarp forest. Like endless rows of shark teeth, in pearl white and luminescent blue, Fox Glacier is like nothing you've ever seen. That is, until you drive 14 miles up the road, where you meet its twin: Franz Josef. Both glaciers extend eight miles into the Southern Alps, and need helicopters and crampons to truly explore them. But that's not a problem—it's an adventure. Franz Josef and Fox villages are ready with every possible snowy outfitter (ice climbing, skydiving, glacier trekking, and so on) and hot springs for your return. Pair your ice with a bit of beach and take the scenic drive to Gillespies to admire the seal colony and relics from New Zealand's mining days. So whether one of you fancies winter and the other summer, you can enjoy the best of both seasons in one locale.

AUSTRALIA

NEW ZEALAND

Westland

WHEN TO GO

Anytime is delightful. For fewer crowds, more sunshine, and stable ice conditions, consider Kiwi winter (June–August); it's typically in the 40s and 50s.

WHERE TO STAY

Te Waonui Forest Retreat: Modern, eco-conscious, and the most luxurious resort around. **Aspen Court Motel:** Updated rooms with kitchenettes and knowledgeable staff, in the heart of Franz Josef village.

GET ROMANTIC

A couples hot stone massage and a private bath await in the rain forest and spa of Glacier Hot Pools.

HONEYTREK TIP

Sign up for your glacier excursions same day. There is a slight risk trips will fill up, but you'll be able to time your flights and ice treks with the best weather. Check the local Department of Conservation office for the most accurate forecasts.

Franz Josef, where the ice meets the rain forest

Helicopter flight over the glaciers and Southern Alps

COUPLES ADVENTURES

Helicopter Grand Tour ▲▲
Call in the chopper to reach the heart of New Zealand's biggest mountains and glaciers. Flying over the impenetrable Fox, Franz Josef, and Tasman Glaciers, circling the more than 12,000-foot Mount Cook, and touching down for a frolic on the ice, you'll experience the purest terrain of the Te Wahipounamu UNESCO World Heritage site.

Minnehaha Glowworm Walk ▲
Trust your night vision and walk the mile loop through the rain forest below Fox Glacier. Treat it like a treasure hunt. Look around fallen trees and ditches, and hundreds of bioluminescent larvae will appear, twinkling like stars.

Fox Ice Climb ▲▲▲▲
Scale the ice walls and blue pinnacles for an intimate and intense glacier experience. After expert guides train and outfit you, helicopter from the

✢ Mighty Fragile

Hiking in Franz Josef's moraine, with its gouged walls dripping with waterfalls, we were reminded how much the glacier is retreating. Franz has lost nearly two miles in length since the 1880s, with one-third of that occurring since 2008. The beauty of the raging rivers and teal lakes can distract from the problems of climate change, but they are signs that the snow is melting faster than it's accumulating. A decade of massive snowfall could spark another era of advance, but we cannot just cross our fingers; we need to do what we can to protect these precious landscapes.

Te Waonui Forest Retreat at the foot of Franz Josef

forest to Fox's frozen oasis (the commute alone is worth it). Dig your ax and crampons into the sheer ice and strike climbers' gold.

Hike Canavans Knob ▲▲
Follow the two-mile trail through a rain forest of ferns, orchids, and rimus tangled in vines. The trees will open up to a lookout over the Tasman Sea and Waiho River flowing with little icebergs. Continue upward to the second viewpoint and go face-to-face with Franz Josef.

TO EXPLORE MORE ON THIS CONTINENT, CHECK OUT:
» **Road Trips: South Island, New Zealand...p. 202**
» **Supernatural: Rotorua, New Zealand...p. 228**

The Waddle

We docked at Booth Island, home to thousands of Adélie, gentoo, and chinstrap penguins. We kept along the path, but the chubby adolescents knew no bounds. Darting in every direction, practicing belly slides, and swimming in circles, they were figuring out life on their own. We bent down to take in their world from eye level and were encircled by curious chicks. They examined us carefully, even giving a nibble on our pants in hopes they were fish flavored.

Penguins finding their way on Booth Island, Antarctica

The frosted Green Mountains from Killington resort

CENTRAL VERMONT
U.S.A.

NORTH AMERICA
Central Vermont
UNITED STATES

Vermont may not be as wild as Patagonia or as steep as the Rockies, but this spunky slice of New England with its maple syrup farms and covered bridges makes up for it in a myriad of ways. With the second smallest state population in the United States, Vermonters are often underestimated—but they are a savvy bunch. It's not by accident that their state remains nearly 80 percent covered in forest and they've built more hiking trails than highways. They have a fierce love of the great outdoors, especially when it's covered in a blanket of snow. One of the snowiest states in America, Vermont knows winter like a best friend. Kids learn to snowshoe in phys ed, and many adults keep a pair in the trunk of their Subaru. It's home to some of the best ski resorts east of the Mississippi, including the skier-run Mad River Glen, and Killington—one of the few in the country to stay open through May. Come to the Green Mountain State and you'll leave with snow in your hair and a smile on your face.

WHEN TO GO
December–April are winter white, with February being the snowiest month. Late March brings spring skiing and maple tapping.

WHERE TO STAY
Mountain Top Inn: On 350 acres, this lakeside resort embraces winter with ice-skating, horse-drawn sleighs, and cozy spaces. **The Woodstock Inn:** In the charming town square, this historic hotel has contemporary rooms, a spa, and Nordic center.

GET ROMANTIC
Bundled up in blankets, ascend Killington Mountain in a snowcat-drawn sleigh to the Ledgewood Yurt. By light of candles and a crackling fire, enjoy a five-course meal of regional delicacies.

HONEYTREK TIP
Enjoy the ultimate Vermont day: Ski the iconic Suicide Six, sample maple syrup at Sugarbush Farm, try the 19th-century recipe at Crowley Cheese, and savor a craft beer at Long Trail Brewery.

Woodstock Inn exudes charming Vermont style.

COUPLES ADVENTURES

Ski Mad River Glen—If You Can! ▲▲▲
Ride the 1940s single chair to the expert terrain of America's only skier-owned mountain. To get the true spirit of Mad River, go on a powder day or "Roll Back the Clock Day," when you can ski for the original ticket price: $3.50.

Follow the Middlebury Tasting Trail ▲
Some of Vermont's finest breweries, distilleries, and wineries are packed into this five-mile stretch. Sip rye whiskey in WhistlePig's barn, a Starlight rosé on the Lincoln Peak porch, and a Sunshine and Hoppiness at the Drop-In Brewing Company.

Cross-Country Ski ▲▲
Chittenden's Mountain Top Inn, one of the oldest cross-country ski areas in the States, offers 38 miles of trails along rolling hills, by lakeshores, and through a birch forest. The Nordic center has all the gear, instruction, and hot chocolate you could want.

Snowshoe Deer Leap ▲▲
Experience two of America's greatest hiking routes, the Appalachian Trail and Long Trail, in just a few miles. Follow the AT through the snowy forest for a vista over the Coolidge Range and Sherburne Pass. Dip onto the country's oldest long-distance trail, before warming up with Guinness stew at McGrath's Irish Pub.

✤ Vermont Is Where the Heart Is

We had been dating for a month when Mike asked me to join his Killington ski house. Considering I had never been to Vermont and barely knew how to ski, committing to a six-month lease (and relationship) was probably a risky move, but I accepted without hesitation. Five ski seasons later, we walked down a snowy aisle in the Green Mountains, with vows to take a honeymoon around the world. No matter where, or if, we ever settle down, Vermont will always be our winter wonderland.

Our outdoor winter wedding at the Mountain Top Inn

TO EXPLORE MORE ON THIS CONTINENT, CHECK OUT:

» On Safari: Churchill, Canada...p. 96
» Ice: Niagara Falls, U.S.A. & Canada...p. 172

TROMSØ
Norway

Tromsø
NORWAY
EUROPE

The Gateway to the Arctic, the Paris of the North, and one of the northernmost cities in the world, Tromsø has many impressive titles. On an island inside the Arctic Circle, with roots as a frontier town, it's a surprisingly sophisticated place. Given its proximity to the polar bears and walruses of Svalbard, it not only attracted hunters, but also esteemed explorers and scientists. Today the city is home to the Norwegian Polar Institute, University of Tromsø, and over 100 nationalities, making for a lively cultural scene (claiming more bars per capita than anywhere in Norway). You don't need to travel far to find the wild alps and dramatic fjords. Away from the downtown lights, auroras burst in neon green and purple, Sami tribesman herd their reindeer, and snowmobiles are the best way to get around. Chase the northern lights, dogsled through the tundra, and warm up with a little Arctic adrenaline.

✈ WHEN TO GO
For northern lights, whales, and snow, visit November–February. On the Gulf Stream, Tromsø doesn't go far below freezing.

⊞ WHERE TO STAY
Thon Hotel Polar: A whimsical boutique hotel in the heart of Tromsø. **Camp Tamok:** Lyngsfjord Adventure's *lavvu* tents and Arctic chalets, plus snowmobiling, reindeer and dogsledding, 50 miles from downtown.

♡ GET ROMANTIC
Hop aboard the dreamy Vulkana Spa Boat. Relax in the Finnish sauna or soak in the saltwater hot tub on deck. Both have panoramic views.

✅ HONEYTREK TIP
Most outfitters provide Arctic outerwear, so don't pack all your ski gear. Pack Yaktrax for Tromsø's icy streets and a tripod for aurora photography.

Northern lights dash over Tromsøya Island.

Lavvu-style tents at the adventure haven of Camp Tamok

COUPLES ADVENTURES

City Walking Tour ▲
Explore the cityscape, an intriguing mix of 18th-century wooden houses, modern ice-inspired architecture, and cozy cafés. Visit the Polar Museum, pop into the Arctic Cathedral, tour the historic Mack Brewery, dine at the trendy Hildr Gastro Bar, and catch live music at the legendary Blå Rock.

Humpback- and Killer Whale–Watching ▲
Catch a boat past the fjords, islands, and snowy mountains to the herring shoals. In recent years, these gentle giants have been migrating here for a winter feast. Humpback sightings are practically guaranteed November to January, and spectacular Arctic landscapes are a certainty.

Chase the Northern Lights ▲▲▲
Check the aurora forecast on *Norway-Lights.com* to maximize your chances for neon skies, then book your chase with the pros. Heading outside the city to wherever the solar winds are blowing, you'll make stops to see them swirl around the sky. For the best odds, consider spending a few nights at a remote lodge or at sea.

Dogsledding ▲▲▲▲
Mush a team of huskies through the Lapland tundra, dipping through snowy forests and over frozen streams. Take turns driving the sled, and whatever you do—hang on! Both Lyngsfjord Adventure and Active Tromsø are pro outfitters with stunning terrain.

✣ Friluftsliv: Free Air Life

A Norwegian word with no English equivalent, *friluftsliv* is a Nordic philosophy for the pursuit of happiness in the great outdoors—the belief that life in the open air is essential to living, that being outside is like coming home. When we went to Sogn og Fjordane to stay at our friend Paal's cabin (a vacation house with no electricity or running water, in a place that receives so much snow, they sometimes have to use a probe to find their roof), the meaning of friluftsliv became clear.

The award-winning Tromsø Library is a cultural hub.

TO EXPLORE MORE ON THIS CONTINENT, CHECK OUT:

» **Rivers: Rhine Gorge, Germany...p. 56**

» **At Sea: Norwegian Fjords, Norway...p. 136**

Massive icebergs float out of Ilulissat Icefjord.

WESTERN GREENLAND

Greenland

BY **DAVE BOUSKILL & DEBRA CORBEIL**

Greenland

Western Greenland

NORTH AMERICA

Eighty percent covered in ice, Greenland isn't on your average traveler's bucket list—and that's exactly why we came here. In the remote North Atlantic Ocean, with the largest polar ice cap outside of Antarctica, it may just be the final frontier of adventure travel. A trip down Western Greenland begins at Ilulissat, a town 155 miles into the Arctic Circle and home to the UNESCO Ilulissat Icefjord, the world's most active calving glacier. To see where the ice cap charges into the ocean, creating avalanches and massive icebergs, is reason enough to come to Greenland, but it's just one of many. Heading south on an expedition ship, your days consist of Zodiac cruising glacier bays, kayaking unnamed fjords, hiking across the Arctic tundra, and getting to know the fascinating Inuit people. Greenland is filled with spectacular scenery, rich culture, and infinite possibilities for adventure.

WHEN TO GO

Visit year-round. June–August offer whale-watching, sailing, and midnight sun. December–March are best for northern lights and winter sports.

WHERE TO STAY

Quark Expeditions: Adventurous ship journeys, heading to remote villages and fjords. **Hotel Hans Egede:** In Nuuk, it's a great base for independent travelers wanting to arrange adventures à la carte.

GET ROMANTIC

Take the boat to Uunartoq, home to Greenland's most blissful thermal pools. Sip champagne in the hot spring as icebergs float by. There's nothing more romantic.

THE PLANET D TIP

Due to Greenland's size and undeveloped nature, it's best to book tours that can help with accommodation and transportation. Try to stay for two weeks or more.

COUPLES ADVENTURES

Jakobshavn Glacier Hike ▲▲
Hike this UNESCO World Heritage site, passing Ilu-lissat's colorful buildings and sled-dog city. A boardwalk weaves through the permafrost, and heads toward the powerful glacier. Moving at a rate of 60 to 100 feet a day, it fills the fjord with 35 billion tons of ice each year.

Kayaking Uncharted Fjords ▲▲▲
Paddle amid brash ice and listen to the crackling. Fjords like Torsukattak and Evighedsfjorden will surround you with high mountains and glaciers plunging into the sea, while nameless fjords await your discovery.

Get Around Greenland Style ▲▲▲
With few roads in the country, dogsledding and snowmobiling are still main modes of transit. Head to the island of Qeqertarsuaq, with its volcanic mountains and dramatic valleys, and you can enjoy both pastimes in the same day. Mush the ancient breed of Greenland huskies through the backcountry, then hop on a snowmobile to chase the northern lights.

Spend Time in Inuit Villages ▲
Try the local cuisine like minke whale and seal in Sisimiut. Visit Paamiut's historic church, and stop at the local fish market. Itivdleq offers the chance to visit with friendly elders and play soccer with the kids. In Greenland, indigenous communities mix the ancient and modern world with grace.

✢ Couples Advice

Adventure lovers tend to be overachievers, busily ticking off their bucket list. They often worry that if they aren't on the go, they're missing out. Though when traveling together, sometimes it's important to "just be." Stop for a few days and do nothing but relax. Take in the beauty of the Earth; watch the sun go down without a camera in hand, and go to the beach without the need to surf or snorkel. Pausing to take a breath will make you realize that you are meant to be nowhere else but here and now.

Abandoned Inuit fishing village near Sisimiut

TO EXPLORE MORE ON THIS CONTINENT, CHECK OUT:

» **On Safari: Churchill, Canada...p. 96**

» **Snow: Central Vermont, U.S.A....p. 166**

POWER COUPLE: *Dave & Deb*

The Canadian couple and founders of *ThePlanetD* *.com* have explored 105 countries on all seven continents. From cycling across Africa to driving a tiny car from England to Mongolia, they inspire adventure in everyone. They have won two gold medals by the Society of American Travel Writers, and are respected adventure travel experts, appearing regularly on TV, radio, and in print.

NIAGARA FALLS
U.S.A. & Canada

The dual-nation falls are the largest in North America and among the most visited in the world, but few people make it there in winter. The freezing temperatures keep tourists away, but that's exactly what makes Niagara so special. Of all the globe's greatest falls (Iguazú, Angel, Victoria, and so on), this is the only one that freezes. See cascades framed with a glacial layer of ice, its boulders entombed in frozen mist, and its trees dripping with icicles. The scene is incredible, especially because you practically have it to yourselves. Known as the "honeymoon capital of the world," it has lured couples since the late 1700s (including relatives of Aaron Burr and Napoleon Bonaparte), and it's keeping up its romantic claim to fame with luxurious spas, top-notch restaurants, and dozens of wineries. Although some attractions close in the winter season, the region is never shy on adventure. Put on your snow boots and hold each other tight; these are falls like you've never experienced.

✈ WHEN TO GO
Canada's Festival of Lights is December–January. January–March have the most ice.

▦ WHERE TO STAY
The Giacomo: Boutique art deco hotel adjacent to Niagara Falls State Park. **Niagara Crossing Hotel & Spa:** In the charming village of Lewiston, New York, with fireplaces and views of Niagara Gorge.

♥ GET ROMANTIC
Dine at the delightful Carmelo's in Lewiston, then stroll the falls, illuminated in a dazzling succession of colors (a nightly spectacular until at least 11 p.m.).

✅ HONEYTREK TIP
Although the flashier Canadian side begs attention, spend time in the au naturel Niagara Falls State Park. Designed by Frederick Olmsted, America's first state park offers 15 miles of manicured trails from the Discovery Center to Goat Island.

Helicopter ride swooping over Horseshoe Falls

Nightly light shows add to the allure of the falls.

Niagara Falls: Fun Facts

More stats and oddities that add to Niagara's claim to fame:

- Daredevils have been tightrope walking over Niagara Gorge since 1859.
- The first person to go over the falls in a barrel was a 63-year-old female schoolteacher.
- Fish travel over the 200-foot falls, and about 90 percent survive.
- Niagara is the birthplace of commercial hydroelectric power, thanks to Nikola Tesla.

COUPLES ADVENTURES

Helicopter the Falls ▲▲
Soar over Lake Ontario, Fort George, wine country, and Niagara River, and loop the falls for stunning views from every angle. The aerial perspective gives a whole new appreciation for this dramatic landscape, especially with your pilot acting as a regional guide. Try National Helicopters for winter takeoffs and the longest flight times.

Snowshoe the Vineyards ▲▲
Start with a Riesling and ice wine tasting to get a little fire in your bellies, then snowshoe the vines, rivers, and forests around Niagara's wine region. For organized tours and on-snow tastings, check out Thirty Bench Wine Makers, and for more independent snowshoe exploration, the Schulze Winery is happy to let you romp around their creekside vineyard.

Journey Behind the Falls ▲▲
Descend 150 feet into the bedrock of Canada's Horseshoe Falls. Walk the windy tunnels and feel the

Canada geese on the banks of the Niagara River

thunder as approximately 740,000 gallons of water fly past the icicle-framed portals every second.

Sample the Culinary Institute ▲
Niagara Falls Culinary Institute is the secret behind Niagara's burgeoning culinary scene. Take a free tour of the impressive 90,000-square-foot space, have a meal at Savor, their fabulous student-run restaurant, or take a mixology or pastry class for a date night. If you're a true foodie, check the Cannon Culinary Theatre schedule for talks by celebrity chefs.

TO EXPLORE MORE ON THIS CONTINENT, CHECK OUT:

» **Islands: North Eleuthera, Bahamas...p. 68**
» **On Safari: Churchill, Canada...p. 96**

The teal Laguna de Los Tres and the iconic Fitz Roy

LOS GLACIARES
Argentina

SOUTH AMERICA

Los Glaciares ARGENTINA

Among the Austral Andes and one of the world's largest ice caps, Los Glaciares National Park is a winter lover's paradise. It harbors frosted peaks, iceberg-filled lakes, and over 200 glaciers, including the legendary Perito Moreno. While many of the world's glaciers are retreating, the fierce Perito advances as much as 10 feet a day. Standing before its three-mile-wide terminus, listening to ice fracture, and watching it calve with cannonball splashes into Lago Argentino (Argentino Lake) is among the most awe-inspiring experiences in South America. Just when you think it couldn't get any better, you arrive at the other side of the park. Mount Fitz Roy, the veritable symbol of Patagonia (the region and the clothing brand), presents itself front and center. Its village of El Chaltén—an oasis of gear shops, vegetarian restaurants, and breweries—exists for no other reason but to access and adore the "smoking mountain." Trails peel off from every corner of town, and you cannot help but follow them. Patagonia's beauty will push your body to hike farther and harder than ever before. Your muscles may not always be so grateful, but your inner trekker will forever thank you.

WHEN TO GO
In highly unpredictable Patagonia, December–March tend to be warmer, sunnier, and less windy. Brave chilly April or November for more park to yourself.

WHERE TO STAY
Hostería Senderos: A cozy contemporary inn, well priced for the level of style and central location in cheerful El Chaltén. **Los Ponchos:** Boutique hotel and self-catering suites at the edge of El Calafate, overlooking Lago Argentino.

GET ROMANTIC
Upgrade your exploration with a three-day glacier-to-glacier cruise. Aboard the sophisticated Cruceros Marpatag, you'll find luxe rooms, gourmet meals, and countless occasions for champagne, from Spegazzini to Upsala. Day cruises are also available.

HONEYTREK TIP
Get in shape for Patagonia. When you see these magnificent mountains and glaciers, you'll want to hike forever. Prepare with a few 10-mile treks on your home trails.

Trekking to the growing glacier of Perito Moreno

COUPLES ADVENTURES

Perito Moreno Big Ice Hike ▲▲▲▲

Skip those "touch the glacier" hikes and get to the heart of this ice field. Leave the sunshine at the base, and enter the wild microclimate of a growing glacier. Navigate the maze of crevasses, duck into blue ice caves, and conquer the rugged terrain with crampons and adrenaline.

Overnight Trek to Laguna de Los Tres ▲▲▲▲

The journey to the base of the granite peaks and turquoise lagoons of the Fitz Roy is arguably the world's best day hike—and even better as two days. Staying overnight at Camp Poincenot gives you time to wait out any clouds (they call it the smoking mountain for a reason), see the peaks radiate in sunrise and sunset, and explore the surrounding Rio Eléctrico valley and glaciers.

Upsala Glacier Adventures ▲

Begin with a boat ride around the bergs of Lago Argentino to the dramatically calving Upsala Glacier. Continue through the canal to Estancia Cristina, a resilient homestead among the ice since 1914. Enjoy the inn's restaurant and gaucho museum, then hike, 4x4, or ride horseback for a higher vantage point of Upsala.

Trek Laguna Torre ▲▲

From the village of El Chaltén, move through southern beech forests toward the 10,262-foot Cerro Torre, the tallest peak in the iconic four-mountain chain. Catch reflections of the ice-capped spire in the lagoon, then head to Mirador Maestri for even better views of the ice cap. It's a huge payout for a relatively easy eight-mile journey.

✢ The Elusive Peanut Butter

It was day #107, country #4, and HoneyTrek attempt #22 to find peanut butter in South America. The ultimate hiking food—creamy, protein packed, and not needing refrigeration—the PB had evaded us. We walked into an El Chaltén market, hopeful this hippie town would understand our plight, and asked the shopkeeper, *"Tiene mantequilla de cacahuete?"* When he responded with, *"Por supuesto,"* we squealed like schoolchildren, practically hugged the man, and bought three jars of trekkers' gold.

Utter joy in the peanut butter aisle

TO EXPLORE MORE ON THIS CONTINENT, CHECK OUT:

» Mountains: Torres del Paine, Chile...p. 40

» Falls: Iguazú Falls, Argentina & Brazil...p. 46

Millions of LEDs at
Nabana no Sato, Japan

Ultimate Winter Festivals

Warm up to Old Man Winter with these entertaining and cultural festivities.

CANADA

1. Carnaval de Québec

Québec holds one of the world's biggest winter carnivals, hosted by Bonhomme (a giant snowman). The festival kicks off at a 300-ton ice palace, followed by mulled wine–fueled parades, and the signature ice canoe race—a 50-team iceberg-hopping event.

JAPAN

2. Nabana no Sato Winter Light Festival

Showcasing Japan's incredible attention to detail, Kuwana City takes its otherwise dormant botanical gardens and brings them to life with over eight million LEDs. From the trippy Tunnel of Lights to sculptural feats like "Mount Fuji at Dawn," it brings everyone out to feel the glow.

U.S.A.

3. Anchorage Fur Rondy

Originating when Anchorage was a miner and trapper town, "The Rondy" carries on the city's pioneering spirit. With competitions like Running of the Reindeer, Dogsledding, Snowshoe Softball, Outhouse Races, and the Beard and Moustache Championship, it's a uniquely Alaskan affair.

RUSSIA

4. Moscow Winter Festival

The capital welcomes the holidays with over-the-top lights, ice sculptures, troika sleigh rides, ice-skating, Christmas markets, and performances in Revolution Square and Izmaylovo Park. A celebration of Russian culture, the winter fest will give you a fuzzy feeling about the motherland.

HUNGARY

5. Busójárás Festival

Dating back to 1526 when villagers tried to frighten off the Turkish army with monster costumes, this UNESCO World Heritage festival continues as a playful attempt to scare away winter. Townspeople dressed as woolly beasts sail the Danube, storm the streets on fantastical horse-drawn carriages, and down *pálinka* brandy to keep the cold at bay.

U.S.A. & CANADA

6. Pond Skimming Cup

The quirky spring skiing tradition of building a pond at the bottom of the slopes and attempting to ski across in costume is now a recognized competition. After qualifying events across North America, ski resorts send their best skimmers to the world cup—to not just make it across but also rack up style points at one of the slopes' best parties.

SWITZERLAND

7. Snow Bike Festival

Mountain bikers and snow-sport junkies come together for the premier winter bike festival. With wider tires and deeper treads, riders take on the Gstaad Alps each January in a four-stage race, the Eliminator slope, and all-around revelry.

CHINA

8. Harbin International Ice & Snow Festival

Taking ice sculpting to China's megalopolis scale, Harbin builds a 150-acre city out of frozen blocks every January. Buildings as high as 15 stories are carved with incredible detail—from replicas of Big Ben to Buddhist temples. Wander the icy world, even alpine ski or polar bear swim.

PERU

9. Inti Raymi

The Inca winter solstice celebration was stifled by the Spanish and observed in secrecy until the mid-20th century. Now this Andean holiday has reemerged with its grandest manifestation in Cusco. A costume-clad procession moves through the ancient Sacsayhuamán fortress, and parties spark up all over town.

GERMANY

10. Rothenburg ob der Tauber Christmas Market

Hosting a yuletide market since the 15th century and playing the part with gingerbread-style houses, this medieval village is a whimsical place to shop for handmade treasures, sip mulled wine, and connect with Santa.

Chapter Nine

JUNGLES & RAIN FORESTS

Walk through an ancient rain forest, past ferns and conifers that have thrived since the age of dinosaurs. Gaze at a towering cedar dripping with moss. Then look closer. This one tree is supporting bromeliads, frogs, birds, and hundreds of other species. The inner workings of a rain forest are mind-boggling. Learn from its indigenous custodians and dedicated naturalists—those who know the secrets of the forest. What starts as a cacophony of humming insects, chirping birds, and rustling leaves soon becomes a symphony. These signs might lead you to a resplendent quetzal, a troop of spider monkeys, or a pod of pink river dolphins. Heighten your senses, including that of adventure, and you'll find a place of endless wonder. Paddle through a flooded forest, climb into the canopy, and take hikes by day and night. Our rain forests are precious, and sadly under siege. Give them the love they deserve.

Ancient rain forest meets the Great Barrier Reef.

DAINTREE
Australia

□Daintree

AUSTRALIA

At more than 100 million years of age, Daintree is one of the oldest rain forests in the world. While much of Australia turned arid, this corner of Queensland remained lush, retaining its ancient ferns, conifers, and primitive flowering plant families (12 of the 19 left on Earth). The flora and fauna are plenty diverse (hello, 12,000 species of insects), though it's the endemic varieties that make Daintree so special. Home to the Boyd's forest dragon, Lumholtz's tree kangaroo, and southern cassowary (a 6-foot, 190-pound bird), rare and unusual are the operative words. Adding to its rich history, Daintree's original inhabitants are still its custodians. Aboriginal Australians are the world's oldest continuous culture, and the Kuku Yalanji people share their traditions as rangers, guides, and artists. Yet another reason to visit: Daintree is adjacent to the Great Barrier Reef, putting two UNESCO World Heritage sites at your fingertips. Rain forest meets beach meets culture. Daintree can satisfy any couple's travel cravings.

WHEN TO GO
Just after the rainy season, May–September offer cooler and clearer months with an average temp of 78°F.

WHERE TO STAY
Daintree EcoLodge & Spa: Fifteen luxurious treehouse villas, focusing on sustainability. Cape Tribulation Beach House: On the seaside of the rain forest, offering laid-back lodging across budgets.

GET ROMANTIC
Enjoy a massage by a rain forest waterfall, or better yet, a spa session *in* the waterfall. Daintree EcoLodge Day Spa uses Aboriginal plant knowledge and a sacred setting for its blissful treatments.

✓ HONEYTREK TIP
Jellyfish and crocodiles are no Aussie joke. If you fancy a carefree swim, try Mossman Gorge's river pools and the swimming hole behind Mason's Store.

The temperamental and exquisite southern cassowary

COUPLES ADVENTURES

Dubuji Boardwalk ▲
Walk under the canopy of fan palms to three different habitats: rain forest, freshwater swamp, and mangroves. This 45-minute stroll ends at Myall Beach with its spindly mangroves, reef-rock pools, and sweeping coastline.

Dreamtime Walks at Mossman Gorge ▲
At the southern end of the park, where the Mossman River flows around massive boulders, you can experience the rain forest through the eyes of the Aboriginal Kuku Yalanji people. An elder will share the jungle's medicinal, practical, and spiritual uses during a 90-minute nature walk.

Four-by-Four the Bloomfield Track ▲▲▲
Take one of the most adventurous drives in Australia, only accessible by 4WD. Weaving between the coast and the rain forest for 19 miles, you'll find secluded beaches, mountain lookouts, waterfalls,

We met a Dutch couple at the hotel breakfast bar. A waffle, two cups of coffee, and a dozen laughs later, we were plotting a road trip from Cairns to Daintree. With less than 24 hours of acquaintance and planning, we loaded into their 1994 Toyota Camry and set off into the wilds of Queensland. Beachcombing, jungle trekking, pond swimming, and telling stories around the bonfire, we had an unforgettable weekend. Sure, road tripping with total strangers is a leap of faith, but the unknown is where the real adventure begins.

Strolling the Dubuji Boardwalk with our new buddies

creek crossings, and a wild ride from Cape Tribulation to Cooktown.

Bird- & Croc-Watching on the Daintree River ▲▲
Cruise down the river to see a few of the region's 400 bird species. Spot little kingfishers, great-billed herons, Papuan frogmouths, or with luck, the massive cassowary. Try to time your boat trip with low tide to see the saltwater crocodiles sunbathing on the banks.

TO EXPLORE MORE ON THIS CONTINENT, CHECK OUT:
» On Safari: Top End, Australia...p. 86
» Ice: Westland, New Zealand...p. 162

KHAO SOK
Thailand

ASIA

Khao Sok □ THAILAND

Karst mountains rise out of the lake and rain forest of Khao Sok National Park. These ancient coral formations, topped with emerald foliage and chiseled with caves, make this one of Thailand's postcard destinations. At the foot of the eye-catching monoliths lies a 100-million-year-old evergreen rain forest, one of the oldest of its kind. Rare palms, wild mangosteens, strangler figs, and liana vines weave a lush ecosystem that is home to tigers, elephants, and tapirs. The park spreads over 285 square miles, with two distinct sections. Khao Sok village is the gateway to the "land side," while the Ratchaprapha Dam is the gateway to the "water side," Cheow Lan Lake. Fringed by over 100 limestone outcroppings and six main tributaries, the teal lake gives the ancient rain forest of Khao Sok that extra sparkle. Take a longtail boat to explore the various coves with their karst islands, expansive caves, and wildlife sanctuaries. Cruise in a canoe or inner tube down the scenic Sok River. Sleep in a floating bungalow, treehouse, or elephant sanctuary. Enjoy the rarity of a chill island vibe in an ancient rain forest.

 WHEN TO GO

December–April are the driest months. In the monsoon season, some of the trails and caves close, though you'll see more mammals and fewer people.

WHERE TO STAY

Our Jungle House: Treehouses centrally located on 25 acres of riverfront in Khao Sok village. Elephant Hills: Luxury safari tents in a remote setting, with an elephant sanctuary (for caring, not riding). *KhaoSok Lake.com:* Local agency offering floating bungalow experiences across prices.

 GET ROMANTIC

Authentic Thai massage is one of the most engaging body treatments, often called assisted yoga. Get limber and invigorated with an in-room or outdoor session.

 HONEYTREK TIP

Resist the urge to book tours in advance. The way to secure the best available treks and lake excursions is to evaluate the options when you arrive. Plus, you'll get better deals.

Longtail boats moored at Cheow Lan Lake's floating bungalows

Bathing elephant in Khlong Saeng Wildlife Sanctuary

COUPLES ADVENTURES

Full-Day Lake Excursion ▲

Book a classic lake tour, heading toward either Klong Long, Klong Ka, or Klong Pey. Start early to see the mist enshroud the karst peaks and the animals out for breakfast. Cruising along the cliffs in your longtail boat, you'll pass the Three Brothers islands, a stunning spot for a swim. Stop for lunch at a floating raft house, take the kayaks out for a paddle, then head to the jungle for a cave hike. *Note:* If you only have one day on the lake, request the Klong Pey route to explore Tham Nam Thalu Cave.

Caving Tham Nam Thalu ▲▲▲▲

Hike through the rain forest, ford rivers, and reach one of Khao Sok's wildest adventures. Using your own strength and a few ropes, spelunk through a subterranean river, climbing and swimming into the far reaches of this stalagmite gauntlet. You'll never forget it.

Hiking the Remote Rain Forest ▲▲

There are a bounty of beautiful hikes through bamboo groves, tiered waterfalls, and mountainsides with rafflesia (the so-called "world's largest flower). Although you can do a few trails on your own, get farther afield with a guide who can lead you on the best trek for your locale, season, and interests.

Khlong Saeng Wildlife Sanctuary ▲▲▲

In the remote northeast corner of the lake, Khlong Saeng is among Thailand's best wildlife reserves. Rare Asian species, like the clouded leopard, Malayan tapir, wild elephant, king cobra, and the sun bear still roam this habitat. Stay the night (or ideally three) in the rustic floating bungalows, wake up to families of white-handed gibbons, and trek the rain forest with a ranger for thrilling encounters.

✦ Traveling With Other Couples

We explored Khao Sok as a group of friends and had a blast. Our secrets for success:

- Determine everyone's trip goals and expectations.
- Divvy up the research (lodging, activities, meals, transportation, and so on).
- Each person write down the top three things they would like to do.
- Do the activities you have in common, and remember it's okay to occasionally split up.
- Schedule a date night where each couple does something special. It will add to your romance and give everyone different stories to share.
- Go with the flow and have fun!

Traveling with our dear friends and fellow couples

TO EXPLORE MORE ON THIS CONTINENT, CHECK OUT:

» Beaches: Railay, Thailand...p. 74
» Architecture: Bagan, Myanmar...p. 106

Our fearless guide paddling the Rio Urubu, Brazil

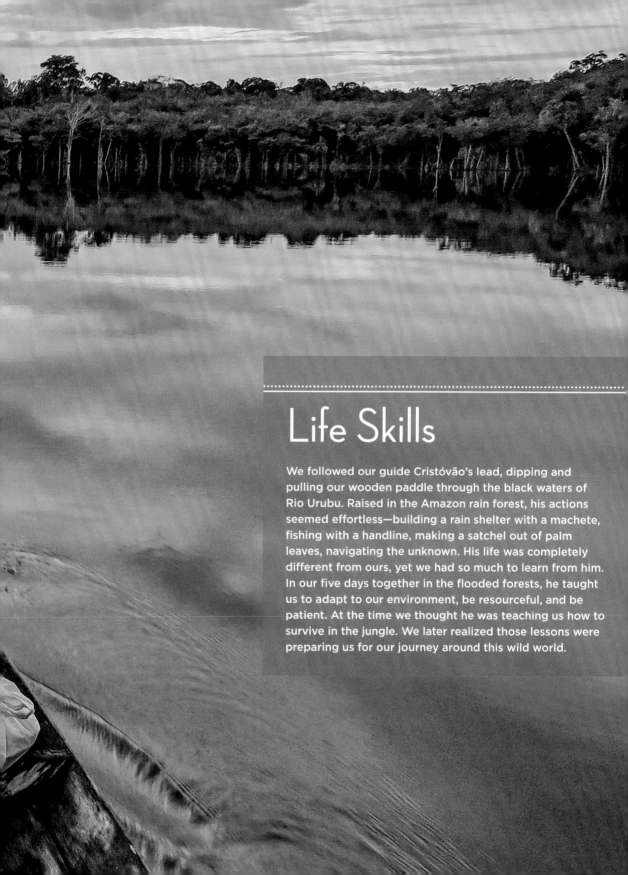

Life Skills

We followed our guide Cristóvão's lead, dipping and pulling our wooden paddle through the black waters of Rio Urubu. Raised in the Amazon rain forest, his actions seemed effortless—building a rain shelter with a machete, fishing with a handline, making a satchel out of palm leaves, navigating the unknown. His life was completely different from ours, yet we had so much to learn from him. In our five days together in the flooded forests, he taught us to adapt to our environment, be resourceful, and be patient. At the time we thought he was teaching us how to survive in the jungle. We later realized those lessons were preparing us for our journey around this wild world.

Hanging bridges connect the cloud forest canopy.

MONTEVERDE
Costa Rica

NORTH
AMERICA
COSTA
RICA
Monteverde □

Sitting on the spine of the Continental Divide, yet only 16 miles from the ocean, Monteverde is uniquely positioned for amazing things. Warm air from both the Pacific and Caribbean condense in the cool mountains and create the cloud forest—the ultimate irrigation system for biodiversity. With some 2,500 varieties of plants, 400 species of birds, 100 species of mammals, and a reputation for having more orchids than anywhere on the planet, Monteverde is so thick with life it can sometimes be hard to appreciate its intricate details. Though if you walk with a local guide, suddenly a three-toed sloth and the resplendent quetzal magically appear. Become attuned to the sounds, smells, and textures of the cloud forest and they'll weave a colorful tale of this ecological dreamland. Santa Elena is the area's lively village, with roads that lead to a slew of nature reserves, ecolodges, day spas, and adventure outfitters. It's a place that's as serene or active as you wish.

WHEN TO GO
Magical mist is a given year-round, though best to avoid the extremely wet August–October.

WHERE TO STAY
Monteverde Lodge & Gardens: Located in Santa Elena, this retreat features excellent food, gorgeous grounds, and talented guides. **Los Pinos:** Fully equipped cabins with walking trails, mountain vistas, and vegetable gardens.

GET ROMANTIC
Learn the art of chocolate making from bean to truffle. Have lunch at Caburé's outdoor café, then take their interactive tour and hand-dip your own dessert.

HONEYTREK TIP
Don't skimp on a guide. Their pro-grade scopes, birdcalls, and trained eyes and ears will be invaluable to your wildlife experience (read: No guide, no quetzal).

A nature-inspired pool at Monteverde Lodge & Gardens

COUPLES ADVENTURES

Monteverde Cloud Forest Reserve ▲

That dreamy mental image of a forest, dripping with mosses, blooming with bromeliads, and blanketed in mist? This is the place. Take a guided hike across Monteverde's six ecological zones, and try to spot a three-wattled bellbird, a dwarf leopard, or a red-capped manakin doing his moonwalk mating dance.

Hanging Bridges and Ziplines ▲▲▲

Ninety percent of life is found in the rain forest canopy . . . get up there! Near the Santa Elena Cloud Forest Reserve, outfitters (both Sky Adventures and Selvatura are fantastic) have connected the treetops with suspension bridges and ziplines for a unique vantage point and extra thrills.

Children's Eternal Rainforest ▲

To preserve Costa Rica's purest rain forests for future generations, 44 countries banded together to create this 50,000-acre private reserve. Monteverde is home to the Bajo del Tigre section with lovely trails, an educational center, audio tours, and guided day and night hikes.

Monteverde Butterfly Garden ▲

Don't let this homespun bug museum fool you; its charming tours could woo an arachnophobe. Learn about the 50 unique insect species on site, walk among fluttering blue morphos, watch the fascinating phases of chrysalis, and hold a rhinoceros beetle.

✢ Fun Bug Facts

Costa Rica is home to over 300,000 species of insects. Meet our favorites:

Golden orb weavers: The females are 10 times the size of their mates and produce silk five times stronger than steel.
Leaf-cutter ants: They can build an underground colony as big as a basketball court.
Ironclad beetles: Their shell is so tough, it can get run over by a car.
Bullet ants: They have a sting said to be 30 times more painful than a yellow jacket's.
Postman butterflies: In the same exact order, they go flower to flower every day (except perhaps on Sundays and holidays).

The diligent postman butterfly on his morning route

TO EXPLORE MORE ON THIS CONTINENT, CHECK OUT:

» On Safari: Tortuguero, Costa Rica...p. 100

» At Sea: Mesoamerican Barrier Reef, Belize...p. 126

OLYMPIC PENINSULA

U.S.A.

NORTH AMERICA
□ Olympic Peninsula
UNITED STATES

Western Washington State gets a lot of flack for "bad" weather, but the rain forests of Olympic National Park make it all worthwhile. The 12 to 14 feet of annual rainfall in the Olympic Mountains yields an intensely lush landscape of moss-draped cedars, towering spruces, and fog-shrouded Douglas firs, some 300 feet tall. The relative rarity of a rain forest in the United States has obvious appeal, though that's just one card in this park's ecological full house. In addition to the mystical Hoh and Quinault temperate rain forests, this heart-shaped peninsula is also nestled amid glacier-capped mountains, wildflower meadows, 13 teal rivers, and 70 miles of rugged coastline. Its diversity of ecosystems is so impressive it has earned status as an international Biosphere Reserve and UNESCO World Heritage site. In theory, you could ice climb, beachcomb, mountain trek, fly-fish, and soak in volcanic hot springs, all in the same day. And we hope you try. No matter your interests, the million acres of national park and 611 miles of trails will lead to excitement.

WHEN TO GO

The hearty can enjoy Olympic National Park all year-round. Those looking for long, sun-filled days should come June–September, or April–May for quieter trails and elk sightings.

WHERE TO STAY

Lake Quinault Lodge: A historic and well-appointed lodge within the park; spring for the Boathouse. **Kalaloch Lodge:** For ocean views, try these cozy cabins along the windswept bluffs.

GET ROMANTIC

Take Boulder Creek Trail to the natural hot springs. Seven pools, some reaching 118°F, are nestled into the forest. (FYI: Skinny-dipping is a common practice.)

HONEYTREK TIP

Even if you're not a camper, spend at least one night in an old-growth forest. Book in advance for a prime riverside spot at Hoh Campground, or go early for same-day booking at the serene Graves Creek.

Hoh Rain Forest's whimsical Hall of Mosses

The coastal side of the dynamic Olympic National Park

COUPLES ADVENTURES

Hurricane Ridge ▲▲
One of the most accessible peaks is also among the most spectacular, especially as an overview of the expansive Olympic National Park. A 17-mile drive brings you to panoramic vistas of the peninsula, Strait of Juan de Fuca, and the glaciated peaks of the Olympic Mountains. The ridge has trails for every fitness level.

Valley of the Giants ▲
Home to some the largest hemlocks, Douglas firs, western red cedars, and a 1,000-year-old Sitka spruce, the Quinault Valley is a humbling place. Start with the educational Quinault Rain Forest Nature Loop, a half-mile trail through this text-book example of a temperate rain forest. Continue hiking on the various connecting trails or keep it mellow with a 31-mile drive around the exception-ally scenic lake.

Hoh River Trail to Five Mile Island ▲▲▲
After a walk through the famous Hall of Mosses, shake the crowds and follow the glacial blue Hoh

✣ **Rain Forest Road Trip: Vancouver Island**

For more mystical temperate rain forests, carry on to Canada's Vancouver Island. From Olympic National Park, drive to Port Angeles and continue by ferry to the charming colonial city of Victoria. Go 100 miles up the east coast to MacMillan Provincial Park's Cathedral Grove and hike among the ancient Douglas firs. Then head southwest for 60 miles until you reach the Pacific Rim National Park, where you'll find sandy surfing beaches and arguably the most beautiful rain forest in British Columbia.

Victoria, gateway to Vancouver Island's rain forests

River to Five Mile Island. Centuries-old cedars weave the canopy, ferns carpet the forest floor, and Roosevelt elk appear in herds the deeper you get. A 10-mile hike will fly by with such flat terrain and beauty largely unchanged for thousands of years.

Tidepooling Beach 4 ▲▲
A rugged beach with massive driftwood, tree-topped sea stacks, and folding rocks, Kalaloch's Beach 4 is stunning and especially impressive when you explore at low tide. Tiptoe around the pools to spy massive green anemones, starfish in sunset hues, and otters splashing about.

TO EXPLORE MORE ON THIS CONTINENT, CHECK OUT:
» **Deserts: Moab, U.S.A....p. 142**
» **Mountains: Mount Rainier, U.S.A....p. 34**

ST. LUCIA
Lesser Antilles

BY NAT SMITH & JODIE BURNHAM

NORTH AMERICA

ST. LUCIA

An East Caribbean island nation, St. Lucia is best known for its dramatic coastal twin peaks, the Pitons. Soaring some 2,500 feet out of the sea, the volcanic spires deserve every bit of attention, though our favorite thing about them is the tropical rain forest they shelter. Seventy-seven percent of St. Lucia is covered in forest, and hiking trails weave through a landscape of wild orchids and giant ferns. Driving along the west coast, winding through the lush mountains and fruit plantations, the views across the mist-covered valleys and beyond to the vibrant blue sea took our breath away. The island is home to one of the rarest endemic tropical birds, the St. Lucia Amazon parrot (aka Jacquot). A blend of Antillean and European influences from former French and British rule, this independent isle has its own distinct and delightful flavor. Come enjoy its photogenic mountains, vibrant coral reef, and one of the most pristine rain forests in the Caribbean.

WHEN TO GO

Peak season is December–April, but sunny May–June have lower prices before the rain kicks in, though even "hurricane season" is often just afternoon showers.

WHERE TO STAY

Crystals St. Lucia: Quirky but elegant, this eco-friendly treehouse property offers incredible vistas. **Ladera Resort:** The only hotel within the Pitons UNESCO area and among the island's most luxurious.

GET ROMANTIC

Sip a rum cocktail from the deck of Chateau Mygo and savor sunset over Marigot Bay, often described as the most beautiful in the Caribbean.

NAT & JODIE'S TIP

En route to Hewanorra Airport, stop at The Reef Beach Café for Piton beers. On the plane, secure a window seat for magnificent views of the Lesser Antilles.

The Pitons rise out of the bay in Soufrière.

COUPLES ADVENTURES

Drive-In Volcano & Sulphur Springs ▲▲
Enter La Soufrière, one of the world's only drive-in volcanoes, and its highly active geothermal park. Dip in the numerous hot springs and lather on the skin-soothing minerals at the bubbling mud baths. Continue pool hopping to Diamond Falls Botanical Gardens.

Northwest Island Food and Fun ▲
Wander Pigeon Island National Park's foothills, beaches, and 18th-century forts. (Don't leave without trying a roti at Jambe de Bois café.) Continue your nibbling and good times at the Gros Islet Friday Night Street Party for a fish fry, music, and dancing in the streets.

Rain Forest Aerial Tram and Zipline ▲▲▲
Fly through the canopy of the island's oldest rain forest reserve, Castries Waterworks. Join Rainforest Adventures' knowledgeable guides on an open-air gondola (built without cutting a single tree) or zipline and Tarzan swing through the trees.

Piton Peak to Beach ▲▲
Hike the challenging Gros Piton for a truly spectacular view of the neighboring nations of Martinique and St. Vincent. (Guides are essential for this four-hour trek.) Reward your efforts with a refreshing swim at nearby Jalousie, aka Sugar Beach, nestled between the Pitons.

✥ Couples Advice

Travel can be stressful, and it's important to remember that your partner might react differently outside his or her comfort zone. Be compassionate and open the lines of communication, especially when things are not flowing smoothly. Getting angry and frustrated in the moment isn't productive, so let it pass and let loose later if you must. Our most vulnerable time traveling is when we are tired or hungry. Emotions can escalate quickly, so be gentle with each other and don't take things personally.

Footbridge into a rain forest full of adventures

TO EXPLORE MORE ON THIS CONTINENT, CHECK OUT:
» **Islands: North Eleuthera, Bahamas...p. 68**
» **Road Trips: Western Cuba...p. 214**

POWER COUPLE: *Nat & Jodie*

As full-time travelers since 2013, Nat and Jodie have lived as locals by house-sitting in 17 countries across the Middle East, Europe, the Americas, and Australasia. Their lifestyle and house-sitting community projects have inspired people around the world, as they share their experiences on *NatnJodie.com*, and encourage slower, more immersive travel.

Jungle lodges nestle into the lush shores of the Napo.

YASUNÍ
Ecuador

ECUADOR   □ **Yasuní**

SOUTH AMERICA

Where the Amazon meets the Andes, the cool waters flow from the mountains, and the equatorial sun shines bright, Yasuní National Park emerges as one of the most biodiverse places on the planet. This UNESCO Biosphere Reserve comprises just 3,800 square miles of the Amazon Basin's 2.9 million, but its species density crushes the competition. In a single hectare, Yasuní is home to more than 100,000 species of insects (that's more than all of North America combined). And in less than 0.2 percent of the Amazon's total landmass, you can find over 33 percent of its bird and reptile species. Still, as you enter the gateway city of Coca, you might think you've come to the wrong place. It's Ecuador's crude oil capital, and rigs and refineries have a presence before you enter the park. Don't let this deter you; let it inspire you to support this precious destination. Cruise down the Napo River into the protected biosphere, and the jungle reclaims the riverbanks with willows, kapok, trumpet trees, and tropical birds on patrol. The region's beauty is unquestionable, and the closer you look, the prettier it gets. Enjoy the forest chatter, watch a spider weave a web, gaze at constellations across both hemispheres, and move slowly. There is life in every step.

✈ WHEN TO GO
It's typically warm, sunny, and humid. Come any time of year; just be prepared for the occasional jungle downpour.

🏨 WHERE TO STAY
The following outfitters offer multiday trips with lodging, meals, and guided activities. **Manatee Amazon Explorer:** A boutique riverboat with kayaks and power canoes for maximum exploration. **Napo Wildlife Center:** The only lodge inside the park and one of Ecuador's finest. **Amazon Dolphin Lodge:** Traditional thatch cabanas in the Pañacocha Biological Corridor.

♥ GET ROMANTIC
Find a comfy spot to lie down and stargaze. Being along the Equator, you'll see constellations from both hemispheres. Look for the North Star, Southern Cross, and your zodiac sign.

✓ HONEYTREK TIP
Wild Yasuní doesn't have much infrastructure for independent exploration. The accessible regions and activities are largely determined by your outfitter. Pick one that maximizes your time and budget.

Parrot feeding frenzy at the clay licks

COUPLES ADVENTURES

Bird-Watch the Parrot Clay Licks ▲

Hundreds of yellow-crowned Amazon parrots and cobalt-winged parakeets gather every morning at the river's mineral-rich cliffs. Vying for a spot in the lunch line, they fly in place, fluttering their colorful wings. Boat there early to watch this spectacular ritual unfold.

Pañacocha Biological Corridor ▲▲▲

Explore the blackwater riverine system with floating forests and a bounty of wildlife. Canoe between trees and hike the patches of terra firma. Keep an eye out for pink river dolphins, white caiman, sloths, howler monkeys, toucans, and piranhas.

Nighttime Walking Safari ▲▲▲

Discover the nocturnal animals and Yasuní's staggering diversity of insects. Walking slowly with a flashlight and shining it from tree to tree allows you to focus on the rain forest's micro-wonders. You'll likely find tree frogs, katydids, praying mantis, and plenty of other surprises.

Kichwa Village Visit ▲

A few indigenous communities, like the Sani and Añangu, welcome visitors into their daily life. Walk around the thatch-roof structures, exotic farms, and schoolhouses, or try a traditional meal like tilapia with hearts of palm, millet beer, and barbequed grubs (way better than it sounds).

❖ Wake-Up Call

Cruising back to Coca, watching the river flow around us and the trees blend into a blur of green, we saw the week's wildlife encounters play back in our minds . . . diving dolphins, leaping monkeys, swooping macaws . . . then an oil barge rumbled past us.

Yasuní needs our help. Tourism is not without its flaws, but in the case of Yasuní, the more visitors they get, the more reasons Ecuador has to protect this precious environment.

Trekking the flooded forests of Pañacocha

TO EXPLORE MORE ON THIS CONTINENT, CHECK OUT:

» **Mountains: Urubamba Valley, Peru...p. 38**

» **Road Trips: Volcano Avenue, Ecuador...p. 212**

MANAUS
Brazil

Manaus □
BRAZIL

SOUTH
AMERICA

The Amazon is the world's largest tropical rain forest, spreading 2.7 million square miles across eight countries, with 60 percent in just Brazil. Often called the "lungs of the Earth," this intensely biodiverse jungle possesses billions of trees, hundreds of thousands of species, and ancient indigenous cultures. To begin your exploration, fly into the Amazonas capital of Manaus. Use its urban infrastructure and ingenuity to your advantage and go deep into the jungle with top-notch guides and unique activities you won't find anywhere else. Founded in 1693, Manaus has always played host to the rain forest's infinite business possibilities—attracting everyone from the Portuguese rubber barons to ecotourism pioneers. Some of the finest jungle lodges, adventure outfitters, and indigenous experiences are found just beyond the banks of its Negro and Solimões Rivers. Plus, Manaus is a just an intriguing place. A port town 1,000 miles from the nearest ocean? A flourishing metropolis in the middle of a jungle? European architecture surrounded by tribal villages? The city has plenty to keep you amused for a few days, while its surrounding rain forest holds immeasurable allure.

⊠ WHEN TO GO
May–November is the dry season, with May–June being the optimal time for clear skies, full rivers, and lush vegetation.

⊞ WHERE TO STAY
Casa Teatro: A cute B&B in Manaus's historic quarter with a fabulous roof deck. **Anavilhanas Jungle Lodge:** Top-notch resort along the Rio Negro's archipelago, including excellent food, activities, and jungle guiding.

♥ GET ROMANTIC
Enjoy a performance at the dazzling Teatro Amazonas. Opera, dance, and classical music in this opulent space make for a glamorous date night (and free if you go early for same-day seats).

✓ HONEYTREK TIP
Eat as many exotic fruits as possible. You may never see them outside of Manaus! Don't be afraid of unidentifiable delights, and seek out the incredible creamy *cupuaçu*.

Rio Negro, the world's largest blackwater river

Downtown blends tribal, colonial, and contemporary.

COUPLES ADVENTURES

Meeting of the Waters ▲
The Encontro das Águas is where the dark Rio Negro and the milky Rio Solimões collide. With different temperatures, the black and tan water don't initially mix, but create a bicolor river that runs for miles. To see this phenomenon, plus frolicking pink river dolphins, take a bus to the Ceasa ferry terminal and charter a boat. (It will be cheaper and more fun than a package tour.)

Jungle Survival 101 ▲▲▲▲
Learn how to forage the forest, build a palm-leaf shelter, whittle a blow dart gun, catch piranhas for dinner, and thrive in the jungle like a Wapixana native. The family-owned Amazonas Indian Turismo's multiday trek and canoe trips will leave you prepared for anything.

Canoe a Flooded Forest ▲▲
With the Amazon River fluctuating as much as 50 feet throughout the year, it can submerge entire

Our around-the-world trip began with a one-way flight to Manaus, Brazil. As we trekked into the rain forest, slept in trees, fished for our dinner, and bathed in piranha-infested waters, we thought, "Maybe we aren't ready for this?" Five days later, we emerged from the jungle, having faced every fear imaginable, feeling like we could take on the world.

Soares, the founder of Amazonas Indian Turismo

forests. Paddle between the trees at dusk or dawn. The tannin-rich water creates the most surreal reflections.

Old-Growth Tree Climb ▲▲▲
Learn the ropes of tree climbing, then scale a 200-foot-tall Angelim tree into the canopy. Singing birds, bromeliads, and a hammock await you. Can be done as a day trip from Manaus or multiday expedition.

TO EXPLORE MORE ON THIS CONTINENT, CHECK OUT:
» Falls: Iguazú Falls, Argentina & Brazil...p. 46
» Dunes: Jericoacoara, Brazil...p. 150

Jungle & Rain Forest Volunteer Opportunities

Head into the field to work with any of these noble conservation initiatives.

All programs are two weeks or less unless otherwise noted.

MALAYSIA

1. Rehab Orangutans

Work in the award-winning Matang Wildlife Centre for injured and orphaned orangutans. Aid the team in improving husbandry standards, providing enrichment for these clever primates, and fostering a positive environment for possible return to the wilds of Borneo.

PUERTO RICO

2. Replant the Rain Forest

Nurture native exotic hardwood species under threat from deforestation. Work on the 1,000-acre Casas de la Selva reserve in the mountains of Patillas, planting seedlings, measuring tree development, and restoring the land as a model of sustainable forestry.

INDONESIA

3. Track Sumatran Tigers

In partnership with World Wildlife Fund, survey the rain forest habitat of the endangered Sumatran tiger. In the Rimbang Baling Wildlife Corridor, scout for tracks, kills, scat, and the cats themselves as you collect data and set up trail cameras for meaningful research.

PERU

4. Play Amazon Ranger

Go on river patrols, document evidence of illegal activity, collect data on flora and fauna, maintain trails, and join the ARCAmazon forest rangers in their work to protect the Madre de Dios rain forest. Analyze findings for a healthier plant and wildlife population.

GUATEMALA

5. Wildlife Rescue

Help rehabilitate and release endangered and exotic species of the Maya Forest, the second largest tropical rain forest in the Americas. Jaguars, margays, kinkajous, scarlet macaws, and howler monkeys are among the patients at the ARCAS Wildlife Rescue Center in Petén.

MADAGASCAR

6. Field Research in Lokobe Rain Forest

In this 4- to 10-week program on the beautiful Nosy Be Island, the Madagascar Research and Conservation Institute will train you to conduct field surveys in the lowland rain forest and implement various catch-and-release methods for studying lemurs, butterflies, reptiles, endemic birds, and more.

THAILAND

7. Care for Elephants

Venture to the mountains south of Chiang Mai, and support elephants formerly used in logging and tourism exploits. Help the BEES community-based sanctuary by providing nourishment, giving baths, and planting grass and trees to preserve their environment.

COSTA RICA

8. Protect Endangered Sea Turtles

Survey Tortuguero's nesting beaches for thousands of green sea turtle eggs. Collect data on the newborn leatherbacks, and assist in the Sea Turtle Conservancy's research and preservation of the four species that call this Caribbean region home.

U.S.A.

9. Eradicate Invasive Tropical Plants

Protect Hawaii's native flora with the Kōkeʻe Resource Conservation Program. Spend your days in the Kauaʻi rain forest, removing disruptive and noxious plants for a balanced ecosystem. Free lodging, flexible commitment, and no fees for participation.

CAMEROON

10. Aid Endangered Apes

Join Cross River Gorilla Program's frontline conservation efforts, surveying the montane rain forest habitat, setting up motion-sensor cameras, and educating the local community on the importance of the Cross River gorilla's and Nigeria-Cameroon chimpanzee's survival.

Otago, New Zealand

*"There was nowhere to go
but everywhere, so just
keep on rolling under the stars."*
—JACK KEROUAC

Chapter Ten

ROAD TRIPS

Windows down, music up, and endless opportunities for adventure—nothing says freedom quite like a road trip. With your own set of wheels, it's no longer about getting from Point A to B; it's the whole alphabet and its varied pronunciations. Discover the nameless places off the tour bus route, meet locals at a farm stand, and find the thrill in whatever is around the bend. Go where you want and stop when you please, be it for the scent of a smoking barbeque in the Southwest U.S.A. or a folk music festival in Northern Ireland. Plan ahead or act on a whim.

Most places in this book could be the beginning of a stellar road trip. We chose the following because the sum of the destinations and the roads in between show off the region's diversity, complete its character, and elevate the journey. Line up your favorite tunes, snacks, mobile apps, and tree-shaped air freshener. It's going to be a wild ride.

WESTERN CAPE
South Africa

AFRICA

Western
Cape □ SOUTH
AFRICA

Dramatic coastline, ancient mountains, wine country, European architecture,
tribal cultures, and wild penguins—the southwest corner of Africa packs a punch. It starts with
Cape Town, the country's first international port, dating back to 1652. The mélange of cultures that graced
its shores has shaped one of the most dynamic and
exotic cities. As cosmopolitan as it is, the heart of
town resides within the iconic flattop peak, Table
Mountain. Rising from the urban grid, such beauty
beckons all visitors to its dramatic summit to take in
the panoramic views of the rugged coastline and rolling vineyards. And when you see this landscape, you'll
know why a road trip is a must.

Hug the west side of the peninsula toward the storied Cape of Good Hope, where the Atlantic and Indian
Oceans meet with fury. Continue along the charming
beaches from Simon's Town to the whale-watching
mecca of Hermanus. Thirsty yet? Point your compass
due north and you'll run into the Winelands' countless
vineyards and world-class restaurants. In less than 300
miles, you will experience three wondrous worlds.

⊠ WHEN TO GO
Beach weather is on tap December–March.
The sweet spot for whale-watching and
warmer temperatures is August–September.

🏨 WHERE TO STAY
Grand Daddy Hotel: In a historic Cape Town
building with a designer Airstream trailer
park on the roof. **Quayside Hotel:** Great
deal and waterfront location near Boulders
Beach. **Le Franschhoek Hotel & Spa:** A luxurious manor in the Winelands' historic
French village.

♡ GET ROMANTIC
Dine at Cape Town's exotic Africa Café, try-
ing gourmet dishes from Malawi, Tanzania,
Ethiopia, and more. Continue to the Tjing
Tjing rooftop bar for a nightcap and divine
date night.

✓ HONEYTREK TIP
Most "universal adapters" don't work here.
Pick up a South Africa–specific model and
you'll be up and running on 230 volts in
no time.

Red aloe flowers surround the Slangkop Lighthouse.

COUPLES ADVENTURES

Cape Town: Art & Foodie Scene ▲
Get a double shot of Cape Town culture with a trip to Woodstock and The Old Biscuit Mill, a historic cookie factory turned arts mecca. Don't miss the Saturday market and over 100 pop-up shops and food stalls, especially the Frying Dutchman and Luke's Rostis.

Table Mountain: The Heart of the Cape ▲▲
Take the cable car or hike up one of the world's oldest mountains, then stroll the plateau, taking note of the incredible flowers (some 1,470 species, 70 percent of which are endemic!) and panoramic cape views.

Boulders Bay: Penguin Colony ▲
Fifteen miles after your essential photo stop at the Cape of Good Hope, you'll find thousands of African penguins waddling around. Try Foxy Beach for the best observation deck and swimming (keeping clear of the penguins, of course).

Cape Whale Route: Betty's Bay to Hermanus ▲
The breeding grounds of the humpback, southern right, and Bryde's whales, False Bay and its string

✣ Welcome to Manhood

"Want to experience a coming-of-age ceremony?" asked the owner of the Mdumbi Backpackers Lodge. We had been in this Xhosa village on South Africa's Wild Coast for all of 10 minutes when we got this invitation. "Sure," we said, having no idea what was to come. Four teenage boys had been living naked in the woods for three weeks, preparing for manhood, and today was their circumcision ceremony. Drums were beaten. A goat was slaughtered. The boys emerged from the woods, swaddled in blankets, looking to be fed—by us. We became a part of a very intimate tribal ceremony, and we will never forget it. Keep driving and, most important, keep an open mind; you never know what invitations might come your way.

Xhosa boys await their coming-of-age ceremony.

of fishing villages offer some of the world's best land-based whale-watching.

Helshoogte Pass: Wine Country Back Roads ▲
Take the idyllic mountain road R310 between the wine regions of Stellenbosch and Franschhoek. Stop at Boschendal's Cape Dutch farmhouse and Delaire Graff's modernist winery for the region's full spectrum of style and vintages.

TO EXPLORE MORE ON THIS CONTINENT, CHECK OUT:
» **Falls: Livingstone, Zambia...p. 54**
» **Deserts: Namib Desert, Namibia...p. 152**

SOUTH ISLAND
New Zealand

AUSTRALIA

NEW
ZEALAND
**South
Island**

Imagine arriving at the shore of a glacial lake, surrounded by brilliant yellow poplars and snowcapped mountains, and saying, "We're home." This is campervanning in New Zealand. Each evening you stop at a gorgeous place of your choosing, enjoy a home-cooked meal with a glass of Marlborough wine, and wake up the next morning to a million-dollar view.

The South Island was made for road trips. It has glaciers, fjords, volcanoes, vineyards, *Lord of the Rings*–style forests, impeccable roads, and very few people sharing it. With only a million inhabitants in a landmass the size of New York State, the South Island feels largely untouched and the ultimate place to connect with nature. Pick up your campervan (or car, if need be) in the "big city" of Christchurch, drive through the heart of the Southern Alps, and cruise along the geological phenomenon of the west coast. Weave though massive mountains toward the shimmering Queenstown-Lakes District, and end at the ocean-flooded valleys of Fiordland. This is our favorite 600-mile route, but really, it's just the beginning of this remarkable country. Keep driving as far as you can.

WHEN TO GO
Come March–April for fall foliage. October–November pop with wildflowers. December–February bring sun and crowds.

WHERE TO STAY
Matakauri: A Relais & Châteaux lodge with unparalleled style, cuisine, and Lake Wakatipu vistas—worth the splurge. **Deer Flat Campsite:** Gorgeous riverside grounds within Fiordland National Park. **Maui Motorhomes:** Luxury apartments on wheels, perfect for freedom camping.

GET ROMANTIC
Pack a picnic and bike Queenstown's Gibbston River Trail through bucolic orchards, gold rush relics, and world-class vineyards. Hydrate at the Peregrine Winery and Gibbston Valley Wine Caves.

HONEYTREK TIP
Download New Zealand's Tourism Radio app. It uses GPS to give location-specific history, tips, and insights as you drive. (It told us about a hidden hot spring we would've cruised right past!)

The road from Queenstown to Paradise

Our guide leads us through Milford Sound.

COUPLES ADVENTURES

Arthur's Pass: Cross the Southern Alps ▲▲
More than a corridor from Christchurch to the west coast, it's a stunning national park with a bounty of road trip–friendly (read: short) hikes, like Castle Hill and Devil's Punchbowl.

Paparoa National Park: Wild Coastal Walks ▲▲
A quick jaunt through the subtropical forest on the Truman Track brings you to a sweeping limestone cove, with a waterfall pouring onto the beach. Down the road, Punakaiki's 30 million years of erosion have carved towers of "pancake rocks," lagoons, and blowholes.

Franz Josef & Fox: Helicopter Grand Tour ▲▲
Fly over the craggy expanse of glaciers toward two of the country's highest mountains. See page 162 for more.

Hawea & Wanaka: Spellbinding Lakes ▲▲
These massive twin lakes are ringed with mountains and connected by just a creek. Wanaka spills over with activities: kayaking, via ferrata, cycling trips, and more, while Hawea excels at utter serenity.

Queenstown: The Adventure Capital ▲▲▲
Take the easygoing skyline gondola for the best views of Lake Wakatipu and the Remarkables mountain range. Then work up to zorbing, flyboarding, jetboating, gorge swinging, or bungee jumping.

Fiordland: Home of the Sounds ▲▲▲
Kayak the legendary Milford Sound, do the Chasm Walk, photograph the upside-down sign at Mirror Lake, and try to count all the waterfalls along Milford Road.

✦ Keep Driving: South to North Island

We spent a month road-tripping both majestic isles, so we cannot help but give more tips: Hike the Catlins' podocarp forests, spot wildlife on the Otago Peninsula, marvel at the Moeraki Boulders, whale-watch Kaikoura, ferry across the Marlborough Sound, hike Tongariro Alpine Crossing, tube the Waitomo Caves, wine taste on Waiheke Island, and ask the friendly Kiwis for their favorite picks!

Sunrise breakfast from our camper at Lake Wahapo

TO EXPLORE MORE ON THIS CONTINENT, CHECK OUT:
» **At Sea: Tasman District, New Zealand...p. 124**
» **Rain Forests: Daintree, Australia...p. 180**

The Wild Way

Turning off the world's longest wine route, we hugged the curves of the South African shoreline. We were on our way to the town of Wilderness and a guesthouse called the Wild Farm; we knew little about either, but their names sounded right up our alley. The paved road faded to dirt and wound its way up a mountain for another 15 minutes. We started to wonder why someone would build way up here, then we reached the peak and its charming farmhouse with panoramic ocean views, and remembered everything gets better off the main roads.

Nothing says freedom like a convertible VW bus: Wilderness, South Africa.

The Virgin River cutting through Zion Canyon, Utah

THE SOUTHWEST
U.S.A.

NORTH
AMERICA
The
Southwest □ UNITED
STATES

The moon, Mars, land of make-believe—the Colorado Plateau and its surrounds have been compared to many things, all of them otherworldly. To drive along its soaring cliffs and hike its plunging valleys is to be transported back in time. Sand dunes from the Jurassic period gradually lithified, then wind, water, and ice sculpted the stone into abstract art. Civilizations dating back thousands of years, followed by the Navajo, Apache, Spanish, Mormons, crystal readers, and adrenaline junkies have created a multicultural mix unique to the Southwest. Drive away from the neon metropolis of Las Vegas and the cityscape will quickly give way to national parks and UNESCO World Heritage sites. Some of the U.S.A.'s most iconic landscapes (Red Rocks, Zion, Bryce, and the Grand Canyon) are wrangled into this magnificent driving loop. So although these destinations might not come as a surprise, the back roads, remote viewpoints, and hiking trails will spin a fresh tale.

⊠ WHEN TO GO
Besides hot and busy June–August, you'll find desert peace and quiet. Snow dusts the cliffs December–February.

⊞ WHERE TO STAY
Zion Lodge: The only in-park lodging, with 28 upscale cabins. **Bright Angel Lodge:** A registered historic national landmark with rustic rooms and luxurious cabins on the rim of the Grand Canyon.

♡ GET ROMANTIC
Find a canyon viewpoint for a sunrise picnic. Cuddle up and watch the rays illuminate the walls, layer by layer.

☑ HONEYTREK TIP
Many of the epic hikes (Narrows, Havasu Falls, etc.) require applying for permits well in advance. Outside of summer, you can often snag a walk-in permit. No matter how it pans out, remember there are plenty more incredible trails.

Havasu Creek flowing toward the Grand Canyon

COUPLES ADVENTURES

Red Rock Canyon, Nevada: Surreal Sandstone ▲▲
Thousand-foot cliffs in sunset hues emerge from the Mojave Desert, surprisingly close to the Las Vegas Strip. Drive the 15-mile scenic loop and rock scramble Ice Box Canyon to the waterfall or take the Calico Hills trail.

Zion, Utah: Staggering Canyons & Cliffs ▲▲▲▲
Hike the narrow cliff-carved trail to Angel's Landing for sweeping views. Rappel down the Orderville slot canyon and swim through emerald pools on a full-day canyoneering excursion. Drive north to Kolob Canyons for a stunning and less traveled path.

Bryce Canyon, Utah: Hoodoo Heaven ▲▲▲
From the visitor center, take the 18-mile scenic drive for a dozen jaw-dropping viewpoints of hoodoos, plateaus, and surreal formations. Hike the eight-mile Fairyland Loop with whimsical scenery well worth your efforts. On a full moon, explore the park with Bryce's Astronomy Rangers.

Grand Canyon, Arizona: Southwest Icon ▲▲
Gaze into the cross section of Earth's crust and see two billion years of geology, running a mile deep. Dig in with a seven-mile hike to Skeleton Point, and stroll the Rim Trail at sunset for a classic panorama.

Sedona, Arizona: Desert Culture ▲
Sedona's natural beauty spreads from its lively city center to Red Rock State Park. Get a dose of culture with Tlaquepaque Arts & Crafts Village and the ancient cliff dwellings of Montezuma Castle National Monument.

✤ Small Town Treasures

We saw a hand-painted sign, "Ernest Shirley Rock Shop," and pulled over without hesitation. It was a dusty treasure chest of petrified wood, trilobites, obsidian, and thousands of mysterious stones. Grandma Shirley woke up from her nap on the quartz cabinet, and pointed us to the yard. Rows of rocks, some dating back 2.5 billion years, funneled us to an "exhibit" of a *T. rex* femur lit with a desk lamp. We arrived with mild interest in geology, but left with coprolite, agate coasters, and a new love of rock hounds.

Ernest Shirley Rock Shop, the gem of Hanksville, Utah

TO EXPLORE MORE ON THIS CONTINENT, CHECK OUT:
» **Deserts: Moab, U.S.A....p. 142**
» **Rain Forests: Olympic Peninsula, U.S.A....p. 188**

COAST
...orthern

North Coast — Northern Ireland (U.K.) — IRELAND — EUROPE

Windswept beauty doesn't stop at the border of Northern Ireland and the Republic of Ireland—though most travelers do. Many driving the famed Wild Atlantic Way exhaust themselves after a thousand miles and never make it to the breathtaking Donegal, let alone cross into the U.K.'s Northern Ireland. Instead of flying to Dublin for your Irish road trip, begin in the fascinating city of Belfast. Drive through the tunnel of intertwined beech trees in Ballymoney, and follow the volcanic cliffs, past whiskey distilleries and medieval castles, to the geological wonder of Giant's Causeway. The coastline's howling wind and crashing waves become the day's soundtrack. That is, until you hear a faint fiddle coming from a stone pub. Laughter, Guinness, and the *craic* flow like a mighty current from Donegal to County Mayo. The Atlantic coast continues to be spectacular all the way south so press on if you can. No matter how long you have for your trip, you'll be glad you made time for the northern reaches of "the Irelands."

WHEN TO GO
Visit May–September to increase the Emerald Isle's odds of warmth and sunshine.

WHERE TO STAY
The Bushmills Inn: With gas-lamp lighting, peat moss fires, and private casks of whiskey, this is Giant's Causeway's coziest choice. **Lough Eske Castle:** Historic accommodations fit for Donegal royalty. **Bunk Campers:** Pick up your self-catering chariot in Belfast and spend the night by the beach, knoll, or anywhere not signposted.

GET ROMANTIC
In the famous Diamond of Donegal lies one of its best restaurants: The Olde Castle Bar. Request a table by the fireplace or with a view of the castle.

HONEYTREK TIP
The Irish love a good festival. Check *DiscoverIreland.ie* and *DiscoverNorthern Ireland.com* to keep track of lively events along your route.

The fantastical shoreline at Giant's Causeway

Kelly's Cellars, one of Belfast's oldest pubs

COUPLES ADVENTURES

Giant's Causeway: Geometric Wonder ▲▲
Explore the sea cliffs, thousands of hexagonal columns, and towering chimneys of this geological fantasy. Start early to enjoy the quiet of the surreal beach and UNESCO World Heritage site.

Dunluce Castle: Medieval Ireland ▲
After a nip of whiskey at the Old Bushmills Distillery, head to a rocky outcropping so formidable, it's home to a former Viking fort and among the most scenic ruins in Northern Ireland.

Fanad Head: Classic Lighthouse ▲
This narrow and lush peninsula, with jagged cliffs on all sides, is topped with an early 19th-century lighthouse. Fanad is what Irish storybooks are made of.

Donegal Sea Stacks: Rock Climbing ▲▲▲▲
Meet the Unique Ascent team in Falcarragh and sail to the vertical islands for one-of-a-kind rock climbing. Explore any of their 150 thrilling routes, with sea breeze at your back and waves crashing below.

✤ Romantic Comedy

I packed a surprise picnic for sunset at the Cliffs of Moher. The wind was intense but "atmospheric," until I attempted to pour Anne a glass of wine and a strong gust showered us with pinot noir. As soon as we toweled off and sat back to enjoy the views, her hat flew off her head and toward the edge of the 390-foot cliff. I lunged for it, she pulled me back, it vanished, and we said a silent goodbye to the beanie. Ten seconds later, we saw a woolly pink blur shoot up and over our heads. The updraft of Moher spat back the hat! For views, drama, and unexpected comedy, there is no better picnic spot than the cliffs of Ireland.

A daring and romantic picnic at the Cliffs of Moher

Sliabh Liag Peninsula: Gaelic Country ▲▲▲
Learn about traditional Irish life at the Glencolmcille Folk Village Museum. Then hike some of the highest sea cliffs in Europe. Test your courage with the Sliabh Liag View Walk, then find your balance (and nerve) for the breathtaking One Man's Pass.

Cúil Irra Peninsula: Ancient Ireland ▲
Discover County Sligo's chamber tombs, ring forts, and passage graves, dating to 4600 B.C., at Carrowmore Megalithic Cemetery, and the massive cairn to an Irish mythical queen on Knocknarea hill.

TO EXPLORE MORE ON THIS CONTINENT, CHECK OUT:
» Mountains: Lauterbrunnen Valley, Switzerland...p. 32
» Architecture: Ghent, Belgium...p. 116

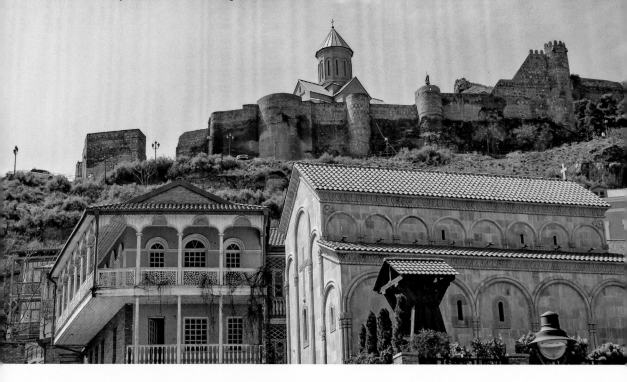

CENTRAL GEORGIA

Georgia

Central Georgia
GEORGIA
ASIA

BY LISA GANT & ALEX PELLING

At the crossroads of Europe and Asia, Georgia has an authenticity and charm unlike anywhere we experienced on our around-the-world road trip. Begin in Tbilisi and revel in the capital's ancient bathhouses and futuristic architecture. Cruise the famous Georgian Military Highway toward the 16,512-foot-tall Mount Kazbek and imagine the traders that followed this winding path between two worlds. Head west to understand the country's dynamic blend of cultures in Borjomi and experience one of the world's oldest wine regions with an Adjarian tasting. Touch the Black Sea and stroll Batumi's promenade adorned with romantic art, before heading into the timeless mountain towns of Svaneti. Adventures can be had at every turn: white-water rafting, horseback riding, heli-skiing, cheesemaking, honey drinking, and more. Possibly the friendliest country we have visited, Georgia lives by its motto: "A guest is a gift from God."

 WHEN TO GO

July–September offer pleasant weather; temperatures vary greatly with elevation.

 WHERE TO STAY

Vinotel: Wine-themed boutique hotel with luxurious rooms and great food. **Castello Mare:** A spa hotel, situated on a sea cliff outside of Batumi. *Note:* Also stay in local homes and wild camp in the rain forests or Batumi Botanical Garden.

 GET ROMANTIC

Bike Batumi's seaside promenade to the motorized "Statue of Love." Cuddle up and watch the folkloric figures, Ali and Nino, move toward each other and become one.

 2PEOPLE1LIFE TIP

Keep your ears open for an impromptu polyphonic serenade. Take a cue from the toastmaster, raise a glass, and yell *"Gaumarjos"* (Cheers), clinking to the nine most important things in life.

COUPLES ADVENTURES

Tbilisi: Capital of Hot & Cool ▲
Trace the Silk Road to the capital's historic Abano-tubani bathhouse district. Under the mosaic-tiled domes filled with sulfurous steam, you will be scrubbed, polished, and feel positively brand new. Cool off with a short stroll on the Bridge of Peace, artfully illuminated with thousands of LEDs.

Borjomi to Vardzia: Across the Centuries ▲
Have a drink at the 19th-century Borjomi Mineral Water Park, an architectural nod to the country's biggest export and blend of cultures. Continue to Vardzia's 12th-century cave monastery. Spread across 19 levels, with 12 chapels and 25 wine cellars, it is still inhabited by monks.

Adjara: Old to New World Wine ▲
Built on the ruins of the 18th-century winery, the Adjarian Wine House is focused on restoring Georgia's 8,000-year-old viticulture traditions. Using ancient methods and varietals, they make an authentic Porto Franco and a mean *chacha* vodka.

Svaneti: Timeless Mountain Towns ▲
At the head of the Enguri Gorge and tucked in the Caucasus Mountains, the four UNESCO-recognized villages of Ushguli are some of the highest continuously inhabited settlements in Europe. Charming churches dating back to the ninth century, adorned with frescoes inside and out, make these mountain towns worth the precarious ascent.

✧ Couples Advice

Remaining a happy couple while living in a 16-foot campervan can be a challenge. We dealt with it by making evening meals a time to reflect on the day, talking about the things that dazzled us, what had gone awry, why we had gotten lost for the 800th time, and what we could do to make tomorrow smoother. We soon found that entering a city at dusk, while hungry and with only a petrol station map, was going to lead to a tiff. Moral of the story: Don't get hangry, and talk it out.

Coffee break at Kvareli Lake Resort

TO EXPLORE MORE IN THIS REGION, CHECK OUT:
» At Sea: Cyclades Islands, Greece...p. 134
» Supernatural: Pamukkale, Turkey...p. 224

POWER COUPLE: *Lisa & Alex*

In 2011 the engaged couple and founders of *2people1life.com* set off in a campervan in search of the perfect place to marry. They drove more than 150,000 miles across 70 countries and held 70 weddings in their five years on the road. Their world tour included roads less traveled through Peru, Morocco, Iran, Malaysia, and Georgia.

VOLCANO AVENUE

Ecuador

ECUADOR Volcano Avenue

SOUTH AMERICA

Driving the Pan-American Highway, the storied road from Alaska to Tierra del Fuego, you'll reach central Ecuador where glacier-capped mountains and smoking volcanoes rise on both sides. Detouring off the main drag and hugging the canyon curves can lead you to a blue crater lake or the base camp of a 20,000-foot peak. The region's beauty is stark, haunting, and humbling. Just when you think only vicuñas and guinea pigs could survive here, you see an adobe-and-straw house tucked into the mountainside, and an indigenous woman in a velvet skirt and bowler cap tilling a field.

Travelers often try to take in the Avenue with a day trip to Cotopaxi or Tungurahua volcanoes, but geological wonders like this beg for a multiday adventure. Being able to pull over for a smoldering volcano, an intriguing trail, or a roadside *cuy* roast makes the freedom of a car invaluable. Pack your best windbreaker and beanie—it's time to slow-cruise Volcano Avenue.

 WHEN TO GO

The climate doesn't vary much along the Equator, though November–February see milder winds.

 WHERE TO STAY

Hotel Samari Spa: Upscale accommodations with Andean flair in Baños. **Hacienda el Porvenir:** A fifth-generation ranch in the Cotopaxi foothills with charming rooms across budgets. **Hacienda Pinsaqui:** Otavalo's grand colonial B&B with a long list of famed guests, including Simón Bolívar.

 GET ROMANTIC

Take in Baños's mountain views from the Luna Runtun hot springs, or try a traditional steam bath at El Refugio Spa Garden.

HONEYTREK TIP

Each day of the week, indigenous communities sell their wares at the different markets along Volcano Avenue. Check your road trip itinerary against the schedule to catch at least one.

The southern stretch of Volcano Avenue, near Alausí

Cotopaxi, a highly active and sacred volcano

COUPLES ADVENTURES

Otavalo: Indigenous Markets to Lakes ▲▲
Famed for its three surrounding volcanoes, extensive craft market, and shamanic rituals, Otavalo is a thriving indigenous city. Wake up early to shop Plaza de los Ponchos, then hike around Cuicocha, a crater lake and the "lagoon of the gods."

Cotopaxi: All-Star Volcano ▲▲▲
Explore one of the highest active volcanoes in the world, towering 19,347 feet and billowing with smoke. Walk among the boulders strewn from recent explosions. Get a panoramic vista of the smoldering giant and surrounding volcanoes with a horseback ride from Hacienda el Porvenir.

Quilotoa: River Valleys to Crater Lakes ▲
Navigate the snaking roads up the chiseled Toachi River Valley. A short stroll to the rim of Quilotoa will reveal a jewel-like lake and contrasting yellow sulfur shores.

Baños: Adventure Capital of Ecuador ▲▲▲
River raft the Class IV Pastaza River, ride the locals' *tarabita* (tram) to Bridal Veil Falls, try the "Swing at the End of the World," dip behind the falls of Devil's Cauldron, and get your fix in this adrenaline-fueled town at the foot of Tungurahua volcano.

Chimborazo: Ascend to Base Camp ▲▲
Drive toward Ecuador's tallest volcano, with its iron red slopes and craggy glaciers, and watch the elevation meter on your GPS climb to 16,000 feet. Grab a hot cocoa at the ranger station, and watch climbers gear up for the next 4,548 feet.

Alausí: Ride the Devil's Nose ▲
Board the antique Trén Ecuador, and ride the switchbacks down to the valley floor. In the early 1900s this engineering marvel was one of the most treacherous routes to the coast, and now it's a two-hour joyride.

✤ Essential Ecuadorian Food

Andean dishes are a delectable blend of hearty meats and exotic produce. Our favorites:

Fritada: Seasoned fried pork with hominy, plantains, and toasted corn.
Llapingacho: Thick, cheesy potato pancakes with tasty peanut sauce.
Cevichocho: Vegetarian ceviche made from lupin beans with a side of banana chips.
Locro: Creamy potato or Andean squash soup, topped with avocado.
Ají: A staple salsa of hot peppers, onion, cilantro, lime juice, and tree tomato.

Anne on the Swing at the End of the World

TO EXPLORE MORE ON THIS CONTINENT, CHECK OUT:
» Lakes: Lake Titicaca, Bolivia & Peru...p. 52
» On Safari: Galápagos, Ecuador...p. 84

Trinidad, one of three UNESCO-listed cities on this road trip

WESTERN CUBA

Cuba

NORTH AMERICA

Western Cuba CUBA

Havana, with its chipping colonial houses, 1950s classic cars, pulsing Afro-Cuban beats, and history as Hollywood's playground, has lured travelers for decades (legally and illegally). Though with the limitations of state-organized tours and confusion about the communist system, few stray far from the capital on their own. They don't know what they're missing. Leaving the Varadero tourists in the dust, drive southwest and the Viñales Valley's karst mountains will emerge from the tobacco fields. The Bay of Pigs will stop sounding like a sad chapter in U.S. history and reveal itself as one of the Caribbean's best snorkeling destinations. The country's famed architecture will be at its finest in the UNESCO World Heritage cities of Trinidad and Cienfuegos. The differences in politics will fade away over arroz con pollo at a *casa particular* (guesthouse). You will take the potholes and cows in the road like a champ, because this is real life in Cuba—its convivial spirit can smooth over anything.

 WHEN TO GO

The sunniest season is November–April, but busiest December–January.

 WHERE TO STAY

Ridel y Claribel: A classic casa particular, a room in this family home offers traditional food and sunset views over Valle de Viñales. **Hotel La Union:** Neoclassical building off Cienfuego's main square, plus pool and rooftop bar. **El Arcangel:** Upscale casa particular run by a lovely family in the heart of Trinidad.

 GET ROMANTIC

Take a dance lesson before leaving Havana so you can move to the Afro-Cuban music at the sultry sessions across the nation.

✅ **HONEYTREK TIP**

Book your rental car well in advance. Download Galileo Offline Maps and get a hard copy of Cuba's Guía de Carreteras. Rules for travel to Cuba are constantly changing. Check the latest guidelines.

COUPLES ADVENTURES

Valle de Viñales: Cigar Country ▲▲
Ride horseback around the karst mountains, and stop to explore the caves and tobacco plantations. Meet generations of growers, and savor a freshly rolled cigar.

Bahía de Cochinos: The True Bay of Pigs ▲
After your obligatory stop at the battle museum, find out what this infamous region should be known for: snorkeling Caleta Buena, bird-watching Zapata's wetlands, and exploring the charming fishing village of Playa Girón.

Cienfuegos: The Pearl of the South ▲
Wander the streets around Parque José Martí and get lost in this UNESCO World Heritage city's neoclassical glamour. Peek into the grand Tomás Terry theater, and catch a seaside cocktail at the Moorish Palacio de Valle.

Topes de Collantes: Dripping With Falls ▲▲
Hike the lush limestone Escambray Mountains to dozens of waterfalls within the national park. Try El Nicho, Salto del Caburní, or Vegas Grande waterfall trails for rewarding scenery and cool swimming holes.

Salto del Caburní waterfall and swimming hole

Trinidad: Colonial Charmer ▲
With pastel houses, cobblestone streets, horse carts, old women knitting lace, and impromptu dance parties, the town of Trinidad is magical. Meander the streets and climb the tower of the Palacio Cantero for the best views over town.

TO EXPLORE MORE ON THIS CONTINENT, CHECK OUT:
» **Beaches: Samaná, Dominican Republic...p. 78**
» **Rain Forests: St. Lucia...p. 190**

Che Guevara lives on in Cuban hearts and highways.

A few of the 75 hairpin turns on Stelvio Pass, Italy

Wildest Roads

Highways, byways, and backroads so unique, the path becomes the destination.

MADAGASCAR
1. Avenue of the Baobabs

Adding to the allure of one of the most biodiverse countries in the world, 800-year-old baobab trees line the road between Morondava and Belon'i Tsiribihina. Drive under these endemic "mothers of the forest," then continue to the famed Baobab Amoureux, a pair intertwined in an embrace.

CANADA
2. Icefields Parkway

Traversing the Canadian Rockies past Lake Louise, Banff, and Jasper, this two-lane road is a catwalk for Canada's prettiest national parks. Glacier-capped mountains tower on both sides of the 144-mile parkway, with emerald lakes nestled in alpine valleys. Keep an eye peeled for grizzlies, moose, bighorn, and caribou.

SOUTH AFRICA
3. Sani Pass

Climbing more than 3,000 feet in less than five miles, this gravel road with gradients up to 1:3 is for 4x4s and adventurers only. Survive the switchbacks and you'll be rewarded with breathtaking views and frosty pints at the purported highest pub in Africa (9,429 feet) in the fascinating Kingdom of Lesotho.

NETHERLANDS
4. Flower Route

No one does springtime like the Dutch. They've been cultivating tulips since 1593, and their gardening and aesthetic talents culminate in a 25-mile stretch of fields, from Haarlem to Leiden. Cruise with the windows down to smell the flowers, and feast your eyes on the sumptuous colors.

ITALY
5. Stelvio Pass

The road from the Swiss to Italian Alps is akin to a pinball course. Start your descent at 9,045 feet, then take the 75 hairpin turns that zigzag down the mountain. Keep an eye out for overachieving cyclists.

NORWAY
6. Atlantic Ocean Road

Winding up and over an archipelago with causeways, viaducts, and eight bridges, this road through Møre og Romsdal county is an oceanside roller coaster. For a real thrill, drive this "Norwegian Construction of the Century" during a storm and through the crashing waves.

BOLIVIA
7. North Yungas Road

Snaking from the snowcapped mountains of La Paz to the rain forest of Coroico, this cliffside road can take your breath away—forever. This 10-foot-wide "two-way" mountain pass has been coined the Death Road, claiming hundreds of lives every year. An alternative road has been built, diminishing traffic and casualties, and leaving the North Yungas a safer yet still thrilling drive. *Note:* This road is also a stellar bike route.

U.S.A.
8. Smugglers' Tunnel

Vermont, a state with so few people it only has one area code, draws visitors the world over for its fall foliage spectacular. Late September through early October, the roadsides are ablaze with crimson, orange, and amber leaves, reaching their pinnacle at the Smugglers' Notch "Autumn Tree Tunnel."

INDIA
9. Mana Pass

Climbing the Himalaya between India and Tibet, Mana is one of the highest navigable roads in the world. At more than 18,000 feet, the air is thin, the views are vast, and the history runs deep along this ancient Tibetan trade route, recently "upgraded" to gravel and dirt.

THE AMERICAS
10. Pan-American Highway

The longest motorable road in the world, from Alaska to Tierra del Fuego, offers the mother of all road trips. This 19,000-mile journey travels through 17 countries and countless cultures, climates, landscapes, and experiences of a lifetime.

Koh Ker, Cambodia

"Nature is painting for us, day after day, pictures of infinite beauty if only we have the eyes to see them."

—JOHN RUSKIN

Chapter Eleven

SUPERNATURAL

••••••••••••••••••••••

Beyond beautiful, the following destinations are so spellbinding, they make you question reality. Exploding mud pools, rainbow-striped mountains, and color-morphing crater lakes are the works of a creative and moody Mother Nature. On a whim, she can set off a volcanic eruption and bring absolute destruction, though once the dust settles, she often leaves a place prettier than she found it.

For adventure travelers, this dance with danger makes these supernatural destinations even more alluring. You scoff at high elevation, long distances, and tenuous passes; the challenge sweetens your reward. Though, if you know where to look, some awe-inspiring sites can come easy. Bask in a hot waterfall in Rotorua, climb the snow white travertines of Pamukkale, and watch the mist roll through the "Avatar Forest." From India to Bolivia, these destinations are beyond your wildest dreams. Though don't take our word for it, go and pinch yourself.

The Altiplano's extreme landscape above 14,000 feet

DEPARTMENT OF POTOSÍ

Bolivia

BOLIVIA

Department of Potosí

SOUTH AMERICA

The perfect cocktail of volcanic conditions, high altitude, and a dash of rainfall turns southwest Bolivia's Altiplano from what could be grim to gorgeous. After you cross the border from Chile, you won't see civilization for days, save for a few resilient tribes and caretakers of the Eduardo Avaroa Andean Fauna National Reserve. Following faint tire tracks from previous 4x4s, you pass neon-colored lakes, boiling mud pools, and smoking volcanoes. You cross 14,000 feet above sea level and stop at Laguna Colorada. As you slowly walk around the pink lake, gawking at hundreds of flamingos mirrored in the waters, you forget about the intense elevation. After a chilly slumber party with your 4x4 compadres, you continue to the aptly named Salvador Dalí Desert, past gardens of rock spires, en route to the main event: Salar de Uyuni. The world's largest salt flat is a land of optical illusions. If you're lucky enough to arrive after a rain shower, it becomes a mirror for clouds, salt laborers, and Incahuasi Island with its cactus forest. Get ready; the beauty of the Andes is about to reach a new extreme.

WHEN TO GO

It's brisk and dry year-round but slightly warmer September–November. January–April bring a bit of rain, but surreal reflections in Uyuni.

WHERE TO STAY

Kanoo Tours: Basic, small-group multiday trips from San Pedro de Atacama to Uyuni (one-way or round-trip). **Luna Salada:** Made entirely of salt, this unique hotel at the edge of Salar de Uyuni perfectly positions you for sunrise and sunset, when the sea of white turns to pink.

GET ROMANTIC

Explore Salar de Uyuni with the help of a private guide, driver, chef, and luxury Airstream trailer. Spend the night in remote corners of the flats, surrounded by nothing but salt and stars.

HONEYTREK TIP

Before your 4x4 trip, acclimatize for a few days in San Pedro de Atacama, and sip plenty of coca tea. While in the Altiplano, drink lots of water, chew coca leaves, and take it nice and slow.

Thousands of flamingos flock to Laguna Colorada.

COUPLES ADVENTURES

Sol de Mañana Mud Springs ▲▲
Reach nearly 16,000 feet in elevation and tiptoe around the cracked earth, boiling with mud. Keep your eye on the geothermal pools; the pressure will burst bubbles into artistic explosions. Arrive early to see the steam rise to its most dramatic heights (more than 150 feet).

Laguna Verde, Blanca, and Colorada ▲▲
Below the perfect cone of the Licancabur Volcano towering more than 19,000 feet, the arsenic-rich waters of Laguna Verde glow a bright blue-green. Pop over to see its milky twin Blanca, then head north to Laguna Colorada. Red algae have turned its waters a burnt sienna and given thousands of James's flamingos even pinker plumes. You could bird-watch these long-legged beauties for hours.

The Uyuni Salt Flats ▲
Drive across the prehistoric lakes, a 4,086-square-mile crystallized expanse. With luminescent white crystals, extremely level surface, and the occasional layer of water, the salt flats are a vision of alternate reality. Have a photography bonanza, playing with the depth of field, posing with props, and catching

✣ The Travel Bond

A Brazilian, Norwegian, Brit, German, and us Americans, piled into a Toyota Land Cruiser for our Altiplano adventure. The first night at the *refugio* in Laguna Colorada, we huddled around the table eating *pique macho* (a Bolivian specialty of chopped hot dogs and potatoes), lingering to swap travel tales and keep warm in this below-freezing accommodation. We laughed into the night and nonstop for the next three days. Years later our 4x4 crew still keeps in touch, because when you share a journey this extraordinary, even a few days together can form a bond for life.

Climbing the cars at Uyuni's Train Cemetery

reflections of the cloudy sky, and you'll see why it's been dubbed "heaven on Earth."

Scale the City of Rocks ▲▲
Upon reaching the paved roads before the town of Villa Alota, you'll spot rock towers dotting the landscape as far as the eye can see. An ancient lava flow created a petrified maze and jungle gym all at once. Play hide-and-seek, climb the formations, spot the animal-like shapes, and be a kid again.

TO EXPLORE MORE ON THIS CONTINENT, CHECK OUT:
» **Deserts: Atacama Desert, Chile...p. 154**
» **Rain Forests: Yasuní, Ecuador...p. 192**

CENTRAL FLORES
Indonesia

A S I A

INDONESIA □ **Central Flores**

This is the kind of magic you hope for in travel—where motorbiking through a lush mountain pass brings you to a timeless village, chatting with locals leads to dinner in a thatch-roof home, listening to music sparks up a traditional dance lesson, and laughing breaks down any language barriers. You'll find this in Flores. This island in Indonesia's Nusa Tenggara archipelago, with crater lakes that change color, deserted sandy beaches, villages untainted by technology, and some of the friendliest people on Earth, has all the right ingredients for unforgettable adventures. But it takes patience and an open mind. This is a place where the average "highway" speed is 18 miles an hour, strong Wi-Fi is a mythical beast, and a hot shower likely requires firewood. Though once you find your Flores rhythm, that slow bus becomes a chance to soak up the countryside and wave back at the smiling faces along your route. Some say Flores is like Bali of the 1970s, and Indonesia's next big thing. It is such a special place, you want to keep it a secret. But you love it so much, you cannot help but share it.

WHEN TO GO
After the rainy season, April–September bring blue skies. Temperatures hover in the 80s year-round.

WHERE TO STAY
Eco Eden Resort: Bamboo bungalows on a quiet beach outside Riung, with a helpful owner for organizing island trips. **Kelimutu Crater Lakes Ecolodge:** As upscale as it gets in Moni, these riverside cabins offer volcano views. **Homestays:** Stay in a Ngada family home for an essential Flores experience; inquire in Bajawa.

GET ROMANTIC
Wander south of Moni village to Murondao Waterfall, a 50-foot cascade plummeting into a serene swimming hole. Bring your suit, blanket, and a couple Bintang beers.

HONEYTREK TIP
Take buses between Bajawa and Moni (a truly cultural experience, often involving goats on the roof). Then rent a motorbike to explore the surrounding villages and gorgeous countryside.

Lakes that change color with the mood of Kelimutu volcano

Steep thatch roofs are a signature of Ngada villages.

COUPLES ADVENTURES

Immersion in Ngada Villages ▲▲▲

Along the slopes of the Inerie volcano, there are a dozen picturesque Catholic-meets-animist villages. Centered around stone altars to connect with the supernatural realm, Ngada villages are other-worldly. Experience daily life, alongside a woman weaving an ikat textile, kids playing ball, and an elder performing a harvest sacrifice. Rent a motor-bike (or arrange a local guide) in Bajawa, start your loop in Bela, continue to Luba, and overnight with a family in Bena.

Sail 17 Islands National Park ▲▲

Brave the bumpy roads to the sleepy fishing village of Riung, the gateway to this palm-filled paradise. Sailing from isle to isle, snorkel with tropical fish, marvel at trees full of sleeping bats, dine on a fresh catch, beachcomb for sand dollars, and rarely see another soul.

A Local Bath at Malanage Hot Springs ▲▲

Around sunset, villagers come for their evening bath at the convergence of a hot spring and cold river. Don't be shy; hop in for a soothing soak and hysterical local interactions. (*Note:* Women should bathe in a sarong.) Walk upstream for a pretty waterfall, or motorbike to the steaming, green branch of the river.

Hike Kelimutu's Tricolored Lakes ▲▲

Hike the 30-minute trail to watch sunrise light up the volcano's three dynamic crater lakes. Depending on the latest chemical reaction between the water's minerals and volcanic gases, the triplets will be a unique color combination of brilliant turquoise, forest green, burnt sienna, chocolate brown, or creamy white.

✦ It Takes a Village

We drove our motorbike toward a Ngada village looking for Ridho, a man supposedly open to hosting travelers. We found his family, and they ushered us in for noodles. After an evening of language charades and tag with the kids, we woke up to see villagers walking with rocks on their heads. We followed them to the pile and offered to help. A woman wrapped a sarong around Anne's head and put a 15-pounder on top. Then she grinned at me and pointed at the behemoth on the ground. We made a few dozen trips and helped them build a house for two newlyweds.

Anne hauling rocks to help build a village home

TO EXPLORE MORE ON THIS CONTINENT, CHECK OUT:
» **Mountains: Cordillera Central, Philippines...p. 26**
» **At Sea: Komodo, Indonesia...p. 132**

The main drag in the Roman spa city of Hierapolis

PAMUKKALE
Turkey

Pamukkale
TURKEY ASIA

Roman ruins and cascading travertines are each impressive in their own right, but together? Out of this world. In the second century B.C., the Romans were attracted to the Menderes River Valley for the healing properties of its hot springs, though the water's calcium carbonite deposits are what make them so impressive to travelers. Flowing over the mountain for millennia, the mineral-rich water has hardened into limestone and coated the mountain like a freak May snowstorm, melting into turquoise puddles. The Turkish word *Pamukkale* translates to "Cotton Castle," and as perfectly whimsical as that is, the ancient architecture and calcified mountain are just the beginning of this fantasyland. In neighboring villages, the travertines turn to red bubbling pools and go deep underground into stunning caves. Impressive Roman ruins (some excavated and some still hidden) are spread all over the surrounding area. Wrap your head around this supernatural place with a hike, a soak, and a paragliding flight—the region has some of the best thermals in West Asia.

 WHEN TO GO
Crowds and heat diminish February–May and September–November.

 WHERE TO STAY
Venus Suite: A freshly renovated, family-run hotel with Ottoman-inspired decor, garden, and pool, at the edge of town.
Ayapam: Modern and airy hotel with views to the travertines and an extensive spa.

 GET ROMANTIC
Explore the Cotton Castle by moonlight. Wade in the warm pools and bask in the glow of the radiant mountain. Few people visit at night, so enjoy the privacy and stay as long as you'd like (just make sure you're inside before the ticket takers go home in the evening).

 HONEYTREK TIP
Even though you cannot wear shoes on the travertines, you're going to want a sturdy pair for exploring on top. Pack a bag that fits your sneakers, lunch, lots of water, sun protection, and a swimsuit to enjoy the pools and antique baths.

Warm water cascades down the travertines.

COUPLES ADVENTURES

Hierapolis Highlights ▲
Explore this ancient Roman city, and imagine the bustling market at the agora, the theatrical performances at the 12,000-seat amphitheater, and toga-clad citizens strolling stone-paved Frontinus Street. Keep walking to the wonderfully preserved necropolis, with its 1,200 carved limestone tombs. Finish your exploration with a soak in Cleopatra's Antique Pool, hot springs filled with marble ruins and water that bubbles like champagne.

Red & White Travertines ▲
The seductive textures, steam, and turquoise waters of Pamukkale's calcified mountain will have you moving from pool to pool for a dip and endless photography opportunities. Complement your iconic white travertine experience with its iron-rich counterpart at the red hot springs in Karahayit village. Rub down in the mud pools for a therapeutic and delightfully local spa experience.

Kaklik Cave & Ruins Road Trip ▲▲
Often referred to as the Underground Pamukkale, these caves have similar geological formations and water features, though being naturally enclosed adds to their intensity. The bulbous rocks surround you, and the waterfalls echo as you move through the narrow passageways. Pair this destination with the impressive Roman ruins of Aphrodisias and Laodicea for a well-rounded day trip.

Paraglide Over the Ancient World ▲▲▲▲
Suit up for tandem paragliding, run down the 1,000-foot-high Dinamit Hill, and let the thermals fill your parachute. Soar over the Roman city, the calcified mountain, and the Anatolian countryside for up to 30 minutes. This region of Turkey has some of the longest flight times and most dynamic scenery.

✣ Our Favorite Meal in Turkey

We were on our way to a picnic, when an antique shop caught our eye. It was filled with tribal rugs, tasseled pillows, and colorful curiosities. We asked the shopkeeper about the origins of a skinny satchel, and he invited us for tea. We got chatting about the nomadic people of Anatolia and the symbolism of different motifs. The conversation was interrupted by my growling stomach. "Are you hungry?" Murat asked. "I have cheese and honey." We had just picked up bread, tomatoes, and olives—the perfect complements for a feast with a new friend.

Our impromptu lunch with an antiques shopkeeper

TO EXPLORE MORE ON THIS CONTINENT, CHECK OUT:

» History: Cappadocia, Turkey...p. 108
» Road Trips: Central Georgia...p. 210

The curious Cerro de los Siete Colores, Argentina

Postcard Perfect

Browsing a gift shop in northern Argentina, we spotted a postcard with a spectacular multicolored peak. *"Donde esta?"* Mike asked the woman at the counter. She told us it was the town of Purmamarca and the Mountain of Seven Colors—just 115 miles north. We rerouted our trip so we could hike to this viewpoint and watch the sunrise illuminate each rock layer of orange, pink, purple, white, red, mauve, and green.

ROTORUA
New Zealand

AUSTRALIA

Rotorua
NEW ZEALAND

I n one of the most volatile places along the Pacific Ring of Fire, and nestled in the basin of a volcanic caldera, Rotorua is bursting with adventures. Being directly over a geothermal hot spot and surrounded by volcanoes poses its risks, but when you are soaking in a forest hot spring, you don't worry about a thing. The Victorians caught a whiff of Rotorua (it's nickname is Sulphur City) and came flocking to the region for its restorative properties. The heart of town is the original Elizabethan-style bathhouse and Government Gardens, with an expansive bowling green, croquet lawn, and pumice promenade. The high sulfur content gives Lake Rotorua a milky blue hue and an undulating, crusty shore. Steam spews from the ground and makes pools of mud bubble like chocolate milk from a kid's straw. Follow the shoreline and you'll reach a Maori village, still using the geothermal energy for cooking, bathing, and heating, as they have for centuries. Rotorua's population is over one-third Maori—among the richest concentrations in the country. Learn about their unique Polynesian culture over a traditional earth-steamed *hangi* feast, visit the sacred Green Lake, try a few of the area's countless activities, and channel its boundless energy.

WHEN TO GO
December–February are the warmest yet busiest months. Consider temperate March–April and October–November, and pack layers for daily temperature swings.

WHERE TO STAY
The Princes Gate Hotel: With 19th-century roots, this upscale retreat has historic charm and an ideal downtown location. Koura Lodge: A 10-bedroom B&B, embracing its secluded lakefront location with inviting open-air spaces and water activities.

GET ROMANTIC
Take the gondola to the Volcanic Hills tasting room for incredible views of Rotorua and excellent New Zealand wines.

HONEYTREK TIP
Before you book one of the many tours in Rotorua, remember that volcanic beauty is all around you, and the least touristy attractions don't cost a thing. Google "free Rotorua activities" and find dozens of incredible and authentic options to keep your costs down.

The Champagne Pool at Waiotapu Thermal Wonderland

Maori art and culture shine bright in Rotorua.

COUPLES ADVENTURES

Geothermal Wonderlands ▲▲

Sherbet-colored pools, boiling at temperatures north of 300°F, fill collapsed craters and help Waiotapu Thermal Wonderland live up to its name. It's a paved stroll between the exploding geysers and mud pits, so for those looking to step up their exploration in a more organic setting, try hiking or sailing Waimangu, the world's youngest geothermal ecosystem. This valley, with steaming crater lakes and neon rivers, didn't even exist until an 1886 eruption.

Living Maori Culture ▲

Stroll the traditional Maori neighborhood of Ohinemutu, where cooking is still done over boiling water vents and hot showers are channeled from the earth. See the ornately carved Meeting House and visit lakeside St. Faith's Church to hear a bilingual service. Locals offer tours, but this is far from a tourist attraction; it's real Maori life. For a "classic" cultural experience offering hangi feasts and *haka* dance performances, Whakarewarewa Living Maori Village is the most authentic on offer.

The Full Range of Hot Springs ▲▲

Try a combination of rustic and luxurious hot springs for a well-rounded Rotorua experience. Canoe to Lake Rotoiti Hot Pools, a locals' hangout only accessible by boat. Hike to Kerosene Creek,

✥ Double the Fun

It's rare Mike and I split up for just about anything (even the grocery store), but Rotorua had so many activities that we had to divide and conquer. We both started at the gurgling mud pits outside Waiotapu Thermal Wonderland, then we parted ways. While I stayed to walk around the Artist's Palette and watch geysers erupt, he went off to hike in the steam of Waimangu's Frying Pan Lake. When we reunited, it was like we hadn't seen each other for days with dozens of photographs and stories to share.

Lawn bowling and bathhouses at Government Gardens

where boiling water combines with a cool stream in a waterfall setting. Splash out at the world-famous Polynesian Spa and enjoy 26 mineral pools, including adults-only and private lakefront options.

Bike Whakarewarewa Forest ▲▲

Cycle the redwood forest, past streams with a psychedelic sheen and lakes in multiple colors. New Zealand's first exotic forest has one of the country's oldest and most extensive mountain-biking networks, hosting numerous world championships. With 56 miles of trails, it has plenty of options for any skill level.

TO EXPLORE MORE ON THIS CONTINENT, CHECK OUT:

» Ice: Westland, New Zealand...p. 162
» Road Trips: South Island, New Zealand...p. 202

The sculpted Indus Valley and Leh city from Shanti Stupa

LADAKH
India

BY SAVI MUNJAL & VIDIT TANEJA

Tucked in the northernmost state of India, Ladakh is known for its otherworldly landscapes—snow-capped peaks, color-shifting lakes, and moonlike valleys—but that's not all. Ladakhi culture is deeply influenced by neighboring Tibet, with Buddhist rituals, prayer flags, and chants giving a spiritual air to daily life.

Driving along the old Silk Road through the barren plateau, dotted with colorful monasteries, is truly the stuff of dreams. Plus, the journey earns bragging rights thanks to Khardung La, one of the highest motorable roads in the world. Wake up for morning prayer with drums and *oms* at Thiksey Monastery, drive through the lunar landscape of Nubra Valley, river raft the wild Indus, and enjoy butter tea with friendly Ladakhi locals. The region offers visitors a rare opportunity to blend authentic culture with extreme sports and decadent luxury. Serpentine mountain passes occasionally translate to bumpy rides. But having braved them, Ladakh has earned a special place in our hearts.

 WHEN TO GO

July–October are ideal. Aim for September's Ladakh Festival. Avoid November–May when snowy roads are often impassable.

 WHERE TO STAY

Chamba Camp: Next-level glamping, with palatial tents and 24-hour butlers, overlooking Thiksey Monastery. **Lchang Nang Retreat:** Cottages in a Nubra Valley fruit orchard with views of the Himalaya.

GET ROMANTIC

Stargaze from the sand dunes of Hunder. Bundle up, lie down, and marvel at thousands of twinkling stars and the Milky Way streaming across the clear Ladakhi sky.

BRUISED PASSPORTS TIP

To access remote Ladakh, foreigners need an Inner Line Permit (reserve the same day at Leh Deputy Commissioner's Office) and a ride. Hire a driver in Leh; their local knowledge is invaluable.

COUPLES ADVENTURES

Cycle Into Thin Air ▲▲▲

Take an organized bike trip down the self-proclaimed "world's highest motorable road" from Khardung La to Leh city. Starting at 17,582 feet in elevation and covering 25 miles, this ride is challenging and rewarding in equal measure.

River Rafting the Indus ▲▲▲▲

Drink in spectacular views of the Zanskar range and Ladakhi riverside villages as you slice through the white water. Riding hair-raising rapids between the villages of Alchi and Khaltse is not for the faint of heart. Ranging from Class II to V, routes can be chosen to match your level of adventure.

Iridescent Lake ▲

Most tourists visit Pangong Lake on a day trip. Stay overnight and watch a gorgeous star show and breathtaking sunrise. Depending on the light and angle, the brackish high-altitude lake seems to change color in a blend of blue, turquoise, green, and violet. Set up a picnic at 14,000 feet, and nibble on samosas as you gaze at the waters stretching to Tibet.

Hike Lamayuru to Hemis Monastery ▲▲▲▲

A teahouse trek through barren plateaus, grassy pastures, and colorful monuments shows the true diversity of Ladakh. Changing elevation from 10,000 to 17,000 feet across the Zanskar range, this challenging multiday hike culminates at Hemis Gompa—among the most impressive Buddhist monasteries in Ladakh.

⁜ Couples Advice

While in a new region, surprise your partner by indulging his or her passions. For a culture vulture, plan a day at a famous museum, treat a foodie to a culinary tour, and delight a wine connoisseur with a vineyard visit. Catering to each other's interests makes for a truly satiating and romantic trip. Plus, these excursions will likely introduce you to a new facet of the region.

The luxurious Chamba Camp and snowy Zanskar range

TO EXPLORE MORE ON THIS CONTINENT, CHECK OUT:

» **Mountains: Annapurna Sanctuary, Nepal...p. 24**
» **History: Fenghuang, China...p. 112**

POWER COUPLE: *Vid & Savi*

Following a love of offbeat and luxury travel, this couple has been to over 500 cities and 70 countries. They're full-time bloggers at *BruisedPassports.com*, with their adventures and photographs featured on major outlets, including Discovery Channel and the *Huffington Post*. Avid road trippers, they recently drove 20,000 miles across a dozen countries.

SIEM REAP
Cambodia

ASIA

Siem Reap ☐ CAMBODIA

The image of Angkor Wat's honeycomb towers reflected in the lotus pond is one of the most iconic of Cambodia, if not all of Southeast Asia. That one temple, although magnificent and beautifully preserved, barely scratches the surface of Angkor Archaeological Park's enchantment. The hundreds of 9th- to 13th-century temples spread across Siem Reap are all the more beautiful in their overgrown and crumbling state. After the fall of the Khmer Empire in the 1430s, the city was abandoned for centuries and almost entirely devoured by jungle, until its excavation by European archaeologists in the 19th century. Much of the growth has been tamed within the 155-square-mile park, but some of the strangler figs are so entwined they have become an integral part of the structures. Whether to fully restore the temples is a topic of much debate, but from a photographic and supernatural standpoint, we say: Keep the trees! Unlike most Western monuments, the park has few guardrails or rules, so you can wander the ruins, climb the rubble, peer over collapsed walls, and choose your own adventure. The temples of Angkor hold as much for archaeologists as for explorers.

⊠ WHEN TO GO

November–March are drier and cooler. The wet season is June–October, though mornings are often sunny with fewer crowds.

▦ WHERE TO STAY

Sofitel Angkor Phokeethra Resort: Between the temples and downtown, this French colonial–style retreat boasts pools, spas, and top-notch service. **Viroth's Hotel:** A centrally located mid-century modern gem with a fantastic restaurant.

♡ GET ROMANTIC

Watch the sunset at Bayon, a temple with 216 larger-than-life stone faces. Oriented to the east, few tourists think to come here for sunset, though that's when the silhouettes pop against the pink sky.

✅ HONEYTREK TIP

Unfortunately, many kids are selling souvenirs around the temples. No matter how persistent or adorable, do not support this child labor. Make a small contribution by renting from the White Bicycles, a non-profit for school scholarships.

Jungle intertwines with architecture at Preah Khan.

Buddhist devotees bring life to the ruins.

COUPLES ADVENTURES

Rickshaw to the Roluos Group ▲
Start your archaeological exploration in chronological order with a 10-mile *remork* (motorbike rickshaw) ride to the earliest temples of Angkor. Although these ninth-century structures are simpler, they set the tone for Khmer style and further your appreciation for the newer and more elaborate complexes. Make extra time for the stepped pyramid of Bakong and the sprawling Preah Ko.

Bayon Jungle Temples ▲▲
Bike to the most overgrown temples in the heart of the park. Ta Prohm is so fantastical, it starred in the film *Lara Croft: Tomb Raider,* while the less visited Ta Som and Preah Khan are just as cinematic, with stone-crushing banyans and serpentine strangler figs. Follow crumbling corridors, peer over walls, and find holy spaces reclaimed by Buddhist devotees.

Get Local in Beng Mealea ▲▲
Only unearthed in recent decades, this remote 12th-century complex has a comparable floor plan and motifs to Angkor Wat, but little more is known as the jungle is hiding the rest. Arrive in the late afternoon when the tour buses have left, climb the ruins with the neighborhood kids, and spend the night with a local family.

River of a Thousand Lingas ▲▲
Behind a veil of white water, Angkor-era designs are carved into the Kbal Spean riverbed. In the upper section, Vishnu appears in the sandstone along with animal depictions. Continuing downstream, hundreds of linga reliefs emerge. Beautiful and bizarre all at once, this a great place for a hike, picnic, and waterfall swim in the rainy season.

✣ River Over Road

Sure, it would have been easier to take the highway from the French colonial city of Battambang to Siem Reap. Buses zip you there in three hours, but we opted for the eight-hour voyage in a wooden boat without seat cushions. Slow-cruising Tonlé Sap lake and river, we passed floating bamboo houses, ladies scrubbing laundry with stones, men casting handmade fishing nets, kids canoeing to school, and a world hidden from highways. This boat may not be the fastest or particularly comfortable, but it offers the most unforgettable way to approach Siem Reap and Cambodian culture.

Kids rowing themselves to school on Tonlé Sap

TO EXPLORE MORE ON THIS CONTINENT, CHECK OUT:

» **Beaches: Tioman, Malayasia...p. 76**

» **Dunes: Mũi Né, Vietnam...p. 144**

Thousands of rock spires fill Zhangjiajie National Forest.

WULINGYUAN
China

ASIA
Wulingyuan □

Remember those floating mountains in the movie *Avatar,* dripping with greenery and swarming with dragonlike creatures? This pocket of Hunan, China, was a key inspiration behind the fantasy flick. Zhangjiajie National Forest Park contains over 3,000 quartzite sandstone towers, with trees and shrubs clinging to its sheer cliffs. When fog fills the valley floor, their bases vanish and you can see where director James Cameron got the idea. (Maybe he didn't use so many special effects after all?) Zhangjiajie is the showstopper in many ways; however, it's just one of four parks that make up the stunning Wulingyuan Scenic Area and UNESCO World Heritage site. The area boasts 560 scenic attractions, from one of China's largest caves to the world's longest glass-bottom bridge, extending over the spire-filled canyon. Head south and take the 24,459-foot-long cableway through the karst landscape to the top of Tianmen Mountain. There you'll reach the "Gateway to Heaven" and more otherworldly surprises. In a country as urbanized as China, it seems to celebrate its natural wonders with extra fervor and flair. Although sometimes we could do without the light show, song, and souvenirs, it's hard not to be awestruck by this geological and cultural phenomenon.

⊠ WHEN TO GO

There is no guarantee you'll avoid fog, rain, or crowds. That said, May–October offer clearer weather, with the shoulder months having fewer tourists.

⊞ WHERE TO STAY

Yuanjiajie Zhongtian International Youth Hostel: Among the few accommodations in Zhangjiajie National Forest, this basic hostel is worth entertaining for its prime location and lack of tour groups. **Pullman Zhangjiajie:** A luxurious Accor Hotel with a pool and hammam perfectly positioned between Wulingyuan's national parks.

GET ROMANTIC

While all the tourists are roaming Zhangjiajie's sky-high walkways, head to the forest floor. Wander the misty stone maze and find a private picnic spot.

HONEYTREK TIP

The Wulingyuan park ticket is good for two days but even then, it's hard to cover all this beauty. Prioritize your sightseeing wish list and utilize the interpark bus system to make the most of your time. Better yet, give yourself three days.

A traditional Chinese pier on Baofeng Lake

COUPLES ADVENTURES

Sky-High Bridges ▲▲
In addition to the Zhangjiajie forest of stone spires, the national park has spectacular bridges spanning the ages. Cross the 400-million-year-old natural rock arch Tian Xia Di Yi Qiao (First Bridge of the World), followed by one of the world's newest, longest, and highest glass-bottom bridges. Hang on tight; both are well over 1,000 feet high.

Hike Sadao Gully ▲▲▲
Follow the trail along the famed Golden Whip Stream, surrounded by steep karst peaks, dense foliage, and swinging monkeys. This gorgeous pass gets its share of Chinese tourists, though take the bridge detour to Sadao Gully and you will practically have this paradise to yourself.

Sail Suoxi Valley Nature Reserve ▲
This reserve is home to natural wonders like the Ten-Mile Gallery cliffs, Yellow Dragon Cave, and Baofeng Lake. All are worth seeing, but it's the rare opportunity to explore Wulingyuan by boat that makes this reserve a must. Sailing across the lake and catching reflections of the soaring peaks in the clear waters doubles their beauty.

A glass-bottom bridge spans Zhangjiajie's Grand Canyon.

Tianmen Mountain's Gateway to Heaven ▲▲
Scale Hunan's most iconic mountain via its cliff-hanging walkways, built some 4,600 feet off the ground. (Adrenaline junkies: Don't miss the sections made of vertigo-inducing glass.) Climb the stairs to the peak's crowning feature, the Gateway to Heaven. The 431-foot hole in the center of the mountain frames the blue sky and passing puffy clouds, while the Tianmenshan Temple adds to the spiritual vibe.

TO EXPLORE MORE ON THIS CONTINENT, CHECK OUT:

» **Mountains: Emeishan, China...p. 28**
» **Rivers: Nam Ou River Valley, Laos...p. 60**

Gas bubbles trapped under icy Abraham Lake, Canada

Supernatural Occurrences

The most spectacular and fleeting natural phenomena; catch them if you can.

VENEZUELA
1. Rapid-Fire Lightning

Where the Catatumbo River empties into Lake Maracaibo, lightning storms are a daily occurrence for over half the year. Winds whip across the lake enclosed on three sides by mountains, creating electrical charges that induce up to 280 strikes an hour—10 hours a day.

ENGLAND
2. Severn Bore Surfing

Running alongside quaint Gloucestershire villages, the River Severn is an unexpected surfer's paradise. When the Atlantic tide rushes upstream and reaches the river's narrowest sections, the two colliding forces curl into a wave that can roll for 30 miles. Time your visit with the tides to see surfers catch this monthly phenomenon.

NORTH AMERICA
3. Monarch Migration

To avoid the cold months, monarch butterflies do a 3,000-mile relay from Canada to Mexico each year. See millions of these orange beauties fluttering by or clustering in trees along their route, or meet them at the finish line in Michoacán, Mexico, at the Monarch Butterfly UNESCO Biosphere Reserve.

MALDIVES
4. Bioluminescent Beaches

During the darkest nights of July–February, many beaches are aglow with electric blue phytoplankton. When these critters crash onto the shore, it activates their bioluminescence, creating a celestial scene. Take a walk through the galaxy.

CANADA
5. Flammable Ice Bubbles

Like the formations in a lava lamp, Abraham Lake is a trippy sight. Methane gas from the basin's decomposing organic material emits bubbles year-round, but in the winter, they become trapped under a sheet of ice, creating an artful skating rink.

TURKMENISTAN
6. Door to Hell

A Soviet drilling mishap in 1971 collapsed a pocket of natural gas, leaving behind a massive crater. To stop the spread of methane, they set it on fire. It's been burning ever since. The 225-foot-wide inferno is a spectacular sight that could extinguish at any time—go soon.

TANZANIA
7. Shifting Dunes

Crawling across the Serengeti Plain at a rate of 16 feet a year, these heaps of volcanic ash should have long since scattered, but their magnetism keeps them united. Throw a handful of sand in the air and watch the particles band together. Look along the fringes, you might find a Maasai's offering to this sacred dune.

MALAYSIA
8. The Elusive Rafflesia

The world's largest flower can take nine months to bloom, only to stay alive a few days. You can see this three-foot-wide, 20-pounder in a number of Southeast Asian jungles, though Mount Kinabalu's high concentration of rafflesia will give you the best chance to spot this red polka-dot parasite.

COLOMBIA
9. River of Five Colors

Caño Cristales is already a vibrant river gorge with jet black rocks, green algae, yellow sand, and aqua-blue rapids. Then come September to November, the riverbed goes psychedelic with the *Macarenia clavigera* plant blooming bright red. Walk through caverns and see these pools turn into a liquid rainbow.

U.S.A.
10. Meeting of Lava & Sea

Glowing lava flows for miles over black molten rock, until it reaches the sea cliffs and cascades into a sizzling spectacular. Since the 1980s, this phenomenon has been happening every few years at Hawaii's Volcanoes National Park. Witness it with a hike, helicopter, or boat.

Kodak Gap, Antarctica

TRAVEL SMART

With dozens of new destinations on your must-see list, it's time to mobilize! Get savvy about travel finances, transportation, lodging, and packing. Discover creative ways to get local, sleuth the best deals, craft unforgettable routes, and make a positive impact along the way. Here's how to travel smarter.

PLANNING A LIFE OF TRAVEL

The world is big, and life is short! Use those vacation days to the fullest, give yourself extra time between jobs, and make the most of unexpected leave. You never want to have a windfall of free time without the means to enjoy it. Consider these steps to make travel more attainable and an integral part of your life.

Start a Travel Fund
Travel is an investment you make in yourself. It can seem like a luxury, so in tighter times, it's often a line item that gets cut. Try this: Create a travel fund and direct 5 percent of your paycheck into that account. Then, when you need a dose of adventure, romance, or a breath of fresh air, money will be less of an obstacle.

Get Your Tools Ready
Although there are often last-minute deals to be had, it's always good to have a long-term strategy for easy and affordable travel. How to get started: Join airline and hotel loyalty programs, and use credit cards that reward your everyday spending (p. 243). Join sharing-economy sites and communities (p. 250). Sign up for travel newsletters, and follow blogs, especially the Power Couples in this book (p. 246). The more you immerse yourself in the travel community, the more opportunities will present themselves. Removing potential roadblocks will position you to seize the day.

Prioritize Your Bucket List
Don't save your travel dreams for later. Write down your list and give it a loose time line. Put your most adventurous things at the top (knees and life can be fickle). Hold yourself to it and accomplish at least one goal every year. Somewhere in that string of dates, create a block for a multimonth journey. More than a vacation, it's an invaluable opportunity to step back from the day-to-day and get a bird's-eye view on life, plus, more thrills, laughs, and memories than you can imagine.

Don't think just about planning your next vacation, but also about the experiences you want in your life and how to make them a reality.

Railay, Thailand, featured in our Beaches to Buddhas itinerary

DREAM ITINERARIES

Think beyond borders and 10-day trips, and go deeper into some of our favorite regions. Explore the seven continents with these epic journeys.

Beaches to Buddhas

Have fun in Bangkok, then transfer from the urban jungle to the evergreen rain forest of Khao Sok National Park (p. 182). Continue south to Phuket, and hop a ferry to the karst peninsula of Railay (p. 74). Rock climb the sea cliffs and snorkel the bioluminescent waters before catching a plane from Krabi to Yangon, Myanmar. Spend a few days exploring this British colonial city with one of the oldest stupas in the world. Continue to the idyllic Inle Lake (p. 48), home to hill tribes and floating villages. For a grand finale, head west to Bagan (p. 106) with more than 2,000 ancient temples.

Ultimate Oceania

Rent a campervan in Christchurch, New Zealand, and discover the glaciers, rain forests, and fjords with a South Island road trip (p. 202). Stop in the Tasman District (p. 124) for a multiday kayak, hike, bike, and wine-tasting extravaganza. Hop a flight to Sydney for an exciting stopover or head straight to Cairns, the gateway to the Great Barrier Reef and the ancient Daintree rain forest (p. 180). Don't leave Australia without getting wild in the outback. Game drive the Top End (p. 86), breaking for wallabies, saltwater crocs, and rock art by one of the oldest living cultures.

Big Ice

From Punta Arenas, Chile, cruise to the frozen continent, Antarctica (p. 160). Kayak around icebergs, hang out in penguin colonies, and take the polar plunge on a 10-day voyage. Returning to Punta Arenas, you'll be in the heart of Patagonia. Torres del Paine (p. 40) awaits with the W Trek, Grey Glacier, and horseback rides between estancias. Cross the border and experience southern Argentina's star park, Los Glaciares (p. 174). Ice trek the ever growing Perito Moreno and watch the sun come up over the iconic Fitz Roy peaks.

African Highlights

Be sure to visit Johannesburg's Apartheid Museum before your safari in Kruger National Park (p. 88), where you can spot the "big five" and some 500 bird species. South Africa is the land of epic road trips, with our favorite covering the wine and whale routes of the Western Cape (p. 200). Give cosmopolitan Cape Town a few days, then fly to Livingstone, Zambia (p. 54), for the thunderous Victoria Falls. Get your adrenaline fix on the swift Zambezi River, then puddle jump to South Luangwa National Park (p. 98) for abundant wildlife and ideal terrain for walking safaris.

Unexpected Europe

Ride the rails across western Europe, beginning in medieval Ghent (p. 116). Admire the Flemish architecture along the canals with afternoon strolls and long bike rides, toasting your days with Trappist beers. Make your way to Cologne, Germany, and continue by train or scenic riverboat to Rüdesheim, passing castles and vineyards of the Rhine Gorge (p. 56). Revel in charming villages and eat Riesling ice cream until you are ready for the Swiss Alps. Pull into the Lauterbrunnen station, then continue by footpath, cable car, or via ferrata ladders to some of Switzerland's most scenic mountain towns (p. 32).

Deserts to Rain Forests

Fly into Las Vegas, Nevada, and road trip to some of the Southwest's most spectacular national parks, including Zion, Bryce, and the Grand Canyon (p. 206). Off-road with a 4x4 or mountain bike in spunky Moab, Utah (p. 142), then sleep in safari tents under the desert sky. Ready for lush landscapes? Catch a flight to Seattle and loop the Olympic Peninsula (p. 188), home to one of the United States's only rain forests. Walk among 1,000-year-old trees, tidepool the sea stacks, and soak in the hot springs. Head southeast to Mount Rainier (p. 34), an active volcano frosted with glaciers. Hike, ski, or frolic among the wildflowers—every season beholds a place of wonder.

Andean Extremes

Fly into La Paz, Bolivia. Spend a few days in one of the world's highest cities, with fascinating indigenous markets and Spanish colonial architecture. Head north to Lake Titicaca (p. 52), the spiritual birthplace of the mighty Inca and home to the Uros floating islands. Continue north to Machu Picchu and the Urubamba Valley (p. 38), or loop south toward the Department of Potosí (p. 220). Road-trip to the world's largest salt flats, teal and pink crater lakes, and ultimately the moonlike Atacama Desert (p. 154). Give yourself three days in San Pedro de Atacama, where adrenaline and luxury find their happy place.

For even more of our favorite itineraries see *HoneyTrek.com/DreamItineraries.*

Dazzling mountain landscape from the Andean Extremes itinerary

IDEAL DESTINATIONS BY MONTH

JANUARY

ANTARCTIC PENINSULA (p. 160)
Warm temperatures, long days,
and baby penguins abound.

FEBRUARY

MANAUS (p. 194)
The Amazon goes wild
with Brazilian Carnival.

MARCH

NIAGARA FALLS (p. 172)
The massive waterfalls freeze
into an ice spectacular.

APRIL

ANNAPURNA SANCTUARY (p. 24)
The Himalayan trails are ablaze
with pink rhododendrons.

MAY

SOUTH ISLAND (p. 202)
Fall foliage + crisp weather - crowds
= ideal road tripping.

JUNE

URUBAMBA VALLEY (p. 38)
Get in the Inca spirit with the
vibrant Inti Raymi festival.

JULY

CRATER HIGHLANDS (p. 92)
Millions of wildebeest and zebra
move across the Serengeti.

AUGUST

IRISH NORTH COAST (p. 208)
The Emerald Isle
shows its sunny side.

SEPTEMBER

TORTUGUERO (p. 100)
Thousands of turtle hatchlings
crawl to the sea.

OCTOBER

NORWEGIAN FJORDS (p. 136)
Enjoy sunshine by day,
northern lights by night.

NOVEMBER

CHURCHILL (p. 96)
The window for polar bear sightings
opens on Hudson Bay.

DECEMBER

NORTH ELEUTHERA (p. 68)
Celebrate the holidays
Junkanoo style.

Wildebeest grazing their way across the Serengeti

MONEY MATTERS

Prepare your spending methods for maximum reward, security, and ease. Make sure the right credit cards and debit cards are in your wallet. Here are our best practices for purchases on the road, plus tricks for avoiding those pesky transaction fees.

Travel Credit Card & Debit Card 101

What to look for in your cards and how to keep them secure while traveling.

Debit Cards: (1) No surcharge for ATM withdraws; (2) refunds any third-party ATM fees; (3) no currency conversion fees; and (4) no monthly service charges.

Credit Cards: (1) No currency conversion fees on international purchases; (2) earns 2 percent cash back or frequent-flyer miles; and (3) provides travel benefits, such as lounge access or free checked bags.

Card Security: Have two unique debit cards and two unique credit cards. Keep them in different places in case one is lost or stolen. Let your lenders know where and when you are traveling so they don't freeze your accounts.

Airline Credit Cards & Programs

Most major airlines and hotel chains offer credit cards with lucrative sign-up bonuses and a variety of perks. Start by joining their loyalty programs (our favorites are United, Southwest, and Marriott). Then sign up for one or two new travel credit cards to start earning point and miles; it's a great way to bring down the cost of your next trip.

Finances Upon Arrival

When entering a new country, skip the currency exchange booths, and withdraw local money from the ATM (use the XE Currency App to crunch the numbers). Take out enough cash for the first few days. That will give you time to get your bearings regarding prices and determine how widely credit cards are accepted.

Using Paper and Plastic

Money practices vary country to country. Wherever you go, you'll be prepared with these tips.

A Myanmar street food feast for 1,600 kyats ($1.20)

Cash: Stock your wallet with one credit card and a day's worth of local currency. Secure the rest in your hotel room. Break a bill at the front desk or corner store to make for smoother purchases about town. Save your U.S. dollars and euros for border crossings and emergencies.

Credit: At reputable businesses, use credit cards over cash. Cards allow you to earn frequent flyer miles, track your spending, and dispute charges if the goods or services are not as promised. Consider reverting to cash if vendors add a 2 to 5 percent credit card fee.

What to Avoid

Currency Exchange Booths: They have hidden fees and your ideal ATM card doesn't.

Prepaid Travel Cards: If this debit card runs dry or charges fees abroad, its supposed peace of mind will likely be negated.

Traveler's Checks: These relics are exchanged at a hefty premium—if they are accepted at all.

BOOKING FLIGHTS

Everyone wants to know the perfect time to book a flight for the best combination of cost and convenience. Airlines keep us guessing by using a complex algorithm to fill every seat at the highest price. Despite their cryptic ways, a variety of tricks, websites, and tools can ensure you don't overpay.

When to Fly

There are two surefire ways to get cheaper flights: Fly midweek and during shoulder seasons. You will see a sizable price reduction, plus increased availability. For example, flight prices from the U.S.A. to Portugal decrease about 30 percent from August to September. And there is an even greater drop in the number of tourists, so you'll have your pick of restaurants, hotel rooms, and beach chairs.

Booking With Money vs. Miles

It pays to have frequent-flyer miles at the ready and be flexible with your method of payment.

Using a Credit Card: Start searching three to four months before your flight, set email price alerts,

A Maasai warrior helps load our bags into a bush plane.

and secure your ticket at least 30 days before departure. If your plans are flexible, you can hold off for last-minute fares, as airlines drop prices to fill remaining seats.

Using Frequent-Flyer Miles: Try to reserve your mileage ticket as early as possible. Seats usually become available 300 to 330 days before liftoff.

Making the Call: Just because you have enough frequent-flyer miles doesn't mean it's the right time to use them. Look for the cheapest cash ticket, then compare that price to the "cost" in frequent-flyer miles (1.5 cents is a fairly common valuation for one mile). Remember, miles are only as valuable as the memories you make.

Cost-Cutting Tips

Don't settle for the first search result. Use these booking tricks to find and seize the deal.

Mind the Fees: When comparing flight costs, be sure you include all fees, taxes, and baggage charges. Some airlines and aggregator sites will insidiously withhold fee information until the final booking page (or even worse, when you arrive to the airport).

Alternate Airports: Some airports charge higher landing fees, which is then folded into your ticket price. Expand your flight search to include nearby airports.

One-Way Benefits: If you want to fly into London on United, spend a few weeks exploring the U.K., and depart out of Edinburgh on British Airways, just compare the cost and convenience. Round-trip tickets aren't necessarily cheaper these days, plus one-way tickets give you the flexibility to mix and match carriers and cities.

Airline Websites: Once you find a ticket on a booking site, visit the airline's website and see if it's available at the same price. If you need to make any changes in the future, it will be easier to deal directly with the source.

For even more of our favorite flight resources, see *HoneyTrek.com/FlightTips.*

OVERLAND TRANSIT

If you ask seasoned travelers for their best stories, public transit probably played a role. From goats on the roof to local kids on your lap, awe-inspiring mountain passes to valleys bursting with wildflowers, overland journeys unfold in full color. Plus, they're cheap, flexible, environmentally friendly, and rarely a bore.

City & Chicken Buses

Western nations have impressive public transportation, though developing countries often have extensive networks too (even if not quite as glamorous). Old-school buses, Jeepneys, and *dala dalas* (share taxis) have frequent departures and unbeatable prices. If nothing else, try them once for the thrill and local banter.

Overnight & Long-Haul Buses

An affordable and flexible alternative to flights, long-distance buses are a great way to get around a country. One key benefit is that reservations can often be made same day, so your itinerary can change as you wish. Plus, the quality of coaches around the world is significantly improving (we've had everything from Wi-Fi to whiskey service). Sleeping on overnight buses also saves precious daylight and can make even eight hours of transit fly by.

Boats

When a body of water parallels your route, see if there is a ferry, dhow, or catamaran heading your way. Waterways and shorelines offer a closer look into a world often missed by roads and flight paths. Plus, a cool breeze and sunshine make any journey more enjoyable.

Motorbikes

Lightweight motorcycles and scooters are hugely popular in island destinations and the whole of Southeast Asia. It's one of the most affordable, efficient, and fun ways to explore remote areas and zip from town to town. If you've never driven one before, try to practice at home and avoid riding in big cities.

Trains

Spacious, scenic, smooth, and nostalgic, train travel is a joy. Whenever possible, hop aboard—whether on the bullet trains of Japan or the colonial rails of Kenya. Book second class for local color and the best snacks. For detailed reviews of specific routes, we always consult the pros at *Seat61.com*.

Routing Resources

Our favorite apps and websites to help you get from Albania to Botswana:

Rome2rio: Discover the transit options, timetables, and pricing for even obscure routes.

Google Maps: Street View and Earth View offer incredible detail when trying to locate a mom-and-pop shop or trailhead.

Maps.me: This free GPS app, with detailed and searchable street maps, works anywhere in the world, without the need for a cell plan.

Train, bus, and plane tickets make great souvenirs.

TRAVEL HACKS

The Power Couples share their top travel tips:

"Book a local guide upon arrival. We did this for Everest Base Camp and couldn't believe how much others paid for the exact same trek. Our epic climb was one-third of their cost, plus it supported the local economy."

—Dave & Deb, The Planet D

"When searching online for flights, be sure to check different country's domains. Swap the .com for .ca, .mx, .de, and so on. Sometimes the price can be significantly less."

—Dalene & Pete, Hecktic Travels

"When you ask a local for a restaurant recommendation, be specific and say, 'Where do *you* eat?' This will help avoid touristy suggestions and send you to a place with an authentic vibe."

—Dan & Audrey, Uncornered Market

"With house-sitting, you stay for free nearly anywhere in the world in exchange for looking after a home and pets. Plus, it gives you the unique opportunity to live like a local."

—Nat & Jodie, Professional House Sitters

"A campervan is the ultimate road trip vehicle. You can see places off the beaten track while having your creature comforts handy. Lodging and food costs go way down, plus, you'll have the added adventure of buying groceries in exotic locales."

—Lisa & Alex, 2people1life

"Make the travel booking sites work for you. Set up flight alerts on several websites to track prices; give this process a couple weeks to ensure you grab a good deal."

—Lina & Dave, Divergent Travelers

"Dry shampoo is a savior on outdoorsy holidays, where hot showers aren't readily available. Besides its obvious use, it also works well as a deodorant or shoe freshener."

—Savi & Vid, Bruised Passports

"TSA PreCheck gives eligible travelers a lane to speed through airport security, while Global Entry will reduce paperwork and shorten lines when returning from abroad. At $100 for five years, this combo offers incredible value."

—Bret & Mary, Green Global Travel

"Wrap 10 feet of duct tape around a pencil for gear repairs. It barely takes up any space, but in an emergency, it will be worth its weight in gold."

—Kris & Tom, Travel Past 50

"Always check in for flights in advance. It may sound obvious but in the rush of it all, it's easy to forget. With this simple task, you can skip the long queues and go straight to baggage drop."

—Lauren & Vaughan, The Travel Manuel

"Eat local. No one should travel to foreign lands to eat familiar foods. Not only will this save you money, but you may find yourself seated next to 'Maria,' who teaches salsa dancing around the corner, where you might dance away the next few evenings."

—Elayna & Riley, Sailing La Vagabonde

House-sitting a villa in Playa Panama, Costa Rica

PACK LIKE A PRO

We all know we shouldn't overpack, but most of us do anyway. Then the moment we are dragging multiple bags up a cobblestone street in the summer heat, we think, "What have I done?" When you don't pack efficiently, it can haunt you the whole trip. Find a balance with style and efficiency.

Look Like You

Pack clothes that make you feel good. If you wouldn't wear convertible hiking pants walking around your hometown, why would you suddenly want to wear them on a daily basis? Lay out your favorite casual clothing, then pick the most versatile, lightweight, and durable items in the group. Having a couple quick-dry pieces is a good idea, especially if you'll be hitting the trails, but that's plenty. You don't want to look like you're climbing a mountain while walking through Mexico City.

Pack Multifunctional Items

Nothing should be a one-time wear (like that bright floral "going out" shirt). Pack versatile clothes, like a dress that doubles as a skirt, and simpler items, so they can be worn numerous times. Add variety with jewelry, scarves, and other lightweight accessories. Three pairs of shoes across styles—dressy, casual, and rugged—are all you need. Footwear should be broken in and comfy enough for walking a couple miles, because a short stroll can often turn into an all-day adventure.

Be Culturally Conscious

Keep in mind that local garb may be more conservative than you're used to. Even in free-spirited places, they don't appreciate tank tops and skimpy shorts in their sacred buildings (where the most impressive architecture is frequently found). Have some demure options in your bag. If you'll be visiting religious places, women should pack a long skirt and a sarong for a quick cover-up. (Anne was turned away at Angkor Wat for shorts above her knees.) *Tip:* Easy slide-off shoes come in handy for temple-hopping.

Go Carry-On

For smoother travel, get your luggage down to carry-on size. You'll bypass the check-in counter, slash baggage fees, have your possessions handy and secure, and breeze past your plane mates at baggage claim. You'll be more nimble, independent, and spontaneous at every stage of your trip. To avoid checking bags, transfer liquids to 3.4-ounce containers, opt for a bladeless multitool, and leave that "what if" outfit at home. If you are going on a cold-weather adventure, wear your bulkiest items on the flight.

Choose the Right Luggage

Before you pick a bag, consider the nature of your trip. The classic rolling suitcase is fitting for urban destinations and posh hotels. The uneven surfaces common in developing countries and the great outdoors might call for a 50-liter backpack. Expecting a bit of both? The wheeled backpack could be the perfect hybrid. Long flights of stairs and gravel roads can pop up anywhere, so there is never a bad time for this option—especially with their sleek new designs.

When it comes to hand luggage, we like the combination of a sturdy all-around daypack, and a thin polyester tote for the beach and shopping. For purses, a shoulder-strap design that zips closed and lays flat against your body is a solid, secure option. If you are into tech, the padded compartments of a camera backpack are great for organization.

Pack It Up

Your luggage is basically a dresser without drawers. Add that same level of organization with packing cubes. Use different colors to divvy up your stuff by category (shirts, pants, etc.) to quickly locate them. Cubes are particularly great for separating dirty laundry and wrangling rogue socks and underwear. Opt for the compression-sack variety for bulky items or longer journeys. If you are going ultralight and want to skip the cubes, rolling clothes is great for a similar grab-and-go. To minimize wrinkles, try flat packing by laying clothes the length of your bag.

TOP 10 TRAVEL ACCESSORIES

No matter the destination, season, or occasion, these are the invaluable items we bring on every trip.

1. Power Strip

A mini surge protector with three outlets and two USB ports allows you to charge many devices at once. This is particularly handy in airports with minimal plugs, and when you have foreign outlets and just one universal adapter.

2. Sarong

This long, lightweight garment has dozens of uses. It's a dress, eye mask, picnic blanket, religious cover-up, satchel, extra layer after sunset, and plenty more.

3. Collapsible Canteen

Unlike a metal or hard plastic water bottle, this vessel packs flat and weighs virtually nothing when empty. Brands like Nalgene are great for their extra-durable materials and wide mouth for easy water purification.

4. SteriPEN Water Purifier

Fill water bottles from any tap or stream. Dip in this ultraviolet light, swirl it around for

Mike purifying river water with a SteriPEN in Japan

50 seconds, and kill 99.99 percent of protozoa, bacteria, and viruses. Not buying water saves us over $1,500 annually, and keeps 1,000 plastic bottles from landfills and oceans every year.

5. Hidden Travel Wallet

A thin, zippered pouch that hangs off your belt and tucks inside your pants secretly and securely stores your cash and cards. It allows you to keep larger sums separate from your main wallet, and offers peace of mind in crowded places or when leaving an ATM.

6. Freezer Bags

Heavy-duty, resealable pouches (à la gallon-size Ziplocs) will waterproof your tech gadgets and documents, contain wet clothes, hold snacks, and help you stay organized.

7. Sporknife

This unified spoon-fork-knife is essential for picnics, meals on the go, or snacks in the hotel room. Durable and lightweight plastic, it can be reused for years.

8. Cable Locks

Flexible luggage locks allow you to secure multiple zippers. Bring one short cable lock for each bag, and one long in case you need to lash your stuff together or anchor it to a fixed object.

9. Your Real Pillow

We know this is a space splurge but, given the importance of a good night's sleep, your own pillow is invaluable. No matter where you spend the night—a five-star hotel or a tent—it will make any place feel like home.

10. Souped-Up Smartphone

Turn your phone into a travel ninja by "unlocking" it (to accept local SIM cards) and downloading these savvy apps: XE Currency converter, Maps.me offline GPS, Wunderground weather forecast, Google Voice calling, and TripIt travel itineraries.

The luxe geodesic domes of EcoCamp Patagonia, Chile

LODGING

We think everyone—no matter whether you're a high roller or flashpacker—should try a range of lodging options. Our favorite stays always have personality and regional authenticity—be it a boutique hotel full of sumptuous details or an Airbnb offered by a house-proud local. Our guiding principles: Spend when it gives you a one-of-a-kind experience (a vineyard loft in Mendoza or a castle in Ireland), and save when it's just a place to lay your head (a hotel near the airport). Stay in a local home at least once in every country; the cultural insight will be invaluable. Use these tips to help you navigate the ever changing world of lodging, and find the best experiences.

Booking Engines

OTAs (online travel agents) are the Internet's one-stop shop. When it comes to lodging, the best deals are often had when you combine your hotel booking with your flight or car rental. Sites like *Travelocity.com* and *Orbitz.com* offer significant discounts for packages, and they price match hotel bookings until 24 to 48 hours before you depart.

Deep-Discount Sites

If you aren't set on a certain hotel and are looking for a bargain, try *Hotwire.com, Priceline.com,* and *HotelTonight.com.* Shop their last-minute deals or name your own price for desired location and quality rating. Although you won't always know the exact hotel until it's booked, you'll realize significant savings for places that match your needs.

Boutique Luxury

For hotels that believe luxury is more than a look—but a feel, with local character, thoughtful design, and personal attention—we turn to a few key collections and curation sites. *RelaisChateaux .com, SLH.com, MrandMrsSmith.com,* and *FiveStar Alliance.com* are among our favorites for special occasions.

Peer-to-Peer Lodging

Renting a local's home—be it a mansion or spare bedroom—is becoming wildly popular thanks to alternative lodging sites like *Airbnb.com* and *Homestay.com.* Opt for a private room within a home to find the best combination of affordability and local interaction. Try Airbnb Experiences to find a host who can teach you to surf, reveal the underground music scene, or navigate the street markets.

CREATIVE WAYS TO GET LOCAL

Get to the heart of the locals scene with these sharing-economy platforms. From gourmet dinner parties in a chef's Buenos Aires loft to harvesting olives in exchange for room and board in Tuscany, these resources are your ticket to immersion.

Barter Lodging

Trade a few hours of your time for room, board, and an invitation into the community.

House-Sitting: There are various websites where travelers can apply to stay anywhere from a château in France to a beach house in Costa Rica, in exchange for routine tasks like walking the dog or just taking in the mail. Sits can be a few days or a few months, and offer a fast track to living like a local. To learn more or get started, see *HoneyTrek.com/HousesittingTips*.

WWOOF: Stay on an organic farm in over 100 countries through *WWOOF.net* (Worldwide

A Portuguese cooking class in a chef's Lisbon home

Opportunities on Organic Farms) and experience how different cultures live off the land. Working four-hour days for a week or more earns you lodging, meals, and new skills. The only cost is the nominal membership fee.

WorkAway: Volunteer at a yoga retreat, cooking school, language center, wildlife sanctuary, or thousands of other opportunities in 150-plus countries with *WorkAway.info*. A few hours of work covers your room, board, and bonding experiences.

Free Lodging

It might sound crazy, but people all over the world host travelers for nothing more than the joy of cultural exchange. Between *Couchsurfing.com*, *TrustRoots.org*, and *BeWelcome.org*, over 10 million people across 200,000 cities are involved in this travel community. Join with an open mind and an equally giving spirit (host, if possible), and you will see that it's not about "free," it's about trust, breaking down barriers, and making friends around the world.

Dining

Shake up your restaurant routine and join a dinner party. Professional chefs and culinary enthusiasts open their homes to share an evening of great food and conversation—whether you cook alongside them or kick back with fellow travelers. Try *EatWith.com* for a gourmand experience and *BonAppetour.com* for something intimate and local.

Tours

Find classic city itineraries and creative excursions—from flea market shopping with an experienced antiques dealer to an artist-led graffiti safari. Both *Vayable.com* and *WithLocals.com* are worth a day on the town.

Transportation

Hop in the car with a verified driver heading your way. Ride-share sites like *BlaBlaCar.com* offer an affordable and personal alternative to rentals.

POSITIVE IMPACT TRAVEL

The choices you make with your time and money can positively affect the places you visit. From shopping to tours to volunteering, here's how you can do your part while doing the things you love.

Tourism for Social Good

When your normal travel activities like dining, shopping, and touring can help nonprofits and marginalized communities, it's an easy win. *Visit.org* is a platform that connects travelers with do-good organizations offering authentic excursions, like an Andean weaving class that benefits a nonprofit for rural Peruvian women. Going out to dinner or shopping in a major Southeast Asian city? Stop by a Friends-International gourmet restaurant or fair-trade shop. This nonprofit trains at-risk youth in the arts and service industries and puts all the proceeds back into the program. Countless tourism-related companies are doing more than earning money. Support them whenever you can.

Voluntourism

Tours that combine classic travel activities like hiking or sightseeing with a volunteering component can be great ways to have both an altruistic and indulgent vacation. Just be aware that some outfitters are capitalizing on the trend of volunteer vacations and crafting marketable projects, rather than ones that truly serve the community's needs. Research their reputation and long-term commitment to the area. World Expeditions' Community Project Travel is an excellent example of a tour company working with local leaders for meaningful change.

Volunteering

Working hand in hand with social and environmental causes can be one of the most rewarding forms of travel, plus it gets you off the tourist track. Begin with some inspiration at *Catalyst.cm,* an online community featuring praiseworthy projects, blogs, and forums. The video library at *LearningService.info* is a fantastic resource for the nuts and bolts of impactful volunteering. To book a project with a trustworthy and affordable organization, consider *VolunteerHQ.com,* whose team personally vets all their programs across 30 countries. For entirely free ways to give back while on the road, check out *TheMuskoka Foundation.org,* an organization we volunteered with in Brazil and Vietnam.

Experteering

Use your professional skills to help social impact organizations. *MovingWorlds.org* connects altruistic travelers with nonprofits and B Corps in need of certain expertise. Search by desired country and length of stay to discover résumé-building and social good endeavors.

Making Smart Choices

- Seek out local guides and tour operators.
- Don't support attractions that exploit animals (elephant riding, dolphin swimming, etc.).
- Be wary of orphanage volunteer programs.
- Buy authentic souvenirs direct from artisans.
- Don't buy products made with animal materials (ivory, fur, coral, etc.).
- Avoid buying plastic (recycling is rare).

Smiling faces—a reminder to support local communities

Celebrating life on
Franz Josef Glacier,
New Zealand

SEE YOU ON THE ROAD

"Bucket list" is often a euphemism for "the dreams I'll get to someday." Why wait?

Travel creates memories you'll enjoy the rest of your life. There isn't a day that goes by that we don't think about a funny moment, beautiful place, or insightful conversation from the road. Travel broadens our perspective. It gives us a moment to look at life with a bird's-eye view. Other cultures show us a fresh approach—whether it's a more inventive way to open a bottle or a compassionate way to structure a government. Seeing a smiling farmer on his oxcart or a potter at her wheel reminds us there are many paths to success and happiness. We are so grateful to have learned this sooner than later.

Look for any and every inspiration to travel. Start with anniversaries and birthday trips—there is no better way to celebrate. Turn a work conference into a long weekend and chance to explore a new region. Attending a destination wedding?

Make use of that flight to an exotic locale. Turn chilly weather into a reason to seek sunshine, and sweltering heat into a quest for snow. Make the most of your vacation days, and carve out blocks of time wherever you can.

More than 75 destinations are featured in this book. While it is entirely possible to visit them all, the most important thing is pinpointing your dream experiences and crafting the journeys to make them a reality. We hope our planning tips and travel hacks have shown that no destination is out of reach for savvy travelers. That taking the local bus can be more fun than a limo. That a cliffside picnic can match the romance of a five-course dinner. And that those wrong turns are just extra adventures, as long as you have each other.

As you turn the final page of this book, begin the next chapter in your life of travel. An unforgettable story is waiting to be written.

"To move, to breathe, to fly, to float,
to gain all while you give,
to roam the roads of lands remote,
to travel is to live."

—HANS CHRISTIAN ANDERSEN

Cappadocia, Turkey

RESOURCES

MOUNTAINS

ANNAPURNA SANCTUARY, NEPAL
Trekking Agencies' Association of Nepal
www.TAAN.org.np
Annapurna Tips & Photos
www.HoneyTrek.com/Annapurnas

CORDILLERA CENTRAL, PHILIPPINES
Native Village Inn
www.NativeVillage-Inn.com
Misty Lodge
MistyLodgeSagada@gmail.com
Cordillera Tips & Photos
www.HoneyTrek.com/Cordillera

EMEISHAN, CHINA
Emeishan Hostel C
www.Facebook.com/emeishan.hostelc
Golden Summit Hotel
www.EMJDJD.com/en
Emeishan Tips & Photos
www.HoneyTrek.com/Emeishan

LAUTERBRUNNEN VALLEY, SWITZERLAND
Hotel Staubbach
www.Staubbach.com
Schilthorn Restaurant
www.Schilthorn.ch
Via Ferrata Mürren
www.Klettersteig-Muerren.ch
Obersteinberg Lodge
Info@Stechelberg.ch

MOUNT RAINIER, U.S.A.
Paradise Inn
www.MtRainierGuestServices.com
Packwood Lodge
www.PackwoodLodge.net

Crystal Mountain
www.CrystalMountainResort.com
Mount Tahoma Hut-to-Hut Trails
www.SkiMTTA.com
Mount Rainier National Park
www.NPS.gov/mora

VIRUNGA MOUNTAINS, RWANDA
Sabyinyo Silverback Lodge
www.GovernorsCamp.com
Mountain Gorilla View Lodge
www.3BHotels.com
Iby'Iwacu Cultural Village
www.CBTRwanda.org
Rwanda Parks & Tourism
www.RwandaTourism.com
Rwanda Tips & Photos
www.GreenGlobalTravel.com

URUBAMBA VALLEY, PERU
Hotel Andenes al Cielo
www.AndenesalCielo.com
Inkaterra Machu Picchu
www.Inkaterra.com
Andean Treks
www.AndeanTreks.com
Peru Travel Information
www.Peru.travel
Urubamba Tips & Photos
www.HoneyTrek.com/Urubamba

TORRES DEL PAINE, CHILE
EcoCamp Patagonia
www.EcoCamp.travel
Hostería Pehoé
www.HosteriaPehoe.cl
Torres del Paine
www.TorresDelPaine.com
Torres del Paine Tips & Photos
www.HoneyTrek.com/TorresDelPaine

LAKES, RIVERS & FALLS

IGUAZÚ FALLS, ARGENTINA & BRAZIL
Boutique Hotel de la Fonte
www.BoutiqueHotelDeLaFonte.com
Sheraton Iguazú
www.SheratonIguazu.com
National Park & Full Moon Tour
www.IguazuArgentina.com
Iguazú Falls Tips & Photos
www.HoneyTrek.com/Iguazu

INLE LAKE, MYANMAR
Pristine Lotus Spa Resort
www.PristineLotus.com
Nawng Kham, The Little Inn
www.Facebook.com/nawngkhamthelittleinn
Red Mountain Estate
www.RedMountain-Estate.com
Inle Lake Tips & Photos
www.HoneyTrek.com/Inle

LAKE TITICACA, BOLIVIA & PERU
Hotel Rosario, Lago Titicaca
www.GrupoRosario.com
Hotel La Cúpula
www.HotelCupula.com
Inka Sailing
www.InkaSailing.com
Lake Titicaca Tips & Photos
www.HoneyTrek.com/LakeTiticaca

LIVINGSTONE, ZAMBIA
Tongabezi Lodge & Livingstone Island
www.Tongabezi.com
Royal Livingstone Hotel
www.Royal-Livingstone.Anantara.com
Falls Microlight Flight
www.LivingstonesAdventure.com
Livingstone Tips & Photos
www.HoneyTrek.com/Livingstone

RHINE GORGE, GERMANY
Breuer Rüdesheimer Schloss Hotel
www.Ruedesheimer-Schloss.com
Hote Im Schulhaus
www.Hotel-Im-Schulhaus.com

Drossel Keller Wine Experiences
www.DrosselKellerei.de
Bacharach Castle, Hostel & Cafe
www.HIHostels.com/hostels/bacharach
Rhine Gorge Tips & Photos
www.UncorneredMarket.com

MEKONG DELTA, VIETNAM
Nam Bộ Boutique Hotel
www.NamBoCanTho.com
Oasis Hotel
www.BenTreHotelOasis.com
Song Xanh Sampan
www.SongXanhCruiseMekong.com
Mekong Delta Tips & Photos
www.HoneyTrek.com/Mekong

NAM OU RIVER VALLEY, LAOS
Nong Kiau Riverside
www.NongKiau.com
Tiger Trail
www.Laos-Adventures.com/23765
Nam Ou River Valley Tips & Photos
www.HoneyTrek.com/NamOu

BEACHES & ISLANDS

KAUA'I, U.S.A.
St. Regis Princeville Resort
www.StRegisPrinceville.com
Fern Grotto Inn
www.KauaiCottages.com
Beach House Restaurant
www.The-Beach-House.com
Island Sails Kaua'i
www.IslandSailsKauai.com
Jack Harter Helicopters
www.Helicopters-Kauai.com

NORTH ELEUTHERA, BAHAMAS
The Cove Eleuthera
www.TheCoveEleuthera.com
Coral Sands Hotel
www.CoralSands.com
The Landing
www.HarbourIslandLanding.com
Harbour Island History Tour
MartinLeeGrant@yahoo.com

Eleuthera Tips & Photos
www.HoneyTrek.com/Eleuthera

ZANZIBAR, TANZANIA
Baraza Resort and Spa
www.Baraza-Zanzibar.com
Zanzibar Coffee House
www.RiftValley-Zanzibar.com
Emerson Spice Tea House
www.EmersonSpice.com
Tangawizi Spice Farm
www.TangawiziSpiceFarm.com
The Rock Restaurant
www.TheRockRestaurantZanzibar.com
Zanzibar Tips & Photos
www.HoneyTrek.com/Zanzibar

RAILAY, THAILAND
Railay Phutawan Resort
www.RailayPhutawan.com
Rayavadee Resort
www.Rayavadee.com
Deepwater Solo Climbing
www.BaseCampTonsai.com
Railay Tips & Photos
www.HoneyTrek.com/Railay

TIOMAN, MALAYSIA
1511 Coconut Grove
www.1511CoconutGrove.com
Ella's Place
www.Tioman.org/ella-place.htm
Grahame Massicks's Scuba
www.Tioman-Scuba.com
Tioman Tips & Photos
www.TheTravelManuel.com

SAMANÁ, DOMINICAN REPUBLIC
Dominican Tree House Village
www.DominicanTreeHouseVillage.com
Sublime Samana Hotel
www.SublimeSamana.com
El Cabito Restaurant
www.ElCabito.net
Samaná Zipline
www.SamanaZipline.com
Samaná Tips & Photos
www.HoneyTrek.com/Samana

ON SAFARI

GALÁPAGOS, ECUADOR
Finch Bay Eco Hotel
www.FinchBayHotel.com
Active Adventures
www.ActiveAdventures.com
Galápagos Tips & Photos
www.HoneyTrek.com/Galapagos

TOP END, AUSTRALIA
Adventure Tours Australia
www.AdventureTours.com.au
Wildman Wilderness Lodge
www.WildmanWildernessLodge.com.au
Mindil Beach Sunset Market
www.Mindil.com.au
Northern Territory Visitors Center
www.NorthernTerritory.com
Top End Tips & Photos
www.HoneyTrek.com/TopEnd

KRUGER, SOUTH AFRICA
Sabi Sabi Earth Lodge
www.SabiSabi.com
Mvuradona Safari Lodge
www.Mvuradona.co.za
Chalkley Treehouse
www.LionSands.com
Sweni Trek, Satara Camp, Shipandani Hide
www.SANParks.org
Kruger Tips & Photos
www.HoneyTrek.com/Kruger

CRATER HIGHLANDS, TANZANIA
Nomad Serengeti Safari Camp
www.Nomad-Tanzania.com
Ndutu Safari Lodge
www.Ndutu.com
Crater Highlands Tips & Photos
www.HoneyTrek.com/CraterHighlands

SAMBURU, KENYA
Elephant Bedroom Camp
www.Atua-Enkop.com
Saruni Samburu & Sera Rhino Tracking
www.SaruniSamburu.com

Joy's Camp
Info@Elewana.com
Samburu Tips & Photos
www.HoneyTrek.com/Samburu

CHURCHILL, CANADA
Frontiers North Adventures
www.FrontiersNorth.com
Seal River Heritage Lodge
www.ChurchillWild.com
Churchill Tips & Photos
www.HeckticTravels.com

SOUTH LUANGWA, ZAMBIA
Nsefu Camp
www.RobinPopeSafaris.net
Mfuwe Lodge
www.MfuweLodge.com
The Bush Spa
www.Bush-Spa.com
Zambia Parks & Adventures
www.ZambiaTourism.com
South Luangwa Tips & Photos
www.HoneyTrek.com/SouthLuangwa

TORTUGUERO, COSTA RICA
Tortuga Lodge
www.TortugaLodge.com
Aracari Garden
www.AracariGarden.com
Sea Turtle Conservancy
www.ConserveTurtles.org
Tortuguero Tips & Photos
www.HoneyTrek.com/Tortuguero

HISTORY & ARCHITECTURE

BAGAN, MYANMAR
The Hotel @ Tharabar Gate
www.TharabarGate.com
Bagan Thande Hotel
www.ThandeHotel.com
Balloons Over Bagan
www.BalloonsOverBagan.com
Bagan Tips & Photos
www.HoneyTrek.com/Bagan

CAPPADOCIA, TURKEY
Museum Hotel
www.MuseumHotel.com.tr
Kelebek Hotel
www.KelebekHotel.com
Kapadokya Hot Air Balloons
www.KapadokyaBalloons.com
Matiana Travel
www.Matiana.com.tr
Cappadocia Tips & Photos
www.HoneyTrek.com/Cappadocia

FENGHUANG, CHINA
Fenghuang Melody Inn
www.FenghuangMelody.com
Fengxiang Jiangbianlou Inn
349 Jinjiayuan, Fenghuang, China
Fenghuang Tips & Photos
www.HoneyTrek.com/Fenghuang

GUANAJUATO, MEXICO
Villa María Cristina
www.VillaMariaCristina.net
Alonso 10
www.HotelAlonso10.com.mx
Mexico Street Food Tours
www.MexicoStreetFood.com

GHENT, BELGIUM
Ghent River Hotel
www.Ghent-River-Hotel.be
Ghent Marriot
www.Marriott.com
Huyghe Brewery
www.Delirium.be
Ghent Tips & Photos
www.TravelPast50.com

SINTRA, PORTUGAL
Tivoli Palácio de Seteais
www.TivoliHotels.com
Sintra Bliss House
www.SintraBlissHouse.com
Tacho Real
Phone: +351 21 923 5277
Park E Bike
www.ParkEBike.com

Sintra Tips & Photos
www.HoneyTrek.com/Sintra

AT SEA

TASMAN DISTRICT, NEW ZEALAND
Abel Tasman Great Walk
www.GreatWalks.co.nz
Abel Tasman Lodge
www.AbelTasmanLodge.co.nz
Wilsons Abel Tasman & Great Taste Trio
www.AbelTasman.co.nz
Gourmet Sailing
www.GourmetSailing.co.nz
Project Janszoon
www.Janszoon.org
Tasman District Tips & Photos
www.HoneyTrek.com/Tasman

MESOAMERICAN BARRIER REEF, BELIZE
Colinda Cabanas
www.ColindaCabanas.com
Maya Beach Hotel
www.MayaBeachHotel.com
Raggamuffin Tours
www.RaggamuffinTours.com

NORTHERN PALAWAN, PHILIPPINES
The Birdhouse
www.TheBirdhouseElNido.com
La Natura Resort
www.LaNaturaResort.com
Tao Philippines
www.TaoPhilippines.com
Waz SUP El Nido
www.WazSupElNido.com

KOMODO, INDONESIA
Bayview Gardens Hotel
www.Bayview-Gardens.com
Dive Komodo
www.DiveKomodo.com
Seraya Hotel
www.SerayaHotel.com
Komodo Tips & Photos
www.HoneyTrek.com/Komodo

CYCLADES ISLANDS, GREECE
AthensWas Hotel
www.AthensWas.gr
Sunsail
www.Sunsail.com
Harmony Mexican Bar and Restaurant
www.HarmonyIos.com
Visit Greece
www.VisitGreece.gr
Cyclades Tips & Photos
www.Sailing-LaVagabonde.com

NORWEGIAN FJORDS, NORWAY
Hurtigruten
www.Hurtigruten.com
G Adventures
www.GAdventures.com
Hotel Union Øye
www.UnionOye.no
Visit Norway
www.VisitNorway.com
Norwegian Fjords Tips & Photos
www.HoneyTrek.com/NorwegianFjords

DESERTS & DUNES

MOAB, U.S.A.
Moab Under Canvas
www.MoabUnderCanvas.com
Hauer Ranch & Trail Rides
www.MoabHorses.com
Castle Creek Winery
www.CastleCreekWinery.com
Redtail Air Adventures
www.FlyRedtail.com
Moab Visitors Page
www.DiscoverMoab.com

MŨI NÉ, VIETNAM
Source Kiteboarding
www.SourceKiteboarding.com
Princess D'Ân Nam
www.PrincessDAnNam.com
Windchimes Kiteboarding
www.Kiteboarding-Vietnam.com
Mũi Né Tips & Photos
www.HoneyTrek.com/MuiNe

DURANGO, MEXICO
Hostal Mexiquillo
www.HostalMexiquillo.com
Hotel Gobernador Durango
www.HotelGobernador.com.mx
Visit Durango
www.VisitaDurango.mx

JERICOACOARA, BRAZIL
La Villa Jericoacoara
www.LaVilla-Jeri.com
Baoba Jeri
www.BaobaJeri.com
Jericoacoara Tips & Photos
www.HoneyTrek.com/Jericoacoara

NAMIB DESERT, NAMIBIA
Sossusvlei Lodge
www.SossusvleiLodge.com
Namib Desert Lodge
www.Gondwana-Collection.com
Alter Action Sandboarding
www.Alter-Action.info
Namib Desert Tips & Photos
www.DivergentTravelers.com

ATACAMA DESERT, CHILE
Awasi
www.AwasiAtacama.com
Terrantai
www.Terrantai.com
Tierra Atacama Hotels
www.TierraHotels.com
Celestial Explorations
www.SpaceObs.com
Atacama Desert Tips & Photos
www.HoneyTrek.com/Atacama

SNOW & ICE

ANTARCTIC PENINSULA, ANTARCTICA
Quark Expeditions
www.QuarkExpeditions.com
One Ocean Expeditions
www.OneOceanExpeditions.com
Antarctica Tips & Photos
www.HoneyTrek.com/Antarctica

WESTLAND, NEW ZEALAND
Te Waonui Forest Retreat
www.TeWaonui.co.nz
Aspen Court
www.AspenCourtFranzJosef.co.nz
Glacier Hot Pools
www.GlacierHotPools.co.nz
Fox Franz Heliservices
www.Scenic-Flights.co.nz
Fox Glacier Guiding
www.FoxGuides.co.nz
Westland Tips & Photos
www.HoneyTrek.com/Westland

CENTRAL VERMONT, U.S.A.
Mountain Top Inn
www.MountainTopInn.com
Woodstock Inn
www.WoodstockInn.com
Killington Resort & Ledgewood Yurt
www.Killington.com
Mad River Glen
www.MadRiverGlen.com
Middlebury Tasting Trail
www.MiddTastingTrail.com

TROMSØ, NORWAY
Thon Hotel Polar
www.ThonHotels.com/Tromso
Lyngsfjord Adventure
www.Lyngsfjord.com
Vulkana Nautic Spa
www.Vulkana.no
Active Tromsø
www.ActiveTromso.no

WESTERN GREENLAND, GREENLAND
Quark Expeditions
www.QuarkExpeditions.com
Hotel Hans Egede
www.HHE.gl
Siku Aput Dogsledding & Snowmobiling
www.SikuAput.gl
Greenland Tips & Photos
www.ThePlanetD.com

NIAGARA FALLS, U.S.A. & CANADA
The Giacomo Hotel
www.TheGiacomo.com

Niagara Crossing Hotel & Spa
www.NiagaraCrossingHotelandSpa.com
Carmelo's Restaurant
www.Carmelos-Restaurant.com
National Helicopters
www.NationalHelicopters.com
Thirty Bench Wine Makers
www.ThirtyBench.com
Schulze Vineyards & Winery
www.SchulzeWines.com
Niagara Falls Culinary Institute
www.NFCulinary.org
Niagara Falls Tips & Photos
www.HoneyTrek.com/Niagara

Hostería Senderos
www.SenderosHosteria.com.ar
Los Ponchos
www.LosPonchosApart.com.ar
Cruceros Marpatag
www.CrucerosMarpatag.com
Hielo & Aventura
www.HieloyAventura.com
Estancia Cristina
www.EstanciaCristina.com
Los Glaciares Tips & Photos
www.HoneyTrek.com/LosGlaciares

JUNGLES & RAIN FORESTS

Daintree EcoLodge & Spa
www.Daintree-EcoLodge.com.au
Cape Tribulation Beach House
www.CapeTribBeach.com.au
Dreamtime Walks
www.MossmanGorge.com.au
Visit Port Douglas & Daintree
www.PDDT.com.au
Daintree Tips & Photos
www.HoneyTrek.com/Daintree

Our Jungle House
www.KhaoSokAccommodation.com
Elephant Hills Rainforest Camp
www.ElephantHills.com

Khao Sok Tips & Photos
www.HoneyTrek.com/KhaoSok

Monteverde Lodge & Gardens
www.MonteverdeLodge.com
Los Pinos Cabins & Gardens
www.LosPinos.net
Café Caburé
www.Cabure.net
Sky Adventures
www.SkyAdventures.travel/monteverde
Children's Eternal Rainforest
www.ACMCR.org/content
Monteverde Butterfly Garden
www.MonteverdeButterflyGarden.com

Lake Quinault Lodge
www.OlympicNationalParks.com
Kalaloch Lodge
www.TheKalalochLodge.com
Olympic National Park & Campgrounds
www.NPS.gov/olym

Crystals Resort
www.StLuciaCrystals.com
Ladera Resort
www.Ladera.com
Chateau Mygo
www.ChateauMygo.com
Rainforest Adventures
www.RainforestAdventure.com
Diamond Falls
www.DiamondStLucia.com
Sulphur Springs
www.SoufriereFoundation.org

Manatee Amazon Explorer
www.ManateeAmazonExplorer.com
Napo Wildlife Center
www.NapoWildlifeCenter.com
Amazon Dolphin Lodge
www.AmazonDolphinLodge.com
Yasuní Tips & Photos
www.HoneyTrek.com/Yasuni

MANAUS, BRAZIL

Boutique Hotel Casa Teatro
www.CasaTeatro.com.br
Anavilhanas Jungle Lodge
www.AnavilhanasLodge.com
Amazonas Indian Turismo
AmazonasIndian@hotmail.com
Tropical Tree Climbing
www.TropicalTreeClimbing.com
Manaus Tips & Photos
www.HoneyTrek.com/Manaus

ROAD TRIPS

WESTERN CAPE, SOUTH AFRICA

Road Trip Route
www.goo.gl/maps/2tzryJEy4cL2
Grand Daddy Hotel
www.GrandDaddy.co.za
Quayside Hotel
www.AHA.co.za/quayside
Le Franschhoek Hotel & Spa
www.LeFranschhoek.co.za
Africa Café
www.AfricaCafe.co.za
The Old Biscuit Mill
www.TheOldBiscuitMill.co.za
South Africa Tips & Photos
www.HoneyTrek.com/SouthAfrica

SOUTH ISLAND, NEW ZEALAND

Road Trip Route
www.goo.gl/maps/y6cqxo5irMF2
Matakauri Lodge
www.MatakauriLodge.com
Maui Campervans
www.Maui.co.nz
Tourism Radio
www.TourismRadio.co.nz
National Parks & Deer Flat Campground
www.DOC.govt.nz
South Island Tips & Photos
www.HoneyTrek.com/SouthIsland

THE SOUTHWEST, U.S.A.

Road Trip Map
www.goo.gl/maps/bfBQvZxGrE42

Zion Lodge
www.ZionLodge.com
Bright Angel Lodge
www.GrandCanyonLodges.com
Zion, Bryce & Grand Canyon
www.NPS.gov

NORTH COAST, IRELAND & NORTHERN IRELAND

Road Trip Map
www.goo.gl/maps/TBeFcbDc4zH2
The Bushmills Inn
www.BushmillsInn.com
Lough Eske Castle
www.SolisHotels.com/lougheskecastle
Bunk Campers
www.BunkCampers.com
Olde Castle Bar
www.OldeCastleBar.com
Unique Ascent
www.UniqueAscent.ie
Glencolmcille Folk Village Museum
www.GlenFolkVillage.com

CENTRAL GEORGIA, GEORGIA

Road Trip Map
www.goo.gl/maps/wtJSiJZFsm12
Vinotel
www.Vinotel.ge
Castello Mare
www.CastelloMare.com
Adjarian Wine House
www.AWH.ge
Georgia Tips & Photos
www.2people1life.com

VOLCANO AVENUE, ECUADOR

Road Trip Map
www.goo.gl/maps/GctsYMXLRMs
Hotel Samari Spa Resort
www.SamariSpa.com
Hacienda el Porvenir
www.TierraDelVolcan.com
Hacienda Pinsaqui
www.HaciendaPinsaqui.com
Luna Runtun
www.LunaRuntun.com
El Refugio Spa
www.ElRefugioSpa.com

Tren Ecuador
www.TrenEcuador.com
Volcano Avenue Tips & Photos
www.HoneyTrek.com/VolcanoAvenue

WESTERN CUBA, CUBA
Road Trip Map
www.goo.gl/maps/iYzvSEcFy2J2
Casa Particular Ridel y Claribel
Ridel326@gmail.com
Hotel La Unión
www.HotelLaUnion-Cuba.com
Casa Arcangel
www.Facebook.com/miguelangeltvc
Galileo Offline Maps
www.Galileo-App.com

SUPERNATURAL

DEPARTMENT OF POTOSÍ, BOLIVIA
Kanoo Salt Flats Tours
www.KanooTours.com
Hotel de Sal Luna Salada
www.LunaSaladaHotel.com.bo
Crillon Airstream Tours
www.Uyuni.travel
Department of Potosí Tips & Photos
www.HoneyTrek.com/Potosi

CENTRAL FLORES, INDONESIA
Eco Eden Flores
www.Facebook.com/EcoEden.Flores
Kelimutu Crater Lakes Ecolodge
www.KelimutuEcolodge.com

PAMUKKALE, TURKEY
Venus Suite
www.VenusSuite.com
Ayapam Hotel
www.AyapamHotel.com
Pamukkale Hijackers Paragliding
www.PamukkaleHijackers.com

ROTORUA, NEW ZEALAND
Princes Gate Hotel
www.PrincesGate.co.nz

Koura Lodge
www.KouraLodge.co.nz
Volcanic Hills Winery
www.VolcanicHills.co.nz
Waiotapu Thermal Wonderland
www.Waiotapu.co.nz
Waimangu Volcanic Valley
www.Waimangu.co.nz
Whakarewarewa Living Maori Village
www.Whakarewarewa.com
Lake Rotoiti Hot Pools
www.LakeRotoitiHotPools.co.nz
Polynesian Spa
www.PolynesianSpa.co.nz
Rotorua Tips & Photos
www.HoneyTrek.com/Rotorua

LADAKH, INDIA
Chamba Camp Thiksey
www.TUTC.com
Lchang Nang Retreat
www.LchangNang.com
River Rafting
www.SplashLadakh.com
Monastery Trek
www.DreamLadakh.com
Ladakh Tips & Photos
www.BruisedPassports.com

SIEM REAP, CAMBODIA
Sofitel Angkor Phokeethra
www.Sofitel.com
Viroth's Hotel
www.Viroth-Hotel.com
The White Bicycles
www.TheWhiteBicycles.org
Siem Reap Tips & Photos
www.HoneyTrek.com/SiemReap

WULINGYUAN, CHINA
Zhongtian International Youth Hostel
www.HIHostels.com
Pullman Zhangjiajie
www.PullmanHotels.com
Wulingyuan Tips & Photos
www.HoneyTrek.com/Wulingyuan

ACKNOWLEDGMENTS

After five years on the road we can whole-heartedly say . . . it's the people that have made our travels so special. Even before we departed, the outpouring of love and support from our families, friends, even bosses, emboldened us. They could've easily told us we were crazy for leaving the security of home, but instead they made us feel brave. When we said, "Mom, we're quitting our jobs to take a multiyear honeymoon," that conversation wasn't expected to go so well. "Dad, we're going to be full-time travel bloggers," a long groan was the assumed response. Oddly enough, they have often told us how proud we make them for charting our own course. Thanks to our entire family for nurturing our dreams.

Traveling full-time takes a village, and we could not be more grateful for all the people who continue to make HoneyTrek possible. Thank you to Pat Howard for babysitting the Saab, sorting mail, and still loving us. To Robin Collins for caring about our where-abouts, with regular emails: "Where are you? Call me! Love, Mom." To Pat Collins for reading every single blog and saving our press clips. To our siblings (Kate, Matt, Ryan, Chel-sea, and Will), for always having our back. To all the friends holding rogue pieces of furniture, we hope you're enjoying them (Hotten-steins, we promise we'll pick up the couch someday). To Jeff Radlin, our dear friend and real estate agent, who comes to the rescue with each appliance snafu. To Andrew Corci-one, for being our Hoboken rock and brain-storm cohort (we will sweep the nation!). To our New York home team for always picking up the good times where they left off. To our Killington crew for helping us become better bloggers and skiers.

To our HoneyTrek fans. Your enthusiasm, curiosity, and personal stories keep us moti-vated to hit the road each day and share our adventures. Those days we need a boost, a heartfelt Facebook comment appears from Jim S., Cindy S., Carol L., Rashaad J., Wynne G., Annie M., Erica V., Paal G., Deb G., Ken W., Steph B., Anna V., Christy C., and the thou-sands of other friends, old and new. Our social media channels have rekindled relationships with childhood pals like the Stolfis and former colleagues like Justin C. They've kept us con-nected to people we've met around the world, from our Maasai guide Bernard to Purisima, the

Buenos Aires seamstress, who has followed us with exuberant emojis since 2012.

To the entire Meet Plan Go and travel blogging community, your friendship, savvy advice, and encouragement through the years have been invaluable. To our Trip Coach students who have made it around the world, you make us so proud. To everyone in the sharing economy who has welcomed us into their homes—to surf their spare bedroom, house-sit their farms, or teach us a new recipe—it's been a pleasure getting to know you: Kat & Willie, Susan J., Ro & Majo, Gareth R., Tena & Alena, Toni L., Dave R., Jeanne & Bill, Neil M., Judith & Larry, and so many more.

To the friends beyond the digital world, although our time together may have been brief, your kindness and character have forever connected us. Pepitome, who took us in for two days when our motorbike broke down in the Thai jungle. Cristóvão, who taught us how to fish for piranha and survive in the Amazon. Kat-san for teaching us to appreciate every grain of rice. To the Achoma villagers for making us smile every time we think about that fateful dance party in Peru. To our students in Tả Phìn village, and mentors at MovingWorlds and Muskoka who remind us to do good as we go.

To everyone who agrees . . . life's a honeymoon! Tom and *Honeymoons.com* for opening doors to romantic locales and giving us a platform to start this love train. Aunt Peggy for introducing us to half of East Africa and being our PR champion. Hayes for representing these fledgling lovebirds. Mey and *Glamping.com* for understanding that adventure pairs perfectly with luxury . . . and that the honeymoon must go on!

Thank you to National Geographic for believing in our story and the wonders of couples travel. Rainer Jenss who lit the spark. Bill O'Donnell who never left our side. Susan Straight for letting our voice shine through. Ellen Neuborne and Michael O'Connor for keeping everything straight. Sanáa Akkach, Nicole Miller, and Moira Haney for making this book so beautiful. To the Power Couples who contributed to this work, you are living proof that love and travel make the world go 'round.

To the couples reading this book, thank you for not just tanning on a beach but for seeing travel as a life-enhancing experience and a journey that's better as two.

Laguna Q'ara, Bolivia. Adventure and romance go hand in hand.

INDEX

ILLUSTRATIONS CREDITS

All photographs by Mike and Anne Howard of Honey Trek.com, unless otherwise noted.

25 (LE), Emily Polar Photography; 34, Jeff Goulden/ Getty Images; 35 (LE), Kevin Schafer/Minden Pictures; 36, Bret Love and Mary Gabbett, GreenGlobalTravel. com; 37 (UP), Bret Love and Mary Gabbett, Green GlobalTravel.com; 37 (LO), Stefan von Bothmer; 42, Matthew Williams-Ellis/Robert Harding; 44, Hugh Sitton/Getty Images; 46, Werner Van Steen/Getty Images; 47 (LE), Alex Saberi/National Geographic Creative; 54, Kelly Cheng Travel Photography/Getty Images; 56, Audrey Scott and Daniel Noll, UncorneredMarket.com; 57 (UP), Audrey Scott and Daniel Noll, Uncornered Market.com; 57 (LO), Audrey Scott and Daniel Noll, UncorneredMarket.com; 58, Duc Den Thui/Getty Images; 61 (UP), Cyril Eberle/Getty Images; 62, JMichl/ Getty Images; 67 (RT), Dennis Frates/Alamy Stock Photo; 72, KucherAV/Shutterstock; 75 (UP), Henn Photography/Cultura Creative (RF)/Alamy Stock Photo; 76, Lauren and Vaughan McShane, TheTravelManuel.com; 77 (UP), Reinhard Dirscherl/ullstein bild via Getty Images; 77 (LO), Lauren and Vaughan McShane, The TravelManuel.com; 85 (LE), Tui de Roy/Minden Pictures; 87 (UP), Gianpiero Ferrari/Minden Pictures; 87 (LO), roboriginal/Getty Images; 96, Pete Heck, Hecktic Travels; 97 (UP), Paul Souders/Getty Images; 97 (LO), Pete Heck, Hecktic Travels; 99 (UP), Thomas Retterath/Getty Images; 100, Javier Fernández Sánchez/Getty Images; 101 (UP), Panoramic Images/Getty Images; 102, Tui de Roy/Minden Pictures; 109 (RT), Imke Lass/Redux; 116, Christian Mueller/Shutterstock.com; 117 (UP), Tom Bartel, TravelPast50.com; 117 (LO), Tom Bartel, Travel Past50.com; 120, Laura Grier/Robert Harding; 124, Stuart Black/Robert Harding; 125 (RT), Andy White; 134, S. Borisov/Shutterstock; 135 (UP), Panos Karapanagiotis/Getty Images; 135 (LO), Riley Whitelum and Elayna Carausu, Sailing La Vagabonde; 138, Global Pics/Getty Images; 140, subman/Getty Images; 143 (UP), Justin Bailie/Getty Images; 143 (LO), Kristin Piljay/Danita Delimont.com; 150, Alex Robinson/Robert Harding; 151 (UP), Leo Sanches/Getty Images; 151 (LO), Oktay Ortakcioglu/Getty Images; 152, Gambarini Gianandrea/ Shutterstock.com; 153 (UP), Lina Stock, Divergent Travelers.com; 153 (LO), Bob King; 155 (LE), Jeremy Woodhouse/Getty Images; 156, John G Ross/Getty Images; 163 (RT), Courtesy of Scenic Hotel Group; 167 (UP), Peter Frank Edwards/Redux Pictures; 167 (LO), Birke Photography; 168, Koonyongyut/Getty Images; 170, Dave Bouskill and Debra Corbeil, ThePlanetD.com; 171 (UP), ThePlanetD.com; 171 (LO), ThePlanetD.com; 173 (LE), noexcuseG/Getty Images; 173 (RT), Jonathan Nicholls/Getty Images; 175 (UP), Keith Levit/Getty Images; 176, Suttipong Sutiratanachai/Getty Images; 178, Pete Oxford/Minden Pictures; 180, David Wall/ Getty Images; 181 (LE), chameleonseye/Getty Images; 182, Alex Hare/Getty Images; 183 (UP), Education Images/UIG via Getty Images; 186, Stefano Paterna/ Robert Harding; 187 (LO), InVision Photography/Getty Images; 188, Konrad Wothe/Minden Pictures; 189 (LE), Dan Sherwood/Design Pics Inc/National Geographic Creative; 189 (RT), Hannamariah/Shutterstock; 190, oriredmouse/Getty Images; 191 (UP), A-Babe/Getty Images; 191 (LO), Dani Heinrich, GlobetrotterGirls.com; 193 (UP), Christian Heeb/Prisma by Dukas Presseagentur GmbH/Alamy Stock Photo; 194, Ed George/National Geographic Creative; 196, BEES Elephant Sanctuary; 207 (UP), Derek von Briesen/National Geographic Creative; 210, Lisa Gant and Alex Pelling, 2people1life; 211 (UP), Lisa Gant and Alex Pelling, 2people1life; 211 (LO), Jonas Seaman Photography; 214, Anne08/Getty Images; 228, Jeremy Bright/Robert Harding; 229 (UP), Toma Babovic/laif/Redux; 229 (LO), David Wall/Danita Delimont.com; 230, Savi Munjal and Vidit Taneja, BruisedPassports.com; 231 (UP), Savi Munjal and Vidit Taneja, BruisedPassports.com; 231 (LO), Savi Munjal and Vidit Taneja, BruisedPassports.com; 235 (LE), Stefan Huwiler/imageBROKER/Alamy Stock Photo; 235 (RT), Oktay Ortakcioglu/Getty Images; 236, Kevin Schafer/ Alamy Stock Photo.

Since 1888, the National Geographic Society has funded more than 12,000 research, exploration, and preservation projects around the world. National Geographic Partners distributes a portion of the funds it receives from your purchase to National Geographic Society to support programs including the conservation of animals and their habitats.

National Geographic Partners
1145 17th Street NW
Washington, DC 20036-4688 USA

Get closer to National Geographic explorers and photographers, and connect with our global community. Join us today at nationalgeographic.com/join

For information about special discounts for bulk purchases, please contact National Geographic Books Special Sales: specialsales@natgeo.com

For rights or permissions inquiries, please contact National Geographic Books Subsidiary Rights: bookrights@natgeo.com

ISBN: 978-1-4262-1839-2

Printed in China

19/RRDS/4

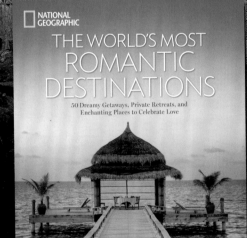